The Fourth Secret of Fatima

Errata Sheet

Page 3, At the end of **footnote 3**, the book publication information should read as follows: Father Paul Kramer's book is *The Devil's Final Battle*. It is published by The Missionary Association, Terryville, Connecticut, 2002, and is available on-line at www.devilsfinalbattle.com – and in print from the web site.

Page 3, In **footnote 5**, the French title of Frère Michel's book is *Toute la Vérité sur Fatima*, published by La Contre-Réforme Catholique. The English version is available from the publisher.

Page 30, In **footnote 44**, the page number reference for the English edition is p. 102.

Page 35, In **footnote 46**, the website address should read as follows: www.vatican.va/holy_father/benedict_xvi/homilies/2005/docu ments/hf_ben-xvi_hom_20050424_inizio-pontificato_en.html.

Page 84, **Footnote 140** should read as follows: Translated from www.vatican.va/holy_father/paul_vi/homilies/1967/ documents/hf_p-vi_hom_19670513_it.html (Italian version).

Page 86, In **footnote 147**, the website information should read as follows: translated from www.vatican.va/holy_ father/john_paul_ii/homilies/1982/documents/hf_jp-ii_hom_19820513_fatima_it.html (Italian version).

Page 132, In **footnote 217**, the book compiled by Father Kramer is *The Devil's Final Battle* and the article is found on pp. 147-165.

Page 136, **Footnote 225** in the book is incorrect. It should instead read as follows: *The Washington Post*, July 1, 2000.

Page 142, In **footnote 240**, the title of the book by Father Alonso is incorrect. The correct title of the book is *The Secret of Fatima: Fact and Legend*.

THE FOURTH SECRET OF FATIMA

Antonio Socci

Loreto Publications

Il Quarto Segreto di Fatima

ISBN 978-1-930278-77-6

First Edition: November 2006
English Language Translation
2009 Loreto Publications

Loreto Publications

P.O. Box 603
Fitzwilliam, NH 03470
603-239-6671
www.LoretoPubs.org

Printed in Canada

THE FOURTH SECRET OF FATIMA

A Fascinating Inquiry Into the Theories
and the Truths of the Most Disconcerting
Mystery of the Twentieth Century

Antonio Socci

DEDICATION

To His Holiness Benedict XVI.

To Yusriani (15 years old), Theresa (16 years old), and Alvita (19 years old), young Christians, throats slit and decapitated by the blows of a machete because of their faith in Jesus.[1]

To Angela Pia, practically moral co-authoress of the book by her prayers.

---

[1] On October 29, 2005 in Indonesia these three Christian students were assaulted by a band of fundamentalist Muslims while going to school (a private Catholic school in Poso). The terrorists held them down, cut their throats, and then their heads. The head of one of them was then thrown in front of the Christian church of Kasiguncu.

"It seems to me that this is the first time Heaven has warned the world of its partial destruction since Our Lord predicted at Jerusalem the chastisement that was threatening it. We are perfectly free to disregard this appeal, but if that should happen, then God have mercy on us all!"

Hamish Fraser

"The moment will come, the danger will be great, it will be thought that all is lost. Then I will be with you."

The Madonna to Saint Catherine Labouré
Paris, 1830

"Out of the mouths of babes and sucklings you affirm your power against your enemies."

Psalm 8

Acknowledgments

I thank Professor Mariagrazza Russo for her precious expertise concerning the text of the Third Secret, which I publish in the Appendix. I thank Dr. Solideo Paolini for his availability to compare notes, his suggestions and the unpublished information he has generously provided to me. I thank besides my Franciscan and Poor Clare "sisters" who sustain me always with prayer. Finally an acknowledgment full of gratitude and prayer also for Frère Michel de la Sainte Trinité, who, with his monumental work on Fatima, has made readily available so many historical documents.

For further information about the author or to contact him, see www.antoniosocci.it

Table of Contents

Chapter 4: The Fourth Secret of Fatima

Chapter 5: The "Secret" Meaning of the Events

Introduction

A surprising discovery

On February 13, 2005 in the Carmelite convent of Coimbra, at the age of 98, Sister Lucia dos Santos, the last visionary of Fatima, custodian of the greatest and most terrible among the secrets of the 20th century, passed away. She died on the 13th day of the month, the same date the Madonna had chosen for the apparitions of Fatima.

Two days later, on my way to Perugia, I stopped for a break at a café on Lake Trasimeno. I took a copy of *Corriere della Sera*, just purchased at the newsstand, and sat by the placid waters, opened it, read and was struck by it. The Catholic writer, Vittorio Messori, had published on the first page an article entitled: "Secret of Fatima, Sealed in Sister Lucia's Cell."

He made some enigmatic nods toward a lot of writings and "letters to Popes" that the visionary had left, and then he spoke of the famous Third Secret revealed by the Vatican in 2000 "that, however, far from dissipating the mystery," according to the Catholic writer, "has given rise to others: on the interpretation, on the contents, on the completeness of this revealed text."

The editorial did not say anything else, and that was a pity; because this "news", tossed off with *nonchalance*, seemed to me a bomb that would have merited a lot more discussion. Also because of the authority of the one who signed it: Messori is a great journalist, exceptionally scrupulous; he is the most translated Catholic essayist in the world and would never have ventured lightly to hint at such "suspicions" concerning the Vatican. In that article it is not said if, when, and how one such as he, very near to the offices of the Vatican,

1

had been persuaded that the official version was not convincing. I do not know his current opinion. Five years before, at the moment of the revelation of the Secret, Messori had not manifested any doubts. I still have his editorial in *Corriere della Sera*, of June 25, 2000, entitled "No Longer Any Fatima Secrets." Everything seemed to line up.

Therefore I reacted to the new article by Messori with a journalistic polemic in which I defended with a sword the rightness of the Vatican (ungenerously above all toward the traditionalists), attacked the writer and liquidated all of his "dietrologies"[1a] concerning unpublished documents. Certainly, I knew that after the fateful revelation of the Third Secret in 2000, doubts, suspicions, rumors, and critical observations had begun to circulate within the curial environment, and that they had found public expression in traditionalist circles. But I had never paid attention to the traditionalist publications because I believed that they originated from a burning disappointment over a Secret that negates all of their "apocalyptic" forecasts.

However, I was struck by an article by a young Catholic scholar, Solideo Paolini, in a traditionalist review in which I myself was mentioned. He entered into my debate with Messori on Fatima and—with a deft polemic—developed a series of arguments that substantially demolished the official Vatican version (which had been mine). In substance—according to Paolini, who immediately after published his thesis in the book *Fatima: Do Not Despise Prophecies*—the Vatican continues to hide the principal part of the Third Secret, even denying its existence because of its explosive contents. Paolini's arguments were serious and his attitude impartial. Other books appeared less well founded and less respectful.

The traditionalists' disputes with the Vatican on the revelation of the Third Secret (of June 26, 2000) have never been analyzed, confronted, and confuted by the ecclesiastical party and are unknown in the lay world—perhaps because their publications circulate almost exclusively in their own environment.[2]

[1a] An Italian idiom for conspiracy theories that look behind (dietro) events for hidden plots.

[2] The Vaticanist Marco Tosatti, with an attention to detail that has distinguished him, summed up in 2002, in the volume *Il Segreto Non Svelato* [*The Secret Not Revealed*], some of the theses, doubts, and theories that had begun to circulate, adding valuable information as we will see.

To me the choice by the Curia and the Catholic media to ignore and say nothing about them did not seem right, especially after having read the extremely harsh tone of their accusations against the Vatican. For example, in a volume assembled by Father Paul Kramer, which combines the works of different authors,[3] the Vatican is denounced for failing to heed the requests of the Madonna of Fatima, and it is affirmed that "the price of the Vatican's indecision could not be greater, and could be paid by the entire human race."[4]

I held that if these suspicions were not dispelled and the accusations confronted, sooner or later the Church would be battered by a tempest analogous to, and perhaps even more forceful, than the one let loose over the "silences of Pius XII" or the theories of Dan Brown.

It seemed to me that the "polemical arms" were ready (even if, for the moment, unknown by the media and the public at large): deposited in traditionalist "arsenals" but at the disposition of whoever would want to launch a heavy attack against the Vatican. For example, the vehement "*I accuse*" of Laurent Morlier under the peremptory title: "The Third Secret of Fatima published by the Vatican is a falsehood." Analyzing this literature—besides that circulating on the Internet—it occurred to me that throughout the Fatima affair there are so many questions without answers as to color it a "detective story."[5] Perhaps the most fascinating and dramatic

---

[3] The author, along with other persons, signs the work with initials (B. Ph., M. Div., S.T.L. Cand.), and with "editorial team of the Missionary Association," and cites (at page xxiii) "the principal sources of the book," often available on the Internet. "With the permission of the authors, Father Paul Kramer and the editors of the Missionary Association have assembled the articles and speeches, adding much additional material." Since the different essays do not carry the signatures of the authors, and for reasons of synthesis, I will have to refer only to Father Kramer inasmuch as he is the curator of this volume, published by Good Counsel Publications, 2002-2004, distributed in Italy by the Association of the Madonna of Fatima (Rome). For further information see www.devilsfinalbattle.com.

[4] Ibid., p. xi.

[5] The "traditionalist" criticisms of the choices of the hierarchy concerning Fatima, from Pius XI forward, are found expressed with exceptional documentation in the monumental work of Frère Michel de la Sainte Trinité, *The Whole Truth About Fatima*," Immaculate Heart Publications. The three volumes, being published between 1989 and 1990, do not treat however of the Third Secret as it was revealed in 2000. For simplicity I will cite these three volumes with the initials of the author FM along with a reference to the volume (v. I, v. II, v. III).

detective story of our times because it involves not only the Vatican, great powers and their secret services, as well as certain obscure apparatuses of power, but also each one of us, and the proximate destiny for all humanity and for the Church.

To explain the Vatican's position and to confute that journalism I sought out representatives of the Curia such as Cardinal Bertone, today the Vatican Secretary of State, who was at the center of the Secret's revelation in 2000 (certainly a delicate and weighty task that merits understanding). While he had gratified me with his personal attention, having invited me to hold a press conference in his former Diocese of Genoa, the prelate did not think it necessary to respond to my request for an interview—a choice he obviously had every right to make, but which nevertheless feeds the fear that there are embarrassing questions and, above all, something serious to hide.

I tried, however, to understand the Vatican's position in order to counter the accusations of the "Fatimists." I investigated the concrete and reliable elements of criticism in the traditionalist literature, unfortunately buried in a mass of theorems, invective, absurdity, and unconfirmed hearsay. I caught certain of their contradictions, dismantled some theses, but in the end I had to surrender—thanks also to the revelations of an authoritative witness who furnished invaluable information. I had not expected the discovery of a colossal enigma, of a mystery that spans the history of the Church of the 20th century, something unutterable, something "chilling" that has literally terrorized different Popes who succeeded each other in mid-century, something that certainly regards the Church, but also the proximate future of us and of our brothers.

Here I recount my voyage into the greatest mystery of the 20th century, and I present the result I honestly reached—a result that seriously contradicted my initial convictions, and that surprised and impressed me. (The reader will note this evolution and change of judgment from the first pages to the conclusion.) I trace finally a hypothesis on the "why" of these events that opens, however, to hope, and allows the Church's divine greatness to shine through alongside the misery of Churchmen (with the limits that all of us have), touching us, as if by hand, with the real and living presence of Jesus Christ and of His Mother—here, today, among us. In our aid. No one, obviously, is obliged to believe in supernatural events like those that happened at Fatima, but no one will be able to say one day that he did not know.

Antonio Socci

October 7, 2006 - Feast of the Blessed Virgin Mary of the Rosary

1. It Happened at Fatima and at Rome...

Mary spoke to the little ones, to children, to those without voice, to those who do not count, in this enlightened world full of pride, of hope and faith in progress, that is also a world full of destruction, full of fear and desperation."

Joseph Ratzinger (Fatima 1996)

Chronicle of a unique event

An extraordinary event, without equal in history, began at Fatima, in Portugal in 1917 and was played out throughout the course of the 20th century. It is something which has already had and can still have consequences of enormous importance for the whole of humanity, not only for Christians. At the center of it all is a secret message that—according to the Catholic Church—the Madonna Herself, on July 13th, 1917, consigned to the little children Lucia dos Santos, Jacinta and Francisco Marto.

The mysterious message—which has become known as the Third Secret of Fatima—was written by Sister Lucia on a simple sheet of paper. In these lines is contained the prophetic warning that the Mother of God, with a most extraordinary initiative, has given to the Church and to the world on the proximate future of humanity, to avert unimaginable tragedies and for its salvation. A Catholic intellectual as great as Jean Guitton spoke of it to Paul VI in these terms: "Holy Father, Fatima is more interesting than Lourdes: it is both cosmic and historical...thus it is linked to the history of salvation, to universal history."

The Fatima event has received on the part of the Church—

which in general is always very cautious concerning supernatural phenomena—a recognition without equal in the history of Christianity and which places this apparition and this message, objectively, above and beyond all of the so-called "private revelations": all of the succeeding Popes have accredited the apparitions with official discourses, acts, and pilgrimages, often evoking biblical comparisons. Paul VI felt Fatima to be an "eschatological" place. He said: "It was as if it was a repetition or annunciation of a scene at the end of time." John Paul II journeyed no fewer than three times to the Portuguese sanctuary. There Pope Wojtyla beatified the two shepherds who died as children (Francisco and Jacinta Marto) and solemnly entrusted the third millennium to the Immaculate Heart of Mary. Finally the third part of the Secret—that for the entire 20th century had fed apocalyptic rumors—was revealed by the Holy See with an official approbation that also has no precedent in Christian history.

As Renzo Allegri has written: "It was the first time that the Church has officially recognized the historic incisiveness of a prophecy whose source was an apparition of the Virgin. A prophecy that Cardinal Sodano has defined as 'the greatest of modern times.'"[6] It even approaches biblical prophecies. A prophecy that obligates the Church, and whose value is not at all "optional," as recognized by John Paul II, pilgrim to the Portuguese sanctuary to give thanks for being delivered from the assassination attempt, who solemnly affirmed: "I am also going toward this blessed place to hear one more time in the name of the entire Church the command that was given by Our Lady, deeply concerned for Her children. Today these commands are more important and vital than ever."[7] Furthermore, the Pope would say, this invitation by the Madonna in 1917 "is more current and even more urgent than before."[8] And above all, the Pope said, "the call made by Mary our Mother at Fatima is such that all of the Church feels obligated to respond to these requests of Our Lady [...] The message imposes an obligation on her [...]"[9]

Decisively weighty expressions, which doubtless clash with the reduction of the Third Secret to a simple and non-binding

---

[6] Renzo Allegri, *The Pope of Fatima*, Mondadori, Milan, 2006, p. 21.

[7] Marco Tosatti, *The Secret Not Revealed*, op. cit., pp. 95-96.

[8] *Teachings of John Paul II*, Vatican Library Edition, 1982, vol. V.

[9] Solideo Paolini, *Fatima: Non disprezzate le profezie*, Edizione Segno, Tavagnacco (Ud), 2005, p. 94.

"private revelation," on a par with so many apparitions and personal supernatural experiences experienced by mystics and saints. First of all, because here it is not mystics who have had apparitions of the Madonna, but normal children. Secondly, because the Virgin entrusted to them a public message directed to the Church and the world, delivering it therefore as a "prophetess"[10] who speaks to everyone of the future and of the life of everyone. Thirdly, because these apparitions have been officially approved by the Church in an extraordinary way. And finally, through treatment reserved to the Third Secret.

In fact, all of the apparitions containing a prophetic message for humanity (from La Salette to the prophetic dreams of Don Bosco, one of which we will cite further on) have been made public informally without engaging the authority of the Church.

But in the case of the third part of the Secret of Fatima, the contrary has happened. Not only did the Holy See (of Pius XII and Ottaviani) decide to keep this text to itself, not only was it the same Holy See (with John XXIII) that decided to disregard the date indicated by the Madonna and by Sister Lucia—1960— decreeing its sequestration, but when—after a long and dramatic deliberation— the Pope personally decided to publish the text (John Paul II did so in 2000), it was announced in the most solemn manner: from the sanctuary of Fatima, before the Pope and the visionary, by the Vatican Secretary of State. And it was even published—on June 26, 2000—with the accompaniment of a theological commentary by the highest doctrinal authority of the Church (next to the Pope), Cardinal Joseph Ratzinger, prefect of the former Holy Office, who presented the text of the Secret and his commentary at nothing less than a press conference televised worldwide. It is really impossible— after all of this—to continue to speak of a "private revelation" and of the relative importance of the Message.

The exceptional words pronounced by John Paul II say exactly the opposite. Let us reread them: "The appeal made by Mary, our Mother, at Fatima is such that the whole Church feels obligated to respond to the requests of Our Lady... The Message imposes an obligation on her..."

The Pontiff was certainly cognizant of the weight of the words

---

[10] See, Joseph Ratzinger, *Mary, Church Rising*, San Paolo, Cinisello Balsamo (Milan), p. 61.

he had pronounced and with which he had dissipated once and for all the nebulous arguments that had so relativized Fatima.[11] In this sense John Paul II was truly the Pope of Fatima. The Pope who more than anyone has understood and made his own the urgency of the Message of the Virgin and, although often misunderstood, the Pontiff who more than anyone accustomed himself to respond to Her positively and to obtain for the Church and the world Her maternal protection.

However, it must be said that all of the succeeding popes since 1917 have recognized Fatima. Also, in order to "validate" the apparitions before the world in a unique manner, and therefore to accredit publicly in a most resounding way the supernatural nature of this event, the Madonna Herself presented the spectacular solar prodigy witnessed by 70,000 people (among which were many journalists and skeptics) in conjunction with the last apparition, on October 13, 1917. A prodigy that the Madonna had preannounced to the children in the course of their previous encounters (which began on May 13th of the same year) to give a public proof to everyone of Her presence.

In the course of these months, with the growth of the pilgrims and the curious who came on the 13th day of each month to the place of the apparitions, also grew the polemics of the secular press and of the attacks of ideological, anti-clerical, and Masonic forces. The authorities, to frighten the little ones, one day arrived to "lock them up in a public prison, declaring to them that later they would come to take them to be boiled alive"[12] (which was in keeping with the rest of the anti-clerical violence that followed later on, destroying even the little chapel constructed in 1919 on the spot where the apparitions occurred).

To the little Lucia dos Santos, frightened by the responsibility she felt weighing on her and the gravity of the Message entrusted to her,

[11] After Fatima and the other great apparitions of the modern era a theological problem was posed for the Church to consider, between the public revelation that terminated with the Apostles and the private revelations reserved to mystics and saints, the status of these intermediate revelations with which the Holy Virgin intervenes in human history to reinforce the faith of the Church and to call the world to conversion. In some cases such apparitions have also illuminated the decision of the Church to proclaim dogma (which was the case with the events of Rue du Bac and of Lourdes for the dogma of the Immaculate Conception).

[12] Luigi Gonzaga da Fonseca, *Le meraviglie di Fatima* [*The Marvels of Fatima*], San Paolo, Cinisello Balsamo (Mi.), 1997, p. 53.

the Madonna promised (on July 13th) that in October there would be a great sign that everyone would see: "In October I will say who I am, and what I want, and I will make a miracle that everyone will see in order to believe." The promise had become public knowledge, and the anti-clerical journals had greatly embellished on the promised prodigy which, according to their advice, could not have been promised, and thus would demonstrate a great deception.

The wait for the unheard-of challenge—that has no equal in history—magnified the curiosity and the interest of the people. Thus that 13th of October an enormous crowd arrived at the Cova da Iria, and many were the disbelieving, with numerous journalists ready to report and deride the anticipated grand delusion of the people and the sensational unmasking of the children. The script was already prepared: popular superstition would be ridiculed and denounced and the faith of the simple would receive a tremendous blow. The parents of the three children were completely terrified because they feared that if nothing were to happen, Lucia, Jacinta and Francisco would be lynched by the crowd, which might feel itself to have been cheated.

Only the three children were calm. And indeed what happened was the most sensational public miracle that has ever taken place— all the more so because, having taken place before the eyes of the modern media and by numerous testimonies from enemies of the Church, it had and has in the global village a planetary proof no miracle has ever had. Above all because it is a preannounced miracle, for which forces hostile to the Church had challenged the Madonna in person.

Yet the Madonna had sweetly acceded to the unheard-of challenge that had been flung at Her. Perhaps because an exceptional time was beginning for the Church and the world. Perhaps because the danger that hangs over the Church and the world was and is exceptional. And She came to Fatima precisely to ward off that immense evil. Therefore She wanted to provide an incontrovertible proof of Her presence, so that no one could say he lacked the gift of faith or that "one can believe or not believe." Here we are dealing with facts for which faith is not necessary, but only the eyes—so much so that the phenomenon was seen by all, and even Hollywood immortalized the extraordinary event in 1952 in the film *The Miracle of Our Lady of Fatima*.

Here, then, is what took place that 13th of October 1917. It suffices to refer to what happened to Avelino de Almeida of the Lisbon daily *O Século*, a secular publication. He had brought himself that October 13th to the remote locality where around 70,000 people had gathered. He had gone to denounce the day as one of the most colossal clerical deceptions ever seen. But on October 15 there was published an article—signed by Almeida the editor himself—which, even from the title, referred to something entirely different: "Extraordinary things! It was as if the sun had danced at noon in Fatima."

The journalist, who clearly remained impressed by these events of which he was an eyewitness, reconstructed those minutes on October 13 as follows: "From the road where the wagons were gathered and where stood thousands of people who did not have the courage to traverse the terrain made muddy by the rain, I saw an immense crowd turn towards the sun which appeared at its zenith cleared through the clouds. It seemed like a disc of silver, and it was possible to fix one's gaze upon it without problems. It did not burn the eyes or blind them, as if there had been an eclipse. Then there was heard a loud cry, and the people nearby began to shout: 'Miracle! Miracle! Marvel! Marvel!' Before my eyes, ecstatic people were amazed […] as the sun shook, performing strange and abrupt movements beyond all the laws of physics." The testimony of Avelino de Almeida, known to come from an enlightened layman, made a big impression and irritated the anti-clericalists around him, who attacked him harshly in other organs of the press. But he confirmed what he had seen.

Naturally, this event was referred to in other journals which had sent reporters there, such as *O Dia*. It was seen also in surrounding villages, even in places many kilometers distant, and the testimonies were disseminated in various publications. There were also such important witnesses as the poet Alfonso Lopez Vieira, who observed the phenomenon from his own home at San Pedro de Moel 40 kilometers from Fatima.[13] This sensational public prodigy seemed to many to be an unheard-of and shocking divine challenge to the century of atheism, apostasy, and anti-Christian hatred. It

---

[13] "This particular," comments Father Valinho, the nephew of Sister Lucia, "demonstrates that it does not involve a collective delusion which struck the crowd present at the apparition" (in Renzo and Roberto Allegri, *Reportage da Fatima*, Ancora, Milan, 2000, p. 167).

was that century that the pontiffs had called "satanic" in its most inhuman expressions of violence. The Miracle of the Sun had given enormous credibility to Fatima and the Message entrusted to the three children.

It was a message that was addressed to the Church and all of humanity and represented something *unique* in two thousand years of Christian history—an element from which it is necessary to conclude that there is evidently something entirely different about the epoch in which we are living, perhaps an "apocalyptic" turning point in the history of humanity. That Message, which contains a series of tremendous prophecies, grave admonitions and urgent requests, was confided by the Madonna in the apparition of July 13, 1917. It can be divided into three parts relating to successive epochs.

Everything began that 13th of July, when the Holy Virgin—for the three children had asked how long they would live—parted the earth and showed them Hell. Here is how Lucia referred to what she saw (this vision constitutes the first part of the Secret):

Saying these last words:[14]

She [Our Lady of Fatima] opened Her hands once more, as She had done during the two previous months. The rays of light seemed to penetrate the earth, and we saw as it were a sea of fire. Plunged in this fire were demons and souls in human form, like transparent burning embers, all blackened or burnished bronze, floating about in the conflagration, now raised into the air by the flames that issued from within themselves together with great clouds of smoke, now falling back on every side like sparks in huge fires, without weight or equilibrium, amid shrieks and groans of pain and despair, which horrified us and made us tremble with fear. The demons could be distinguished by their terrifying and repellent likeness to frightful and unknown animals, black and transparent. This vision lasted but an instant. How can we ever be grateful enough to our kind heavenly Mother, Who had

---

[14] The words of the Madonna that She had just pronounced were these: "Sacrifice yourselves for sinners, and say many times, especially whenever you make some sacrifice: 'O Jesus, it is for love of You, for the conversion of sinners, and in reparation for the sins committed against the Immaculate Heart of Mary.'" Quote from Fr. Louis Kondor, SVD, ed., *Fatima in Lucia's own words* (Fatima, Portugal: Postulation Centre, 1976), p. 162.

already prepared us by promising, in the first apparition, to take us to Heaven. Otherwise, I think we would have died of fear and terror.

Here begins the second part of the Secret [Author's note]:

You have seen hell where the souls of poor sinners go. To save them, God wills to establish in the world devotion to My Immaculate Heart. If what I say to you is done, many souls will be saved and there will be peace. The war is going to end; but if people do not cease offending God, a worse one will break out during the reign of Pius XI. When you see a night illumined by an unknown light, know that this is the great sign given you by God that He is about to punish the world for its crimes, by means of war, famine, and persecutions against the Church and the Holy Father.

To prevent this, I shall come to ask for the Consecration of Russia to My Immaculate Heart, and the Communion of Reparation on the First Saturdays. If My requests are heeded, Russia will be converted, and there will be peace; if not, she will spread her errors throughout the world, causing wars and persecutions against the Church. The good will be martyred, the Holy Father will have much to suffer, various nations will be annihilated. In the end, My Immaculate Heart will triumph. The Holy Father will consecrate Russia to Me, and she will be converted, and a period of peace will be granted to the world. In Portugal the dogma of the Faith will always be preserved etc. Do not tell this to anybody. Francisco, yes, you may tell him.

Where Lucia wrote "In Portugal the dogma of the faith will always be preserved etc"[15] the Madonna revealed the third part of Her Message which, however, could not be revealed with the other two. This text remained mysterious until June 2000. If the first two parts of the Secret already revealed terrifying scenes (the first eschatological, the second historical), why was the third part kept hidden for decades? This question has been repeated a thousand times. Evidently—if one may draw an inference—because it is even more serious and disturbing. But what could be more frightening

---

[15] This phrase was not reported by Lucia in her Third Memoir, but emerges instead in her Fourth. It has always been held to be an anticipation of the Third Secret, probably its beginning.

than what had been preannounced in the second part (that is, the Bolshevik Revolution, the Second World War, terrible persecutions of the Church, the annihilation of various nations)? In fact, during the course of the twentieth century there was consummated the most immense massacre of Christians ever seen in 2000 years of Church history,[16] not only by totalitarian Communism and Nazism, not only by Islamic regimes, but also by laicist Masonry.[17]

From the silence imposed on the Third Secret, it was deduced that something even worse could happen. Because of this, the so-called Third Secret of Fatima has accompanied the entire second half of the twentieth century like an apocalyptic nightmare. Its prophetic value had also been accredited by the fact that what the Madonna had predicted on July 13, 1917, in the second part of the Secret, had come true. Indeed—as it has been said (and I wish to repeat)—there had been preannounced: the Russian Revolution, the Second World War with horrendous genocides (beginning with the Shoah), the planetary expansion of Communism, the terrible persecutions of the Church, and the greatest martyrdom of Christians in the Church's two-thousand-year history.[18] Therefore—it has been asked—what could possibly be contained in the "third part" that is more disturbing? What is so unspeakable as to induce the Holy See to keep it under lock and key?

The shadows of 2000

When, in the year 2000, for the Great Jubilee and the beatification of the two shepherds of Fatima, John Paul II—overcoming great

---

[16] See Antonio Socci, *I nuovi perseguitati*, Piemme, Cassale Monferrato, 2002.

[17] Concerning this, the historian of the Lodge, Ernesto Galli, has written: "Until contrary proof, to conceive of a Mexico without God is to conduct a ruthless hunt for Catholic priests and peasant Cristeros. They were certainly not Communists but rather bourgeois of an immaculate liberal-Masonic pedigree." (*Corriere della Sera*, May 14, 2000). One could add to this the case of the Spanish Civil War, where many anti-Catholic forces coalesced to exterminate thousands of unarmed and innocent Christian martyrs.

[18] An objection has been placed: that we are dealing with an after-the-fact prophecy. But this is not a convincing objection because, as we will see, the children had already anticipated the events which had been preannounced. See Luigi Gonzaga da Fonseca, *Le meraviglie di Fatima*, op. cit., p. 311; and Solideo Paolini, *Fatima*, op. cit., p. 92. John Paul II himself said at Fatima on May 13, 2000: "The Lady of the Message seemed to read, with a special perspicacity, the signs of our time."

resistance—finally made public the by now legendary Third Secret, the text disappointed many expectations.

In the press some expressed serious doubts about the completeness of the Secret and its interpretation, and Cardinal Ratzinger himself began his theological commentary as follows: "A careful reading of the text of the so-called third 'secret' of Fatima, published here in its entirety long after the fact and by decision of the Holy Father, will probably prove disappointing or surprising after all the speculation it has stirred. No great mystery is revealed; nor is the future unveiled. We see the Church of the martyrs of the century which has just passed represented in a scene described in a language which is symbolic and not easy to decipher."[19]

There were those who asked on the spot why the Church had kept the secret for so long, permitting the spread of uncontrollable rumors and fears, if it contained "no great mystery" nor parted "the veil of the future." But there were also those who hypothesized that it did not involve the Third Secret in its completeness and that the most disturbing part still remained—and perhaps would always remain—secret. Further, this text did not resume at all the known beginning, namely, that phrase of the Madonna concerning Portugal following the "etc". So an air of suspense remained. No clarification had been given on what followed those words of the Madonna. Over time, therefore, critical voices broke through with more developed arguments, news, suppositions. Above all, in traditionalist circles there is by now a widespread conviction that the Vatican is hiding from the world a tremendous and unspeakable secret. We will see what their theses are.

For now, however, let us read the text of the Third Secret of Fatima as it was revealed by the Vatican on June 26, 2000:

> ... After the two parts which I have already explained, at the left of Our Lady and a little above, we saw an Angel with a flaming sword in his left hand; flashing, it gave out flames that looked as though they would set the world on fire; but they died out in contact with the splendour that Our Lady radiated towards him from her right hand: pointing to the earth with his right hand, the Angel cried out in a loud voice: 'Penance, Penance, Penance!'. And we

---

[19] *The Message of Fatima*, San Paolo, Cinisello Balsamo (Mi), 2000, p. 32 (hereafter *TMF*).

saw in an immense light that is God: 'something similar to how people appear in a mirror when they pass in front of it' a Bishop dressed in White 'we had the impression that it was the Holy Father'. Other Bishops, Priests, men and women Religious going up a steep mountain, at the top of which there was a big Cross of rough-hewn trunks as of a cork-tree with the bark; before reaching there the Holy Father passed through a big city half in ruins and half trembling with halting step, afflicted with pain and sorrow, he prayed for the souls of the corpses he met on his way; having reached the top of the mountain, on his knees at the foot of the big Cross he was killed by a group of soldiers who fired bullets and arrows at him, and in the same way there died one after another the other Bishops, Priests, men and women Religious, and various lay people of different ranks and positions. Beneath the two arms of the Cross there were two Angels each with a crystal aspersorium in his hand, in which they gathered up the blood of the Martyrs and with it sprinkled the souls that were making their way to God.

Tuy-3-1-1944.[20]

It goes without saying that this text was revealed in a rather singular way. On May 13, 2000 at Fatima, Cardinal Angelo Sodano,

---

[20] The most disconcerting reactions were those originating from the so-called "Catholic world." The theologian Enzo Bianchi (*Corriere della Sera*, May 15, 2000), without even having read the text, and before it was published, on the basis of the announcement by Cardinal Sodano adjudged: "A God that had given a prophecy on the persecution of Christians in this century, forgetting the Shoah, with the death of six million Jews, does not exist." Evidently, Bianchi, besides having judged the third part of the Secret without having read it, also ignored the second part, where the Shoah is clearly prefigured. And he must have little knowledge or consideration of the enormous dimensions of the slaughter of Christians in the twentieth century, which he seems to consider a little secondary fact. Quite surreal was the reaction of Oscar Luigi Scalfaro, who commented on the announcement and the anticipation by Sodano by stating that he was right never to have believed that the Third Secret "prophesied enormous woes and terrible disasters." Evidently, the vision of a city in ruins full of cadavers and an unprecedented massacre of bishops and Christians, Pope included, contained nothing worrisome for the ex-president of the Republic. Which certainty concerning the Third Secret he obtains from the fact that "the Madonna is our mother and," according to him, "a mother does not prophesy woe to her children." (*La Repubblica*, May 14, 2000) Perhaps the Mother of Christ, who appeared at Fatima—having warned humanity of this tragedy and before it (in the second part) other catastrophes such as the Second World War, the Shoah, and the Communist persecution—was not behaving as a mother? The opposite is true.

at the conclusion of the ceremony for the beatification of Francisco and Jacinta Marto, read a speech in which he announced in the name of the Pope that the so-called Third Secret would finally be published. Sodano did not read the text of the Secret, but instead anticipated his interpretation, as Andrea Tornielli noted: "Before entering into the merits of the contents he wished to establish in people's minds an interpretation which according to him was the correct one."[21] It is not clear why the interpretation would have been by the Secretary of State, who is not a doctrinal authority.

Sodano's interpretation is as follows: "The vision of Fatima regards above all the struggle of atheist systems against the Church and Christians and describes the immense suffering of witnesses to the Faith in the last century of the millennium. It is an interminable Way of the Cross guided by the Popes of the 20th century…the 'bishop dressed in white' who prays for all the faithful is the Pope. He also, hobbling toward the cross among the bodies of the martyrs [...] falls to the ground apparently dead, under a burst of gunfire."

In substance the contents of the Third Secret would be a prophetic reference to the attack on John Paul II perpetrated on May 13, 1981, precisely on the feast day of Our Lady of Fatima. After saying this, Sodano explained that the text would be published in the near future, as soon as the commentary that the Pope had entrusted to the Congregation for the Doctrine of the Faith was ready. In fact, on the following June 26, Cardinal Joseph Ratzinger held a press conference during which he read this comment by Sodano while publishing the Secret along with a series of other very important documents which have given rise to certain polemics. The material begins with an introduction to the Vatican dossier by Monsignor Tarcisio Bertone, at that time Secretary of the Congregation for the Doctrine of the Faith and today Vatican Secretary of State.

The first of his (Bertone's) writings, the "Introduction," to which we will return, shows immediately, and at first glance, some strange incongruities which have aroused some questions and doubts—first of all, because of a logical contradiction. In fact, Bertone informs us that "John Paul II requested the envelope containing the third part of the 'Secret' after the attack on May 13, 1981," reading it precisely "on July 18, 1981." And "he [John Paul II] thought immediately of

---

[21] Andrea Tornielli, *Il segreto svelato*, Gribaudi, Milan, 2000, p. 9.

18

consecrating the world to the Immaculate Heart of Mary"[22] which was realized (the first time) with the "Act of Entrustment performed in the Basilica of St. Mary Major on June 7, 1981."

Notice the dates. As Father Kramer objects: "How is it possible that the reading of the Third Secret prompted the Pope to consecrate the world to Mary on June 7, 1981 when—according to the affirmation of Archbishop Bertone—the Pope would have read the Third Secret no earlier than July 18, 1981, more than six weeks later?"[23]

As a matter of fact, it is amazing that in the official reconstruction, which was certainly very precisely reread and polished, and pondered down to the last comma, there remained such a nonsensical contradiction. How can it be explained? It is unimaginable that it involves an oversight, as if there would have been a mistake in the date, given that such a text would have been read and corrected a thousand times and that errors could not escape notice. This does not involve merely a date, but an historical/psychological transition in the life of the Pope (having just read the Third Secret, the Pope "thought immediately" of the consecration requested by the Madonna). And it is equally unimaginable that Monsignor Bertone would furnish false information, let alone information that would have been a falsehood without any motive or purpose. Therefore, we find ourselves before a first mystery, whose probable solution we will discover in the following chapters.

Moreover, it is also striking that Bertone continued to call an "entrustment" the "consecration" requested by the Madonna at Fatima. (Many theologians, as if they were Protestants, rebel against the idea of a consecration to Mary. Nevertheless, Pope John Paul II spoke of a "consecration"). Above all, Bertone continues to speak of it as an entrustment-consecration of the world, whereas the Madonna at Fatima requested instead a specific act: the consecration of Russia (requested in the second part of the Secret), and Sister Lucia always said that this involves Russia and not the world.[24] This is strange

---

[22] Msgr. Pavel Hnilica has testified: "When he left the hospital, he [the Pope] told me verbatim: 'I understand that the only solution to save the world from war, to save it from atheism, is the conversion of Russia according to the message of Fatima,'" in *30 Giorni* [*Thirty Days*], March 1990.

[23] Father Paul Kramer, *The Devil's Final Battle*, The Missionary Association, Buffalo, 2002-4, p. 180.

[24] See Solideo Paolini, *Fatima*, op. cit., p. 125. Also, during the press conference of June

and dramatic, because until now the different Popes, while wishing to do it, have not succeeded in carrying out the simple act that the Madonna requested.[25]

For decades there prevailed political and diplomatic preoccupations on the part of those who besieged the Pope with warnings that the act requested by the Virgin would be an open provocation to the Soviet Communist power. Then, to the advocates of *Ostpolitik* were added those who—making ecumenical dialogue into a dogma—have feared an apocalyptic rupture with the Russian Orthodox Church. Finally, many theologians have turned up their noses at talk of a "consecration" to the Immaculate Heart of Mary, because they do not wish to offend Protestants who do not hold Mary worthy of the dignity of a "consecration." As if this were not enough, there is also the practical impossibility of convincing all the bishops that they should unite themselves in this unanimous act by all of the Church (perhaps only an order of the Pope, in the name of obedience, could induce them to do it). The fact remains that the Popes of the 20th century have not succeeded (in certain cases while wishing it with all of their hearts, as did John Paul II, in other cases because of indifference) to grant this simple request of the Madonna expressed by Her in 1917.

The other element that has prompted discussion in the "Introduction" made by Monsignor Bertone relates precisely

---

26, 2000, and thus in the most formal setting, Monsignor Bertone, presenting all of the documents published by the Holy See pertinent to the Third Secret, declared verbatim: "In this line of citations we turn to the question of the so-called 'Consecration of the world to the Immaculate Heart of Mary', a special act of devotion requested by the Mother of Jesus on July 13, 1917" (*L'Osservatore Romano*, June 26-27, 2000). On that day Monsignor Bertone knew quite well that Sister Lucia had specified many times that the Madonna had requested the consecration of Russia and not of the world and he knew well the age-old controversy concerning these two different consecrations. Therefore why did he put between quotation marks and attribute to the Madonna that formulation which he knew quite well had been negated by Sister Lucia? Why did he not simply state the truth?

[25] Bishop Pavel Hnilica, personal friend of Pope Wojtyla and a great follower of Fatima, has explained well the particular centrality of Russia (and of the Communist question) in the design of Mary: "One day, returning from Fatima, where I had met Sister Lucia, I recounted to Mother Teresa what the visionary had told me. It was that the Madonna of Fatima, in various apparitions, both the official ones in 1917 and private apparitions to Sister Lucia in the following years, expressed an interest in Russia at least twenty-two times. 'This insistence,' I said to Mother Teresa, 'is proof of the Madonna's extraordinary solicitude for the Russian people.'" (Renzo Allegri, *Il papa di Fatima*, op. cit., p. 305.)

to the "consecration". Was it realized by Pope John Paul II in St. Peter's Square on March 25, 1984? As Bertone writes: "Sister Lucia personally confirmed that this solemn and universal act of consecration corresponded to what the Virgin wished ('Yes, it was done, as Our Lady had requested on March 25, 1984': letter of November 8, 1989). All further discussion, therefore, and all further petitions are without foundation."

This extremely important passage also contains many oddities. The mode of citing the document that would prove the approbation of Lucia is disconcerting: "Letter of November 8, 1989." Which letter? Addressed to whom? Published where? There is not even a footnote. Why? And why was a photocopy not produced, as with all the other writings of Lucia that were cited? How can this anomaly be explained? No respectable publication, book, or essay, not even a student thesis, would ever cite a document this way—much less when we are dealing with a document of capital importance, the sole testimony concerning something essential.[26] And the official Vatican publication of the Third Secret of Fatima is far more important than any book.

At any rate not even Monsignor Bertone defines the ceremony of March 25, 1984 as a "consecration of Russia." This is very significant. Remaining vague, he speaks of "a solemn and universal act of consecration." Yet it is precisely this lack of a specific object (Russia) that is one of the two reasons Sister Lucia has repeated a thousand times—since the consecration done by Pius XII—that there has not been a response to what the Virgin of Fatima requested. Further, concerning the solemn act of 1984 Sister Lucia repeated: "There was not a participation of all the bishops and there was no mention of Russia. Many bishops gave no importance to this act."[27]

The Pope, as a matter of fact, is the first to show his awareness of the problem. He probably wanted and willed that act [the 1984

---

[26] There is also the controversial interview of Sister Lucia by Carlos Evaristo on October 11, 1992 (during a meeting with non-Portuguese ecclesiastics) in which the visionary supposedly confirmed that the consecration in 1984 was that requested by the Madonna. However, it is significant that not even Monsignor Bertone cited it. This interview was at the center of a harsh polemic and a series of objections.

[27] Interview published in September 1985 by *Sol de Fatima*, periodical of the Spanish chapter of the Blue Army. For her other analogous declarations on this event see also Father Paul Kramer, *The Devil's Final Battle*, op. cit., pp. 127-129; and Solideo Paolini, *Fatima*, op. cit., p. 126.

ceremony] as an approach—a spiritual preparation for the more quarrelsome—toward the true consecration he hoped to be able to do in the future. A close collaborator of the Holy Father, Bishop Paul Josef Cordes, was vice president of the Pontifical Council for the Laity when he made this revelation in 1990: "It was 1984, and during a private lunch with the Pope I spoke of the consecration he had done. I recall that he thought, some time before, of mentioning Russia in the prayer of benediction. But at the suggestion of his collaborators he had abandoned the idea. He could not risk such a direct provocation of Soviet leaders. I also recall how this renunciation of the public benediction of Russia weighed heavily on him."[28]

At any rate John Paul II himself, perfectly aware that there had still not been a "consecration of Russia" that day, wanted to say so in the very midst of his solemn prayer. He departed in fact from the written text and added these words off-the-cuff: "Mother of the Church [...] illuminate especially those peoples of whom You are awaiting our consecration and our entrustment."

This does not mean that the consecration of 1984 was not accepted by Heaven and has not obtained its beneficial effects (as happened with Pius XII, as we will see) but the Pope knew from the first—and said so—that it was not the consecration requested at Fatima, and that it would not be able to have the effects promised there by the Madonna (in particular the conversion of Russia). The Pope's words were reported as such, the day after, by *L'Osservatore Romano* (March 26, 2004) and Bertone himself cited them, invoking that speech. It is therefore evident that if the Madonna is still awaiting the consecration that means it has not been done. The Pope knew this and declared it from the first. Indeed, even after the act of 1984 Sister Lucia, as she had done before, made it known that there had not been the "consecration of Russia" the Madonna was awaiting.

Why then, in the text by Monsignor Bertone, does Sister Lucia in the year 2000 seem to say the contrary? And why would she be saying this by way of a letter that the visionary supposedly wrote five years after the consecration, in 1989—and not by hand but with a computer that, as far as we know, Sister Lucia did not know how to use. According to objections that undermine the credibility of the

---

[28] In *30 Giorni*, March 1990.

letter, there is also a major error that Sister Lucia absolutely would never have made. There one reads—according to Father Kramer—that Paul VI supposedly consecrated the world to the Immaculate Heart of Mary during his pilgrimage to Fatima.[29]

Can one base such an important pronouncement by Sister Lucia on a letter so much in "dispute", neither published nor reproduced, whose addressee and current location are not mentioned, a letter that denies all the preceding declarations of the visionary? Can one base oneself solely on a letter not written in the hand of Sister Lucia and whose authenticity has never been personally confirmed by the sister? To put an end to the polemics and objections and to be able to say truly that "all discussion and all further petitions are without foundation," Monsignor Bertone had an extremely efficacious and (for him) extremely easy way to proceed that should have banished all doubts—a unique, memorable, and historic occasion: to question Lucia.

A very strange encounter

It is a brilliant spring morning, April 27, 2000, when the high Piedmontese prelate crosses the silent and sweet-smelling threshold of the Carmel of Coimbra. He carries with him in a dark briefcase a letter from the Pope for Sister Lucia, entrusted to him by the Secretary of State, in which the Holy Father explains the Archbishop's mission. Monsignor Bertone is welcomed with great cordiality and kindness by the sisters, made to feel at home; a few words, a coffee, and then, with the aid of a walker, Sister Lucia arrives. Although very old, she appears to the prelate "lucid and serene" (his words).

Monsignor Bertone has before him the living witness of Fatima, she who has written with her pen the entire Secret of Mary. He could undo all of the doubts, clarify all of the disquieting questions. Sister Lucia can explain everything. The prelate could (if he wished) ask her directly, with extreme ease, if that letter from 1989 was written by her and if the act of 1984 is "the consecration of Russia" requested by the Madonna at Fatima. He could (and should) ask her to deny formally the many declarations attributed to her in which she had said that the consecration had not been done. And, above

---

[29] Father Paul Kramer, *The Devil's Final Battle*, op. cit., pp. 104, 125.

all, he could and should have asked Sister Lucia directly if she had ever written what follows the fundamental phrase of the Virgin "In Portugal the dogma of the faith will always be preserved," or, in other words, whether there were any subsequent words of the Madonna in the Fourth Memoir where the "etc" is substituted.

Monsignor Bertone is there for this. But surprisingly the prelate does not pose any of these questions. Not even one. Nothing at all. Or at least nothing that appears in the account (not signed and verified by Bertone himself) that is contained in the "Fatima dossier" of the Vatican. Now, it can be asked: Why does the Archbishop, two months later, in the "Introduction" of this dossier, cite as proof—the only proof, moreover—a purported letter from Lucia, not signed, of disputed authenticity, whose addressee is unknown and that contradicts all of the other declarations of the visionary, when he had at his disposal Sister Lucia herself and could have requested of her directly, first hand, a formal declaration, perhaps even recorded by video camera, exhibiting it to all objectors and to the world?

No explanation is forthcoming. To tell the truth, the anonymous account of this meeting, which is appended to the Vatican dossier but is not countersigned by Sister Lucia—the umpteenth oddity—cites very few phrases attributed between quotation marks to the visionary. From an interview that "lasted many hours," as it was then described by Cardinal Bertone,[30] the account attributes to Sister Lucia things that could be expressed in a maximum of three minutes. And the rest? What was said to the sister and by the sister in the remaining "many hours"? No record has ever been produced.[31] It is known only, from Bertone himself, that that meeting "was important, so that the Pope could make the decision to publish the

---

[30] In Aura Miguel, *Totus Tuus: il segreto di Fatima nel pontificato di Giovanni Paolo II*, Itaca, Castel Bolognese, 2003, p. 147.

[31] To speak the truth, in August of 2006, that is, six years after the publication of the Vatican dossier and a year-and-a-half after the death of Sister Lucia, on the eve of the elevation of Bertone to Secretary of State, the prelate hinted for the first time during an interview at the existence of a record of which there had never before been any mention. A journalist had asked: "Are there catastrophic revelations concerning the future (in the secret of Fatima) or has everything been revealed and accomplished?" The Cardinal responded: "I have met Sister Lucia many times, and I have had in my hands the minutes that she signed on this subject. There are no further revelations on Fatima, and the so-called Third Secret has been entirely revealed." (*Il Giornale*, August 29, 2006). It is not clear what minutes Cardinal Bertone is referring to, nor is it clear why they have never been published.

secret."[32] This means that it was as decisive as a "verdict."[33] And it is necessary to recognize that this too is rather important information.

Why in fact was there a need for such a long meeting in order to decide on the publication of the text of the vision? What type of "verdict"—that is, of safe conduct or of reassurance—did Sister Lucia have to render? It was in 1944 that she wrote the third part of the Secret, requesting, according to the indications of the Virgin, that it be revealed in 1960. Since that date she had continued to request its disclosure. Therefore, what more was required of her? Why would they impose upon her—a nonagenarian—a long meeting of "many hours"?

Furthermore, the meeting must have been extremely taxing if one considers the length and the fact that it served to help the Vatican to decide whether to publish or not publish the Secret. Was there perhaps a risk that she was not in agreement with "that" type of revelation of the Secret? Was it desired that she give her approval to a partial revelation that would bury (forever?) the part with the words of the Madonna, and would interpret the vision as a reference to the past? From that meeting, on the other hand, might also have emanated the Vatican's decision to give the Sister permission to publish her book of meditations, *The Appeals of the Message of Fatima*, which contains a phrase rightly emphasized by Marco Tosatti because it provokes a great deal of reflection: "I leave entirely to Holy Church the liberty to interpret the sense of the Message because this pertains to her competence; therefore, I humbly and happily submit myself to what she will say or what she wishes to correct, modify, or declare."[34]

Is it perhaps this "obedience" that was requested of the Sister during that meeting of April 2000? Are we dealing with an amenability to silence or "correction"? At the margins of these questions, there is an extremely "strange" bit of news noted by Paolini. On June 26, 2000, the day the publication of the Secret was effected with a sensational internationally-televised press

---

[32] Aura Miguel, *Totus Tuus*, op. cit., p. 147.

[33] The Portuguese journalist, Aura Miguel, in his book *Totus Tuus*, that begins with an introduction by none other than Monsignor Bertone, writes that the Pope "took the definitive decision (to publish the secret) only when Monsignor Bertone returned from the Carmel of Coimbra with the "verdict of Sister Lucia" (p. 147).

[34] Sister Lucia, *The Appeals of the Message of Fatima*, Libreria Editrice Vaticana, Citta del Vaticano, 2001, p. 22.

conference at the Vatican featuring the Prefect of the Holy Office, this headline appeared in *Corriere della Sera*: "Sister Lucia will not watch the revelation of the Secret of Fatima on TV." Even more stupefying than the headline is the explanation given in the body of the article by Sister Maria do Carmo, custodian of the convent: "We watch TV, but only on exceptional occasions. The press conference on the Secret of Fatima is not such an occasion."

And what would be "exceptional cases" for the Carmelites of Coimbra? Perhaps the finals of the world soccer championship? It is difficult to respond. We turn therefore to the account of the meeting of April 27, 2000, which was conducted in order for the Vatican to decide whether to reveal the Secret. Among the very few phrases attributed to Sister Lucia, one in particular attracts attention for the umpteenth logical contradiction it contains. Let us read that entire passage:

> Since Sister Lucia, before consigning the sealed envelope containing the third part of the "secret" to the then Bishop of Leiria-Fatima, had written on the external envelope that it could be opened only after 1960[35] by the Patriarch of Lisbon or by the Bishop of Leiria, His Excellency Mons. Bertone asked her: "Why only after 1960? Was it Our Lady who fixed that date?" Sister Lucia replied: "It was not Our Lady. I fixed the date because I had the intuition that before 1960 it would not be understood, but that only later would it be understood. Now one can understand better."

These few lines from the "minutes" arouse a tempest of questions. First question: If the Secret was destined for the Patriarch of Lisbon and the Bishop of Leiria, as is said officially here, why did the Vatican decide to keep it to itself? What reason drove such a decision?

---

[35] In this official document of the Holy See it is thus explicitly attested that Sister Lucia wrote on the Third Secret envelope the date by which it should be disclosed. Therefore, it seems surprising that one of the people who had a hand in the entire Fatima affair at the highest level, the Secretary of John XXIII, Monsignor Loris Capovilla, was able to declare in a book that Pope John knew nothing of that date: "The fact is that no one spoke to him of it, no one hinted at that deadline." (Mario Roncalli, *Giovanni XXIII nel recordo del segretario Mons. Loris F. Capovilla* [*John XXIII as Remembered by Secretary Monsignor Loris F. Capovilla*] (San Paolo: Alba, 1994), p. 116. Pope Roncalli read the Third Secret on August 17, 1959 and, if what the Vatican document affirms is true, he inevitably also read what Sister Lucia had written on the envelope. Yet again a resounding and surprising discordance on such delicate subjects.

In an official and conclusive Vatican dossier on the Third Secret, one would expect a definitive explanation. The "Introduction" by Monsignor Bertone says that the sealed envelope, "originally in the custody of the Bishop of Leiria" (to whom it was addressed and who had given Lucia the order to write it), "was delivered on April 4, 1957 to the Secret Archive of the Holy Office." The formulation is ambiguous because it leads one to think that the Bishop of Fatima wished to deliver everything to the Vatican, when instead it was the Holy Office, beginning in 1957, that ordered all of the writings of Lucia to be sent to Rome, and "also the Secret, above all the Secret."[36]

What was the reason? Bertone says: "To better safeguard the 'secret.'"[37] An incredible response. Was the custody by the Bishop not secure? It would have been an insult to the Bishop—especially in 1944, the Vatican itself having said that it was not opportune to send everything to Rome at that time. Given that for well nigh 13 years the Secret had been kept at Leiria, why would that no longer have been proper on the vigil of the date the Madonna had indicated for its publication? The answer is simple: Because the Bishop of Leiria, Monsignor da Silva and the Patriarch of Lisbon, Cardinal Cerejeira, following the indication given by the Madonna through Sister Lucia, had already announced that they would disclose the Third Secret in 1960. It was to prevent this that the Holy Office intervened. Because in the Vatican it was decided to "protect the Secret"—that is, to "bury it"—in a safe.

It is an absolutely unheard of procedure, all the more so given that the first and second parts of the Secret were not safeguarded in the Vatican, and were published in a manner rather different from the text of 2000, without an official act of the Holy See.

The first two parts of the Secret, unfortunately in an incredibly "retouched" form that favored the USSR for political and war-related reasons,[38] were published in April 1942 in the fourth edition

---

[36] An accurate reconstruction of the affair is found in FM, v. III, pp. 479-484.

[37] *TMF*, op. cit., p. 4.

[38] This fact agitated the chancelleries and secret services of the belligerent countries. The pact of alliance between Nazi Germany and the USSR had just been broken. The latter had become an alliance of Western nations for which the publication of the words of the Madonna concerning Russia acquired an explosive significance. The historian Father Robert Graham, an American Jesuit, reconstructs what happened as follows: "In the part 'if My requests are granted, Russia will convert and peace will be had. Otherwise, she will propagate her errors throughout the world,' for the word 'she' was

(printed in Vatican City) of the *Marvels of Fatima* by Padre da Fonseca, a Portuguese Jesuit of the Pontifical Biblical Institute in Rome. This work contained ample selections from the four Memoirs of Lucia.[39] In May 1942 Don Luigi Moresco published *The Madonna of Fatima* with the same "retouched" version of the first two parts of the Secret. Finally, on October 13 of the same year the complete and correct text of the Memoirs was published in Portugal in the third edition of the book *Jacinta*, with the approval of José Galamba de Oliveira and the semi-official approval of the Portuguese Church,[40] but always in a non-official manner, so to speak.

If these two parts were published while being so "explosive," and moreover under incandescent historical circumstances (there was a full-blown world war in progress and the revelation concerning Russia had arrived right after Russia had joined the Allied front),[41] why not the same for the "third part," as to which the Vatican kept the text and the secret to itself? What unmentionable contents could it have had? It is possible that it involves only the text of the Secret revealed in 2000? That text would not seem to justify such alarm, nor such a dramatic intervention on the part of the Holy See.

Is one referred, therefore, to another text? Is that where the "dynamite" is? Evidently, yes. Cardinal Ottaviani, who was head of the Holy Office, stated explicitly on February 11, 1967 why that decision had been made ten years earlier: "To prevent something of so delicate a nature, not destined for public consumption (sic!) from falling, for any reason whatsoever, even accidentally into

---

substituted the vague expression 'impious propaganda' which could also refer to Nazi Germany." Father Graham further explains that "instead of the request for 'the consecration of Russia' one reads 'consecration of the world.' Inadmissible naiveté, if naiveté… is what it involves. I agree that there was a war, but this does not justify changing the words of the Madonna." (In Stefano Impaci, "And the Virgin promised…", *30 Giorni*, March 1990).

[39] Fonseca observes that "the Secret was made public during the war when prudence and 'censorship' required the avoidance of whatever could wound the sensibilities of the two parties in conflict" (*Le meraviglie di Fatima*, op. cit., p. 311).

[40] Galamba's book had a preface by Cardinal Cerejeira and a prologue by Monsignor da Silva.

[41] In FM, v. II, pp. 753-755, a profound significance is accorded to this temporal coincidence, which allows one to understand that the "inspiration" felt by Sister Lucia to reveal the words of the Madonna concerning Russia precisely in the summer of 1941 must have been to warn against an alliance with Russia.

alien hands."[42] But if the Madonna had appeared at Fatima so sensationally to give precisely a message "so delicate" and urgent for humanity and for the Church, how can we Catholics "silence Her" and censor Her, holding that Her message was "not destined for public consumption"? Is it not an act of supreme pride to pretend ourselves more prudent than She who is venerated as "Virgin Most Prudent," and wiser than She who is described as "Seat of Wisdom"? How is it possible that political considerations or human fear have prevailed over the obedience due to Heaven?

Second question: Sister Lucia had always said, from time immemorial, that it was the Madonna who indicated to her the date of 1960 for publication of the Secret, and this involves clear and certain declarations of the visionary.[43] Why, then, would the visionary suddenly put the lie to her own prior statements in 2000, telling Monsignor Bertone that the date was her own idea? And why would the prelate not have asked the reason for the preceding declarations? Why did he not object to her having uttered for years a lie attributing to the Madonna an idea that was really her own, and in the bargain deceiving the Holy See (because she had asked them to listen to the Madonna)? If Monsignor Bertone, always intelligent and attentive, did not ask her for these clarifications, there must have been a reason. Moreover, that the choice of 1960 as the term to reveal the Secret

---

[42] FM, v. III, p. 483. The Vatican's decision could have arisen from a trip to Fatima in May 1955 by Cardinal Ottaviani himself, who was rather unsympathetic to so-called "private revelations." He was involved in a long meeting with Sister Lucia where he must have come to understand well the nature of the Third Secret, returning to the Vatican with the conviction that it was necessary to avoid its publication at any cost.

[43] The text most cited and never refuted was published in 1952. It is that of Canon Barthas, who on the 17th and 18th of October, 1946, was able to speak with the visionary concerning the Third Secret. In the published account one reads: "When will the third part of the Secret be revealed? Already in 1946 Lucia and the Bishop of Leiria answered me concordantly without hesitation or comment: 'In 1960.' And when, in my audacity, I finally asked why it was necessary to wait until then, I obtained the same answer from one as from the other: 'Because the Blessed Virgin wishes it so.'" Casimir Barthas, *Fatima. Merveille du XXe siècle* [*Fatima. Marvel of the 20th Century*] (Fatima editions: Toulouse, 1952), p. 83; cited in Laurent Morlier, *Il Terzo Segreto di Fatima...*, op. cit., p. 48). Later, in 1960, the same author will confirm: "Lucia affirms that Our Lady wishes that it be published after the beginning of 1960" (*Dalla Grotta alla Quercia-verde*, 1960, pp. 108-109, op. cit.; cited in Morlier, p. 49). Also, Father Valinho, the nephew of Sister Lucia, affirms: "The report of the secret was accompanied by a letter in which Sister Lucia said that the Madonna had said that the Secret could be revealed only after 1960" (in Renzo and Roberto Allegri, *Reportage da Fatima*, op. cit., p. 127).

was from the Madonna and not from Lucia is also certain for a logical reason: that on July 13, 1917 the Virgin in person forbade disclosure of the third part of the Secret—"Tell this to no one"— and Lucia would never have dared to establish a date on which it could be made known to everyone. Only the Madonna, who had imposed secrecy on the message, could have done it. In fact, the first two parts of the Secret were revealed by Sister Lucia in 1941 only when and "because I have (had) permission from Heaven."[44] (That is, she had been given permission in one of the apparitions of the Madonna after 1917.)

Furthermore, how could a cloistered Portuguese nun who at the time of the apparitions did not even know how to read or write, and who thought that "Russia" (named by the Madonna) was an unknown woman, be able to trace political-ecclesiastical scenarios so as to foresee that in 1960 what is depicted in the vision would be "more clear"?

Third question: Sister Lucia had requested that the Secret be revealed in 1960 or after her death if that should come first. Why did Monsignor Bertone, while questioning the visionary, overlook this subordinate condition and not ask her to explain it?

Fourth Question: In a Vatican dossier in which Lucia is asked who had decided upon the date of 1960, one would equally expect from the Vatican an explanation of why, concerning that date, it was decided not to listen to the request of the visionary (or of the Madonna). Why instead is no explanation found?

Fifth Question: Why would Sister Lucia say that in 1960 the Third Secret would be clearer if it is a text that prophesies an assassination attempt that will happen in 1981?[44a] If the text of the Third Secret is the one revealed in 2000 and there is not another part that remains secret, what is there in this text that would be more clear in 1960? In the description of the vision published in 2000 there is nothing that would become more comprehensible in 1960. Why, then, did

---

[44] *Memorie di Suor Lucia* [*Memoirs of Sister Lucia*] (Secretariado dos pastorinhos: Fatima, 2000), p. 104.

[44a] Editorial Note: Following his interrogation of Sister Lucia in 1955, Cardinal Ottaviani revealed that when he asked her why 1960, she replied: "Because then it will seem clearer (*mais claro*)." In answer to the same question from Canon Barthas in 1946, Lucia replied simply: "Because Our Lady wishes it so." *See Documentation Catholique*, March 19, 1967, Col. 542; cited in FM, v. III, p. 725, and Canon Barthas, *Fatima, Merveille du XXe siècle* (Fatima-Editions, 1952), p. 83.

Cardinal Bertone not ask the visionary to explain herself? Why did he let drop a question of such great importance at the very moment he had been sent to Coimbra precisely for an interpretation of the Third Secret?

The mystery definitely thickens. But there are other, even more serious questions.

2. The life of this Pope is in danger

Wolves (more or less gray)

Joseph Ratzinger could have been killed very easily that day, without obstacles or risks. It was October 16, 2004, only 180 days before his election as Pope. It dawned on me immediately, as I passed the parish church of Santa Giustina Belluno, catching sight of a little road that climbs up the slopes of the mountain, crossing over a beautiful green meadow. Along the sides were some splendid chestnut trees, blazing with autumn and the rays of the setting sun. Up there at that cabin in the mountains, the house of the Pope Luciani Center of the Diocese of Belluno, I had to meet with Cardinal Ratzinger. (Later he and I would present a book together, *Faith, Truth, and Tolerance*, at a press conference).

Suddenly, while ascending slowly in the car, I rounded a curve and caught sight of the figure of a slight and solitary man, a priest: it is him, at the side of the field, twenty meters ahead and walking. All alone. (I noticed that, following some meters behind, was the trusty Don George.) He proceeded with slow step, Basque beret on his head, looking at the mountains, happy, breathing the fresh air. He seemed almost like a mountain parish priest.

His solitude impressed me. And also his serenity. I smiled, we waved at each other. But above all it made me wince—a thought went through me like lightning—the idea of his vulnerability. That totally defenseless man on that path was he upon whom, in those sorrowful and prolonged months of papal disability, rested the reality of the universal Catholic Church.

It was a dismaying moment. In times of spreading terrorism (and not just Islamic terrorism), in times in which almost unknown

33

undersecretaries travel with an escort, the most important man for universal Christianity (after the Pope), was here alone, on an isolated little road, exposed to any possible danger or aggression from any group with evil intentions. A fragile man, meek, and completely defenseless. It was precisely that man who would become in a few days the Vicar of Christ.

Cardinal Ratzinger had habitually lived and traveled without an escort, without any "human" defense. In fact even when I met him in St. Peter's Square, years ago, he was alone and without an escort. (I knew then that every morning, for years, anyone could meet him traversing the Bernini colonnade, walking toward the Congregation for the Doctrine of the Faith where he worked.)

Certainly Someone had visibly protected him during those years in order to entrust him one day to His barque. And it was equally evident that Cardinal Ratzinger—while knowing quite well his exposure and the enormous amount of risk he incurred—serenely entrusted himself to a "different" protection. This singular confidence is even more impressive today, in the face of the mission to which (surprisingly) he has been called. (It has been noted, in fact, that he cherished the idea of turning old in his study and of the private life.) It is clear that this man knows well the threat, ever greater, that now hangs over his head. He hinted of it with few but unequivocally dramatic words at the end of the installation Mass on April 24, 2005: "Pray for me, that I may not flee in fear of the wolves."

To which "wolves" was he referring? Gray wolves have never been seen in action in the Vatican. Or was he thinking of wolves of another color? At any rate wolves there are in ambush, considering the solemn drama of a homily at the beginning of the pontificate in which he inserted that prayer. Of what is the Pope thinking and what does he fear?[45] What terrifying threats does he feel hanging over him that he would reveal his fears publicly, in a celebration before the world—he, a man always so measured and reserved? And is it not strange that no one has noticed a phrase so dramatic? The rest of the homily—to reread it attentively—is entirely a meditation on the martyrdom to which the Vicar of Christ is called. No one

---

[45] In the Gospel, Jesus puts us on our guard against false prophets who are like wolves dressed as sheep: "Beware of false prophets who come to you in garments of sheep but inside are rapacious wolves." (Mt. 7:15).

seems to have noticed that during that solemn Mass of installation Benedict XVI arrived finally at the point of indicating precisely martyrdom as his own "pastoral program."

Martyrdom: A program?

He began by repeating twice that "we are not alone in life nor in death," then he spoke of his calling.[46] Finally he pronounced these words which no one seemed to have caught as a sign of awareness of what can be expected and as a declaration of readiness for martyrdom. Yet they cause us to reflect seriously:

> Dear friends! At this moment there is no need for me to present a program of governance.... My real program of governance is not to do my own will, not to pursue my own ideas, but to listen, together with the whole Church, to the word and the will of the Lord, to be guided by Him, so that He Himself will lead the Church at this hour of our history. Instead of putting forward a program, I should simply like to comment on the two liturgical symbols which represent the inauguration of the Petrine ministry....

> The symbolism of the pallium is even more concrete: the lamb's wool is meant to represent the lost, sick or weak sheep which the shepherd places on his shoulders and carries to the waters of life.... He is the good shepherd who lays down his life for the sheep. What the pallium indicates first and foremost is that we are all carried by Christ. But at the same time it invites us to carry one another. Hence the pallium becomes a symbol of the shepherd's mission...

> When the shepherd of all humanity, the living God, Himself became a lamb, He stood on the side of the lambs, with those who are downtrodden and killed.

---

[46] "And now, in this moment, I the weak servant of God must assume this inconceivable task, that really exceeds all human capacity. How can I do this? How will I be able to do it? You all, dear friends, have just invoked the entire litany of the saints, represented by some of the great names in the history of God with men. In this way, in me also is revived this awareness: I am not alone. I do not have to carry by myself what in reality can never be carried alone. All the saints of God are there to protect me, sustain me and carry me." (See www.vatican.va)

This is how He reveals Himself to be the true shepherd: "I am the Good Shepherd ... I lay down My life for the sheep," Jesus says of Himself (Jn. 10:14ff). It is not power, but love that redeems us.... God, Who became a lamb, tells us that the world is saved by the Crucified One, not by those who crucified Him. The world is redeemed by the patience of God. It is destroyed by the impatience of man. One of the basic characteristics of a shepherd must be to love the people entrusted to him, even as he loves Christ whom he serves. "Feed My sheep," says Christ to Peter, and now, at this moment, He says it to me as well. Feeding means loving, and loving also means being ready to suffer. Loving means giving the sheep what is truly good, the nourishment of God's truth, of God's word, the nourishment of His presence, which He gives us in the Blessed Sacrament. My dear friends -- at this moment I can only say: Pray for me, that I may learn to love the Lord more and more. Pray for me, that I may learn to love His flock more and more -- in other words, you, the holy Church, each one of you and all of you together. Pray for me, that I may not flee for fear of the wolves....

Wolves and fear. Also, the day after his election, during the concelebration in the Sistine Chapel, he had begun by confessing fear before that which he expected. But this does not involve only understandable dismay before an immense task, but rather a concrete and particular fear of "wolves" before which the alternative was dry and dramatic: one can only "flee" or face martyrdom.[47] From its beginning, in sum, Benedict seems to have given to his pontificate the horizon of martyrdom. For the entire first year, moreover, he has done nothing but return to this theme. The Vaticanist for *Espresso*, Sandro Magister, commented thus on the consistory of March 24, 2006: "The first consistory of Benedict XVI with the old and new Cardinals will be remembered for its extremely marked crimson color. The Pope has given a strong importance to the significance of this color in the cardinalate attire. He has likened it to the red of the

---

[47] Significantly, the Pope concluded that homily by reaffirming his engagement to fidelity to Christ, and entrusting this intention to the Virgin: "To sustain this promise I invoke the maternal intercession of Mary most Holy, in whose hands I place the present and the future of my person and of the Church." A request for patronage not at all routine or devotional, but rather significant in this context and in view of Fatima.

blood that pours from Christ on the Cross."[48]

Here are the Pope's words: "It will signify for you a more intense participation in the mystery of the Cross and in the sharing of the sufferings of Christ. And we are all really witnesses of the sufferings of today, in the world and also in the Church." Two days later, on March 26, at the Angelus the Pope returned to the significance of the crimson when speaking of the Christian people: "The sacrifice of life is a distinctive characteristic of cardinals, as attested by their oath and by the symbolism of the crimson, which has the color of blood."

Then the Pope remembered the martyrs and persecuted Christians in every part of the world: "By a providential coincidence, the consistory takes place on the 24th day of March, on which are commemorated the missionaries who in the past year have fallen on the frontiers of evangelization and in the service of man in different parts of the earth. The consistory has been, therefore, an occasion for feeling ourselves nearer than ever to all of those Christians who suffer persecution because of the Faith… my thoughts turn, in a particular way, to those communities which live in countries where religious liberty is lacking… and which are teeming with conditions of great difficulty and suffering."

On May 7, 2006, during the Mass of ordination of fifteen deacons for the diocese of Rome, he returned to the theme of the "Good Shepherd," harshly attacked by "careerism" in the Church, the "attempt to procure for oneself a position through the Church: to serve oneself, not to serve others," while instead "the only legitimate assent toward the ministry of the pastor," the Pope underlined, "is the Cross… the pastor gives his life for the sheep… To give life, not to take it. It is in just this way that we can experience liberty."

Benedict XVI's decision to limit the issuance of documents during his pontificate and to concentrate his teaching in normal pastoral interventions, evidently written with his own pen, gives a special significance to the content of these interventions and messages. Throughout the series of insistent reminders of martyrdom there is something which recalls the words of John Paul II at Fulda in November 1980, six months before the attack by Ağca: "We must prepare ourselves to suffer great trials at a time not long from now, which will require from us a willingness to part with our lives…"

---

[48] Sandro Magister, www.espressonline.it, March 28, 2006.

Benedict XVI has not explained the reason for his continuous and grave meditation on martyrdom, on the necessity of being ready to give one's life, but objectively—rereading these interventions from the first year of his pontificate—one cannot avoid remembering the text of the most sensational public prophecy in the two thousand years of Christianity, officially recognized by the Church: the so-called Third Secret of Fatima, which contains precisely the vision of a Pope who "at the foot of the big Cross he was killed by a group of soldiers… and in the same way there died one after another, Bishops, Priests, men and women Religious, and various laypeople of different ranks and positions."

It is evident that the apocalyptic event prophesied here with such solemnity by the Madonna of Fatima has a gravity absolutely unique in the history of the world and of the Church, where there are not lacking persecutions, immense massacres, and even attempts on the life of the Pope. But who is, therefore, the Pope of the Third Secret?

A prophecy already realized?

Contrary to what is believed and what the mass media have repeated, the authority of the Church has never officially identified John Paul II as the Pope killed in the Secret, nor the prophetic vision of that assassination as the failed attempt in St. Peter's Square on May 13, 1981.[49]

It is necessary to recognize, however, that this interpretation, by now accredited as the official one (Renzo Allegri has built it up in his book *The Pope of Fatima*) had its "input" from the words of Cardinal Sodano, Secretary of State of the Holy See, when, on May 13, 2000, he announced that within a few days there would be published the "legendary" text of the Third Secret.[50]

---

[49] To be considered "mythological" is the rumor, published in many parts, of a prophecy of the assassination attempt made by Padre Pio in the famous meeting in 1948 with the young Wojtyla. The Pope himself, approached three times on the subject, has always tersely denied it entirely. (Andrea Tornielli reconstructs the affair quite well in *Il segreto di Padre Pio e Karol Wojtyla* [*The Secret of Padre Pio and Karol Wojtyla*] (Piemme: Casale Monferrato, 2006), pp. 57-74.

[50] The only ecclesiastic to have explained it explicity was Monsignor Rino Fisichella in the introduction to *TMF*, where he writes as follows: "According to the words of Cardinal Sodano, which also find the agreement of Sister Lucia, the third part of the message

If the "preventative interpretation" of Sodano was indubitably intended to suggest precisely this reading (with a series of surprising twists of the text), it has to be said that the prelate has never precisely formulated such an identification, and that he has proposed his interpretation with a shower of "[it] seems" that render it simply a respectable hypothesis, not binding on anyone.[51] It is enough to say that after Sodano's announcement *L'Osservatore Romano* also seemed to back away from the question. Indeed, the title of the full-page article was: "The Church has placed on the lamp stand the shepherds Francisco and Jacinta, two flames which God has lit to illuminate humanity in its hours of darkness and fear." The *Corriere della Sera* noted that an event was brewing and the day after published this headline: "*Osservatore Romano*: No headline concerning the prophecy."

Here are the precise words of Sodano:

> The vision of Fatima concerns above all the war waged by atheist systems against the Church and Christians, and it describes the immense suffering endured by the witnesses to the faith in the last century of the second millennium. It is an interminable Way of the Cross led by the Popes of the twentieth century.

> According to the interpretation of the "little shepherds," which was also recently confirmed by Sister Lucia, the "bishop clothed in white" who prays for all the faithful is the Pope. As he makes his way with great effort towards the Cross amid the corpses of those who were martyred (bishops, priests, men and women religious and many lay persons), he too falls to the ground, as if dead, under a burst of gunfire.

> After the assassination attempt of May 13, 1981, it

---

of Fatima was fulfilled on May 13, 1981, when John Paul II was gravely wounded." As we will see, Cardinal Sodano has never officially made this identification, much less has this thesis ever had the consent of Sister Lucia. I add, however, that Fisichella's introduction is quite interesting, and also contains an affirmation which suggests the contrary: "Yet it is permitted to us to think that this type of prophecy cannot be considered fulfilled [...]. We can regard it therefore as opening to the future and illuminating it [...]. The Fatima prophecy, therefore, remains open." (*TMF*, Paoline edn., pp. 8-9).

[51] Speaking of the Madonna's protection of John Paul II, he says: "It is a protection that *seems* also to touch upon the so-called third part of the 'Secret' of Fatima." And then: "The events to which the third part of the 'secret' of Fatima refers now *seem* to belong to the past." (The italics are mine.)

appeared evident to His Holiness that it was "a motherly hand which guided the bullet's path," enabling the "dying Pope" to halt "at the threshold of death." On the occasion of a visit to Rome by the then Bishop of Leiria-Fatima, the Pope decided to give him the bullet which had remained in the jeep after the assassination attempt, so that it might be kept in the Shrine. At the behest of the bishop, the bullet was later set in the crown of the statue of Our Lady of Fatima.

This text is at the origin of widespread interpretations today. What immediately presents itself is a macroscopic twisting: The Pope in the vision, according to Cardinal Sodano, "falls to the earth as if dead." Yet, with all due respect, it has to be recognized that the Third Secret says something quite different: The Pope in the prophetic vision "is killed," and this is vastly different from being wounded. At any rate, the rest of the scene of the vision of Fatima, which seems to evoke a situation of war and destruction, does not have any point of contact with the scene in St. Peter's Square on May 13, 1981—neither the protagonists nor the "soldiers," let alone the "arrows." The attack in 1981 stands with respect to that vision exactly as the other attempts suffered by popes—for example, the attack on Paul VI on November 27, 1970, when he was stabbed in the abdomen by a lunatic in Manila.[52]

Given this, we can see other critical points in the "preventative interpretation" by Sodano. The "vision of Fatima" in its essence does not regard "above all" the "struggle of atheist systems against the Church," but the eternal salvation of souls (related to the vision of Hell and the recommendations of the Virgin for prayer and penance to avoid it).[53] Secondarily, it also regards—but as an historical consequence of disobedience to this exhortation—the struggle of atheist systems against the Church.

Sodano interprets that ascent to the Cross as the way of the cross of the "Popes of the twentieth century," and the tremendous persecutions and sufferings of Christians in that century. This

---

[52] Pius XII was also subjected to plans for deportation by the Nazis (*see* Giorgio Angelozzi Gariboldi, *Pio XII, Hitler e Mussolini*, Mursia: 1988, pp. 193 ff.) and plans for assassination.

[53] "The essential point of the 'secret' is not war; neither was its aim to satisfy our curiosity, but rather the eternal welfare of souls." (Luigi Gonzaga da Fonseca, *Le meraviglie di Fatima*, op. cit., p. 45.)

interpretation seems plausible, but we find it already contained in the prophecy of the Madonna that constitutes the second part of the Secret of Fatima, which has already been known for decades. The matter involves, therefore, understanding whether the vision pertaining to the Third Secret is only a repetition, in images, of the Second Secret and can now be referred to the past, or if instead it concerns distinct facts (as Sister Lucia has written officially) that must still happen.

It is clear that Sodano embraces the first hypothesis, holding that the vision indicates the martyrdom of Catholics of the 20th century (above all in the Communist revolution of 1917) culminating with the attack on the Pope in 1981, and that there would not be any epilogue. However, to sustain this thesis it is necessary to force the text of the Secret, turning on its head the temporal sequence of events. In fact, Sodano speaks of a Pope who prays for the "souls of the corpses of the martyred," whereas the text of the Secret speaks only of "bodies" in the city in ruins. Sodano then makes a second twist, identifying these "bodies" with "bishops, priests, religious, nuns, and numerous members of the laity." Therefore—according to him—these "bodies" would have been the Catholic martyrs of the 20th century. It is a twisting that turns the text upside down. The motive is evident: It is wished to connect chronologically the martyrdom of Catholics before the attack on the Pope in 1981, and to identify the attack with the image of the stricken Pope in the Secret.

But the text of the Third Secret says something entirely different. It speaks of "corpses" in the destroyed city who have need of the prayers of the Pope, which would not make any sense if it involved martyrs for the faith, and then describes the assassination of the Pope (who is dead, not "as if dead") by soldiers, and only afterwards speaks of the martyrdom of religious "one after the other." Therefore, Solideo Paolini is right to observe that "the martyrs of which the texts speaks are martyred *after* the Holy Father has reached the end of the Way of the Cross, so that the bloodbath of Catholics "follows this violent death of the Roman Pontiff."[54] Consequently, this would appear to be a tragedy that must still happen, there not having occurred, since 1917, facts of this kind.

But let us turn to the central thesis of the Secretary of State.

---

[54] Solideo Paolini, *Fatima*, op. cit., pp. 242 and 246.

After having said that the Pope in the vision "falls to the ground as if dead," Sodano says that after the attack on May 13 it "appeared clear" to John Paul II that the Madonna had intervened to prevent the bullet from being fatal. Hence, the identification between the Pope killed in the Third Secret and the attack of May 13 is not formulated openly, but only implicitly suggested through the "correction" of the text of the Secret ("as if dead"). The identification is evaded, and one passes immediately to the sensations of Pope Wojtyla after the attack.

It is certainly understandable and right that John Paul II attributed his salvation—indeed miraculous—to the protection of the Madonna of Fatima, whose feast occurred on precisely that day (the anniversary of the first apparition).[55] And I believe that any Catholic shares the perception of the maternity of Mary, especially toward a Marian pope and thus a favorite. It remains, however, to explain how one can identify the attack on May 13 with the vision of the Third Secret. This identification is so difficult that, in fact, the Cardinal does not make it explicit.

And neither has Sister Lucia ever made this identification. I have not found a single word of hers that can be thus interpreted. In truth, she calls Sodano's thesis into question by having "even recently" identified "the bishop dressed in white" with "the" Pope in general, not "a" Pope in particular. But this identification is already contained in the text of the Secret ("we had the impression that it was the Holy Father") and, therefore, there was no need to confirm it. Or was there? And why was there a need to confirm something so obvious? Perhaps there is a reason. We will discover it further on. Meanwhile, suffice it to ask ourselves who is the Pope that "is killed" in the vision. Sodano seems to call the sister into question by suggesting that she shares his interpretation of the Third Secret— that is, the identification with John Paul II.

In reality, he is referring to the meeting (cited above) that took

---

[55] Professor Crucitti adds that he observes something "absolutely anomalous and in-explicable." The bullet had moved from the Pope's stomach in a zigzag, avoiding the vital organs. It came within a hairsbreadth of the central aorta: if it had reached it, the Holy Father would have died from loss of blood even before arriving in the hospital. It avoided the dorsal spine and all the other principal nerve centers: if it had struck them, John Paul II would have been paralyzed. "It seems," the professor concludes, "that that bullet was guided so as to avoid irreparable damage." (Renzo Allegri, *The Pope of Fatima*, op. cit., p. 271.)

place the previous month, on April 27, 2000, between the sister and an envoy from the Holy See, Monsignor Tarcisio Bertone. Except that in this interview Lucia does not at all confirm the identification of the Secret with the attack of May 13. Quite the contrary.

Bertone—it must be noted well—had been sent to Coimbra, in Portugal, to pose to Sister Lucia precisely "some questions concerning the interpretation of the third part of the Secret." However, that question (on the attack of May 13 as the presumed contents of the Secret) and the sister's answer were not reported in the two little pages of the "minutes" that were then published in the Introduction to the Secret.[56] Here are the essential lines:

> When asked: "Is the principal figure in the vision the Pope?", Sister Lucia replied at once that it was. She recalled that the three children were very sad about the suffering of the Pope... Sister Lucia continued: "We did not know the name of the Pope; Our Lady did not tell us the name of the Pope; we did not know whether it was Benedict XV or Pius XII or Paul VI or John Paul II; but it was the Pope who was suffering and that made us suffer too."[57] As regards the passage about the Bishop dressed in white, that is, the Holy Father—as the children immediately realized during the "vision"—who is struck dead and falls to the ground, Sister Lucia was in full agreement with the Pope's claim that "it was a mother's hand that guided the bullet's path and in his throes the Pope halted at the threshold of death."

Here there is another evident logical leap. Why does one pass from the bishop dressed in white, "shot dead," to Sister Lucia who "shares the affirmation of the Pope" concerning the protection of the Madonna. In the middle there is a hole into which falls the following question: Is the bishop dressed in white who is killed John Paul II, shot by Ali Ağca? Why was this question not asked when it is the very heart of the problem? And if it was asked, why is it not reported? What exactly were the questions by Bertone, and what

---

[56] The brief report will be published together with the text of the discourse by Sodano, the theological commentary by Cardinal Ratzinger, and various documents.

[57] Although there are very few literal words of Lucia reported in the document, what seems to transpire from these is a clear wish by Lucia not to support with her own name the identification of the Secret with the attack in 1981. In fact, she confirms that the "Bishop dressed in white" is the Pope, but she adds she does not know which pope it would be.

were the verbatim answers by Sister Lucia? Why have they not been produced? Would that not have been much simpler and clearer?

We might think that perhaps Sister Lucia was not up to responding, that given her advanced age she was not in the physical condition or did not have the lucidity to give the necessary clarifications. But in that case the Vatican envoy certainly would have declared it, and would never have invented a nonexistent or unreliable interview. Instead, the official account attests precisely that "Sister Lucia was lucid and serene," therefore, perfectly able to respond. As in fact we could see on our television sets on the 13th of May 2000.

If Bertone's mission was to "ask some questions on the interpretation of the Third Secret" (as one reads in the accompanying letter from John Paul II), he would certainly *not* want to know from Lucia if the "bishop dressed in white" was a Pope, seeing that this had already been written in the text of the Secret. Neither would he be interested in asking her if she shared the certainty of Karol Wojtyla that he was protected, on May 13, 1981, by the Madonna (which, obviously, any Catholic would share). Thus, what was important was to know whether Lucia agreed with the identification between the Pope killed in the Third Secret and the Pope wounded in the attack by Ağca. Why is there not a trace of this question in the synthesized account published in the Vatican dossier? Yet that was the aim of the mission. If Sister Lucia's answer had been a "yes," it would have been absurd not to report it. It would have enormously accredited the "Sodano hypothesis." Instead, that "yes" is not there. What can be concluded? One could deduce that the visionary thought "no." Also because among the few quoted words of Lucia reported in the document, there is a decisive phrase where Lucia affirms: "I wrote what I saw, the interpretation is not mine to make." A significant phrase which—one can think—allowed her to avoid the (pressing?) request to legitimate "that" interpretation.

But is it possible that Lucia, unlike Sodano, holds that the Third Secret was not fulfilled with Ali Ağca on May 13, 1981, and that it must still be realized? It seems that that is exactly the way things stand, at least to read the letter that the sister sent to John Paul II on May 12, 1982. This involves a very particular document that— as we will see—has ended up at the center of a little "detective story."

It was published officially by the Vatican precisely in the "Introduction" in *The Message of Fatima* signed by the then Archbishop Bertone, and therefore by the most official source. It is worthwhile to report all of the words attributed to Lucia, and then we will comment on the resounding information they provide. Lucia writes on May 12, 1982:

> The third part of the secret refers to Our Lady's words: "If not [Russia] will spread her errors throughout the world, causing wars and persecutions of the Church. The good will be martyred; the Holy Father will have much to suffer; various nations will be annihilated" (13-VII-1917).

> The third part of the secret is a symbolic revelation, referring to this part of the Message, conditioned by whether we accept or not what the Message itself asks of us: "If My requests are heeded, Russia will be converted, and there will be peace; if not, she will spread her errors throughout the world, etc".

> Since we did not heed this appeal of the Message, we see that it has been fulfilled, Russia has invaded the world with her errors. And if we have not yet seen the complete fulfillment of the final part of this prophecy, we are going towards it little by little with great strides. If we do not reject the path of sin, hatred, revenge, injustice, violations of the rights of the human person, immorality and violence, etc.

> And let us not say that it is God who is punishing us in this way; on the contrary it is people themselves who are preparing their own punishment. In His kindness God warns us and calls us to the right path, while respecting the freedom He has given us; hence people are responsible.

The curious thing is that Bertone cites this letter as confirmation of the official interpretation. But logic shows the contrary. This important text by Lucia tells us many things. In the first place, that the Third Secret also speaks of Russia and her errors, like the second part (something that is not found in the text of the vision published in 2000). In the second place, Sister Lucia, who wrote the letter in 1982, does not even remotely refer to the assassination attempt of Ağca (which happened the year before, in May 1981) and therefore does not at all hold that it is the fulfillment of the Secret, but on the contrary affirms *apertis verbis* [explicitly] that "the final fulfillment of this prophecy" has not yet occurred.

In substance Lucia totally denies the assumption upon which the "Introduction" by Monsignor Bertone is founded, according to which the prophecy was already realized, with the final epilogue represented by the attack of 1981. According to the Sodano-Bertone interpretation, everything would be consigned to the past and the revelation of the Secret "closes a period of history."

Bertone's citation of Lucia's letter to sustain his thesis appears, frankly, peculiar. It seems an accident, a strange goal scored against one's own team. But there is more. There is a detective story. In fact, a note produced by the Holy See includes a photocopy of the handwritten letter by Sister Lucia. Whoever reads the Portuguese text written by the Sister with her own pen, as Father Kramer notes, discovers that the text as cited by Bertone expunges an explosive phrase: "that you are so anxious to know." In all of the versions produced by Bertone and furnished by the Vatican (English, Italian, and Portuguese), the phrase here reproduced in italics, and which one reads in the photo-reproduced handwritten text, is missing:

In English: "The third part of the secret, *that you are so anxious to know*, is a symbolic revelation…"

In Portuguese: "A terceira parte do segredo, *que tanto ansiais por conhecer*, é uma revelação simbólica…"

In Italian: "La terza parte del segreto, *che volete ardentemente conoscere*, é una rivelazione simbolica."

Why has Monsignor Bertone omitted without explanation (and even without alerting the reader with ellipses) that phrase of Lucia's? And why does he sustain that this letter is "a letter to the Holy Father"? Lucia speaks of enquirers who "ardently wish to know the secret" in 1982, while John Paul II, according to all official reconstructions, had already read it by that date; and, moreover, "at any time", notes Father Kramer, "he could have read the text kept in the Vatican archives."[58] Therefore, he could not have had a burning curiosity.

So, to whom is that letter really addressed? Who would have ardently wished to know the secret in 1982? Or, if it really is addressed to the Pope as the official version says, and as I believe

---

[58] Father Paul Kramer, *The Devil's Final Battle*, op. cit., pp. 312-313.

(not believing it sensible to presume a lie), what was it that the Pope wished to know in 1982 regarding the Third Secret that he had not already read before? Are we confronted with a resounding official lie[59] or rather a mystery to decipher? It is also difficult to believe that it is a lie because the Vatican itself published the letter among the attachments to the Third Secret. It was not at all held back. Moreover, the publication actually reproduces the letter photographically, so that anyone would be able to gather that that phrase was missing from the translation. Whoever would have wanted to "falsify" the letter certainly would not have reproduced it thus, for that would have been truly clumsy. Yet, no explanation was furnished for this incredible "cancellation." In this case also, we will discover the reason further on.

For now, we will note that this involves a mystery which will become more complicated. At any rate, there are still further resounding incongruities in the introductory text by Bertone to which we will turn in sequence—a text which also carefully avoids affirming that the attack in 1981 is the realization of the prophecy contained in the Secret. But the element that most provokes thought is what we have said: Sister Lucia, in her letter, does not even consider the attack in relation to the Secret, but on the contrary writes to the Pope in May of 1982 (or to other mysterious addressees): "If we have not yet seen the complete fulfillment of the final part of this prophecy, we are going towards it with great strides."

If the attack of 1981 is really the complete fulfillment of the Secret, and if it is something that has by now been consigned to the past, already realized, how could Sister Lucia have written those words? Here the mystery deepens. Our attention is drawn to an interesting and mysterious phrase that John Paul II uttered to Vito Messori in the book-interview *Crossing the Threshold of Hope*. The book was published in 1994 and hence was written many years after the attack of 1981. The Pope was, in fact, recalling the attack: "Therefore, when I was shot by the assassin in St. Peter's Square, I did not pay any heed at first to the fact that it was precisely the anniversary of the

---

[59] Regarding this Morlier is extremely harsh and always very categorical: "This detail by itself unmasks the fraud. It is clear that the Vatican has suppressed this part of the phrase from all translations of this letter to induce us to believe that the document was addressed precisely to 'the Holy Father,' while in reality it was not... the question is important: Why was this passage eliminated from all of the translations?" (*The Third Secret of Fatima...*, op. cit., p. 219.)

day on which Mary had appeared to the three shepherds in Fatima, in Portugal, revealing to them those words which, by the end of the century, seemed to be moving toward their fulfillment."[60]

It is amazing that these words of the Pope have passed without observation. We find in them at least two important revelations. The first is that thirteen years after the attack—that is, "at the end of the century"—John Paul II held that the Fatima prophecy had yet to be realized completely, and he said this with an expression that recalls almost literally that of Sister Lucia in the 1982 letter just mentioned. The second revelation is that, as the Pope informs us, the prophecy whose fulfillment is approaching was expressed by Mary with *"words"*—something that, if taken literally, has an explosive significance, as we will see shortly.

But now let us sum up the events just considered. On May 13, 2000, Cardinal Sodano announces that the famous Third Secret of Fatima will soon be published, and at the same time will do something else: anticipate the theological interpretation of that extremely delicate text (which would not exactly have been his affair). A Vaticanist, Andrea Tornielli, hence expresses the perplexity of so many: "What happened at Fatima on May 13, 2000 represents therefore something unique in the history of the Church. A correct interpretation was offered even before the text to be interpreted was provided."[61]

The other paradoxical aspect is that this interpretation is explicitly *suggested* by Sodano and Bertone, but is not openly declared by either of them. Nor is it found explicitly in the Vatican texts. Besides, it is resoundingly denied by the same letter of Sister Lucia that the Vatican will publish with the text of the vision. Finally, Cardinal Ratzinger—Prefect of the Congregation for the Doctrine of the Faith—is charged with supporting this lame interpretation with a theological commentary on the text of the Secret.

Ratzinger leaves us free

The press conference by the Cardinal will take place a month-and-a-half later, on June 26, 2000: It is in this setting that the

[60] Karol Wojtyla and Vittorio Messori, *Crossing the Threshold of Hope*, Mondadori (Milan, 1994), p. 243.

[61] Andrea Tornielli, *The Secret Revealed*, op. cit., p. 13.

Secret will be published. Cardinal Ratzinger was not able to make a free theological comment on the text, but had to move within a preconceived idea. In fact, the prelate-theologian insistently declared that the interpretation was by the Secretary of State and that he is only giving points of reflection within the confines of a pre-determined interpretative framework. He begins thus: "Before undertaking an attempt at an interpretation, the essential lines of which can be found in the announcement made by Cardinal Sodano on May 13…"

After he has made an excursus on the theme of private revelations, he gets to the point and begins with these words: "We thus arrive at the third part of the 'secret' of Fatima… As emerges from the documentation provided, the interpretation which Cardinal Sodano offered in his statement of May 13…"[62] He then proceeds, stating explicitly the limits of his commentary: "In what follows therefore, we can only attempt to provide a deeper foundation for this interpretation…"

And finally, on the crucial point, he cites directly the words of Sodano, referring to him: "Above all we must affirm with Cardinal Sodano: 'The events to which the third part of the secret of Fatima refers now seem part of the past.'"

This, according to Ratzinger, is what "we must affirm." On the crucial point the Prefect of the former Holy Office identifies the Pope who ascends toward the cross with "different Popes who, beginning with Pius X until the current Pope, have shared the sufferings of the century and strove to go forward through so much anguish along the path that leads to the cross. In the vision, the pope too is killed along with the martyrs…"

We are at the final event. Marco Politti observes that concerning the "vision of the slain pope […] in no part of the document he signed and presented on live television did the Cardinal affirm that

---

[62] Ratzinger here adds that Sodano's interpretation was "presented personally to Sister Lucia. Concerning it, Sister Lucia above all observed that to her had been given the vision but not its interpretation. The interpretation, she said, was not given to the visionary, but to the Church. After reading the text, however, she said that this interpretation corresponds to what she had experienced and that on her part she thought the interpretation was correct." In Italian the adjective "correct" [*corretta*] would not necessarily imply that Sister Lucia agreed with that interpretation. Rather, it remains the fact that from the meeting with Monsignor Bertone it does not result that Sister Lucia ever approved or defined as "correct" the interpretation that identifies the Secret with the attack of May 13, 1981.

it refers to the attack by Ali Ağca. The theologian finally resorts to a question…"[63]

Here is the question to which Cardinal Ratzinger resorts: "When, after the attempted assassination on May 13, 1981, the Holy Father had the text of the third part of the 'secret' brought to him, was it not inevitable that he should see in it his own fate? He had been very close to death, and he himself explained his survival in the following words: '…it was a mother's hand that guided the bullet's path, and in his throes, the Pope halted at the threshold of death.' That here 'a mother's hand' deflected the fateful bullet only shows yet again that there is no immutable destiny, that faith and prayer are forces which can influence history and that, in the end, prayer is more powerful than bullets and faith more powerful than armies."[64]

According to Politi, this is "an elegant trick" by the Cardinal. But let us examine some particulars. To prescind from the Third Secret, that John Paul II believed that he was protected by the Madonna is sacrosanct; and certainly all of us Catholics are, and had already been, certain of this before the vision was revealed. Quite different, however, is the problem of a "prophecy" not yet fulfilled. The objection was raised: "Is it possible that a *Secret* so famous, so anticipated, so feared, and so opposed, consists of such a soap bubble; that the *secret* was an assassination attempt that everyone *already knew* 19 years ago? That the *secret* was a prophecy of the death of a pope…who does not die? The Madonna did not know that She Herself would divert the trajectory of the fatal bullet? And why, while knowing this, would She have preannounced that which would not happen?"[65]

Thus, one remains perplexed. And it is also curious that Ratzinger begins a commentary that is supposed to support identification of the Third Secret with a prophecy of the attack on the Pope with these words, which seem to say precisely the opposite: "No great mystery is revealed, the veil of the future is not parted."

Besides, one cannot avoid noticing the particularity of the Bavarian Cardinal's expression by which he repeats Cardinal

---

[63] *La Repubblica*, June 27, 2000.

[64] *TMF*, p. 42.

[65] From "Preface" by the Italian editor, in Lorent Morlier, *The Third Secret of Fatima…*, op. cit., p. 5.

Sodano's thesis, not with a clear affirmation, but with an elegant rhetorical question ("Should not the Holy Father...?"). But what could the prelate say? What role had Ratzinger in this entire affair? Father Paul Kramer—another traditionalist author who is quite polemical with the Vatican, in certain cases beyond due limits—notes that after the reform of the Roman Curia carried out by Villot following the Council, the Congregation for the Doctrine of the Faith—that is, the highest doctrinal authority (then and now second only to the Pope)—was placed under the Secretary of State; the political authority governs the Church with a power sometimes imposed even on the Pope himself (one of the many follies of the post-conciliar period).[66] From this Father Kramer concludes that, concerning Fatima, Ratzinger "could not do other than to comply with whatever opinion Sodano had."[67] Except that, on the other hand, the German prelate is accused of the contrary. In fact, in the anonymous pamphlet *Against Ratzinger* of a progressivist inspiration, the author sustains that the Bavarian Cardinal contradicted and corrected the Pope many times, and also that "after the revelation of the Third Secret of Fatima [he] reduced the 'holiness' of the pontiff to its proper perspective, sharply curbing the enthusiasms of the Secretary of State, Angelo Sodano."[68]

Two opposing accusations, both biased. Cardinal Ratzinger in fact seemed driven by another and higher concern. The daily *La Repubblica* thus headlined its commentary: "The difficult truth from which the Cardinal must protect the Holy Father."[69] In fact, he was seeking to protect the Holy See in the difficult conditions in which he found himself. What were these circumstances? It is necessary to reconstruct the background of that revelation of the Secret in order to understand them. John Paul II wanted to reveal the text, giving

---

[66] To support this judgment, Father Kramer cites the review *The Latin Mass*, January, 2002, where "the journalist Alessandro Zangrando reports an intervention by the Vatican Secretary of State to block publication in *L'Osservatore Romano* of the Pope's praise for the traditional Latin Mass." (Father Paul Kramer, *The Devil's Final Battle*, op. cit., p. 118).

[67] Ibid.

[68] Anonymous, *Contro Ratzinger* (*Against Ratzinger*), ISBN Edizioni, Milan, 2006, p. 77.

[69] In this commentary one reads: "The Cardinal was right when, with consummate honesty, he preannounced on the eve of its disclosure that the Secret would be reduced to its proper perspective. Very much so [...] Where was the necessity of so much secrecy?" (*La Repubblica*, June 27, 2000).

it the interpretation cited above; in 1999 he had already decided to do it, and Bishop Serafim of Fatima anticipated it. The attitude of the Curia is not clear. According to Luigi Accattoli, a Vaticanist with *Corriere della Sera*, "We can imagine that Ratzinger made the prudential objections that were habitual for him."[70] Probably the prudence suggested by Ratzinger related above all to the "interpretation." To link the Church officially to that interpretation of the vision of the Third Secret—that is, to its identification with the attack of 1981—could have been extremely imprudent.

When the Pope arrived in Fatima on May 13 for the beatification of Francisco and Jacinta, something strange happened because the expected revelation of the Secret was announced, as the Pope wished, but was deferred for several weeks. And it was Cardinal Sodano who announced it. It seems to have been the Vatican spokesman, Navarro-Valls, who very opportunely advised that it should not be the Pope in person who gave the announcement and the interpretative key: "Because he was implicated personally in the prophecy, as it involved a private revelation different from the revelation of the Bible."[71]

The fact that the revelation had been deferred because an adequate theological commentary had not been prepared (even though there had been ample time to do it since 1999), leads one to think that publication was in doubt until the end.[72] The reason for this is unknown, but it *is* known—and it was seen—that precisely in those final days there was a meeting between Monsignor Bertone and Sister Lucia in order to break the deadlock over publication— or better, publication of a sort that would involve an annexed interpretation. Indeed, Sodano gave the announcement along with a "preventative interpretation" of the vision which tried to confine the explosive force of that prophecy to the past, so as to neutralize it.

Therefore—it is said—Cardinal Ratzinger was charged with developing the theological commentary that would accompany the text of the Secret. He—while feeling obliged to move within the

---

[70] *Corriere della Sera*, May 14, 2000.

[71] Ibid.

[72] The first signal that something had happened arrived with a cryptic announcement by Cardinal Ratzinger on May 11, 2000, two days before the ceremony, when he said to journalists: "This Pope is unpredictable, he is used to surprises. He could reveal the Third Secret, even if the aim of his trip to Fatima is the beatification of Francisco and Jacinta Marto." (In Andrea Tornielli, op. cit., p. 14.)

"Sodano thesis"—strongly downplayed its significance, saying on the one hand to *La Repubblica,* on May 19, 2000, that "the Third Secret of Fatima will be placed in its proper perspective,"[73] and on the other hand providing two precious lifeboats. Because the Cardinal stressed that concerning the Fatima visions there are no "official definitions, nor obligatory interpretations."[74] By so doing, thereby silently demoting the Sodano thesis to a mere hypothesis not at all binding on the faithful[75]—a hypothesis that is certainly legitimate, but alongside other "attempts at interpretation" which can also be well-founded[76]—Ratzinger affords a great liberty, and also opens up a frank dialogue between Catholics.

In the second place, responding to a respectful but pointedly critical letter from Bishop Pavel Hnilica on the theological commentary, the Cardinal affirmed that he did not at all wish "to attribute exclusively to the past the contents of the Secret in a simplistic manner."[77] Therefore, the Cardinal Prefect of the former Holy Office avoids yet again the Church (adventurously) taking on the burden of an interpretation that is not only legitimately open to objection, but which—in this case—seems to leak water from every part, as some journalists have not failed to note. For example, the day after the press conference for the presentation of the Secret, in an editorial headlined "Mystery Half Revealed," *La Repubblica* declared: "The celebrated 'Third Secret' cannot be reconciled with the dramatic events of May 13, 1981. There is no Pope who is struck

---

[73] Mario Pirani has underlined "the sharp dialectic of positions" which he noticed: "It is enough to compare the words of Cardinal Sodano, which assimilate to Holy Scripture the five little pages written by Sister Lucia in 1943 [...] almost as if it concerned a new revelation, with the unequivocal declarations of Cardinal Ratzinger," who has insisted precisely that "revelation terminated with Jesus Christ" (*La Repubblica,* May 22, 2000).

[74] *La Repubblica,* June 27, 2000.

[75] See "The Third Secret of Fatima Is Not a Dogma of the Faith," interview of Cardinal Ratzinger in *La Repubblica,* May 19, 2000.

[76] The Prefect of the former Holy Office also repeated to journalists that "Catholics are free to believe or not to believe apparitions," private apparitions "are certainly not essential for a Catholic," and so one "can disbelieve apparitions" such as Lourdes or Fatima (*La Repubblica,* May 19, 2000). From this it can be deduced that all the more are Catholics not held to believe in a hypothetical interpretation of this or that sign in a given apparition.

[77] The correspondence was published in the review *Pro Deo et Fratribus* (November-December, n. 36-37/2000). It is accessible at the website of the Catholic Alliance: www.alleanzacattolica.org/temi/fatima/fatima_hnlica_ratzinger.htm.

down 'as if dead.' The scene is another. A pope killed by 'soldiers who shoot him with bullets and arrows.' It does no good to invoke the language of symbols and metaphors. No one will be able to put it into the heads of the people that the prophecy is mistaken. It is not an allusion; it points entirely elsewhere."

But where? Evidently toward a pope who has yet to arrive. Who? Is it perhaps Pope Benedict himself who is the Pope of the Third Secret, or someone—perhaps still unknown—who will arrive in the next few years?

Who is the Pope of the Secret?

Concerning the Pope of the Third Secret,[78] we know something else, through the vision of one of the three children of Fatima, Jacinta (today beatified by the Church). The episode was described in Lucia's Third Memoir, dated August 31, 1941.

> One day we spent our siesta down by my parents' well. Jacinta sat on the stone slabs on top of the well. Francisco and I climbed up a steep bank in search of wild honey among the brambles in a nearby thicket. After a little while, Jacinta called out to me:
>
> "Didn't you see the Holy Father?"
>
> "No."
>
> "I don't know how it was, but I saw the Holy Father in a very big house, kneeling by a table, with his head buried in his hands, and he was weeping. Outside the house, there were many people. Some of them were throwing stones, others were cursing him and using bad language. Poor Holy Father, we must pray very much for him."
>
> I have already told you how, one day, two priests recommended us to pray for the Holy Father, and explained to us who the Pope was. Afterwards, Jacinta asked me:
>
> "Is he the one I saw weeping, the one Our Lady told us

---

[78] That it concerns a particular Pope is obviously debatable. Concerning this, see FM, v. III, pp. 715-716 and Laurent Morlier, *The Third Secret of Fatima...*, op. cit., pp. 70-78. At any rate, even the Vatican interpretation in *TMF*, while speaking of the "Popes of the twentieth century," then indicates John Paul II, a single Pope, as the Pope of the Secret.

about in the Secret?"

"Yes, he is," I answered.

"The Lady must surely have shown him also to those priests. You see, I wasn't mistaken. We need to pray a lot for him."

At another time, we went to the cave called Lapa do Cabeço. As soon as we got there, we prostrated on the ground, saying the prayers the Angel had taught us. After some time, Jacinta stood up and called to me:

"Can't you see all those highways and roads and fields full of people, who are crying with hunger and have nothing to eat? And the Holy Father in a church praying before the Immaculate Heart of Mary? And so many people praying with him?"

Some days later, she asked me: "Can I say that I saw the Holy Father and all those people?"

"No. Don't you see that that's part of the Secret? If you do, they'll find out right away."

"All right! Then I'll say nothing at all."[79]

This dramatic scene seems to belong together with the Message of Fatima, either in the second part where the suffering of the Pope is spoken of, or in the third part where there is announced the assassination of a Pope, an immense martyrdom of Christians and worldwide devastation. Lucia indeed confirms that this vision [of Jacinta's] forms a part of the Secret. But does she mean the first two parts of the Secret or the third? Does it refer, therefore, to the past, to the Popes of the twentieth century, or does it regard the future, the Pope of the Third Secret?

Jacinta never revealed anything when she was alive, as Sister Lucia had invited her cousin to remain silent. The first two parts will be revealed by Sister Lucia herself in her Memoir of August 31, 1941; and this would explain why Lucia herself also reveals Jacinta's vision there. Logic, therefore, leads one to believe that this vision concerns the first two parts of the Secret. But it is also true that Jacinta "sees" an event that even today has not yet occurred; therefore, it would have something to do with the Pope of the

---

[79] Fr. Louis Kondor, SVD, ed., *Fatima in Lucia's own words* (Fatima, Portugal: Postulation Centre, 1976), pp. 108-109.

Third Secret, if we do not wish to interpret the vision in a symbolic manner, as if it referred metaphorically to the painful affairs of the Popes of the twentieth century, who certainly underwent no little suffering. Yet such an interpretation would certainly be plausible, and thus it would be necessary to recognize as justified the official construction by Sodano who, concerning the Third Secret, speaks of a symbolic vision.

It is necessary, however, to admit—if we consider the symbolic visions of the Old and New Testaments[80] to which Sodano refers[81]— that what is described by Lucia truly appears to be of a different nature, having very little of the symbolic, and that it seems rather to prefigure a precise historical event that has yet to occur. Therefore, it is difficult to unravel.

At any rate—to return to the Third Secret revealed in 2000— it is certainly possible to read that vision in a symbolic manner if one can accept that it does not describe "in a photographic sense the details of events." But when one affirms that the "symbolic vision" also contains a concrete prophecy to be applied, in detail, to the precise historic event of the attack on the Pope, one falls into a contradiction. To accept this strained interpretation, it would be necessary at least that the prophecy had proved to be correct. Instead, it is not so.

Is it therefore necessary to conclude that the attack on the Pope of May 13, 1981 is not contained in the Third Secret of Fatima? This seems to me to be the most reasonable conclusion, even if that event nevertheless forms part of a broader prophecy by Mary on the times in which we live. My hypothesis is that, in fact, the bloody event in St. Peter's Square really was preannounced by the Madonna, not at Fatima, but rather at La Salette, another of the great apparitions of the Virgin Mary in the modern age recognized by the Church. La Salette is, in certain verses, an anticipation of Fatima.[82]

---

[80] For example, in the 37th Chapter of Ezekiel (the field of bones which reassumes flesh and comes to life), or Chapter 10 of the Acts of the Apostles (the vision of Peter) or any of the prophetic images of the Apocalypse.

[81] "That text contains a prophetic vision similar to those found in Sacred Scripture, which do not describe photographically the details of future events, but synthesize and compress against a single background facts which extend through time in an unspecified succession and duration. As a result, the text must be interpreted in a symbolic key." *TMF*, p. 30.

[82] For its history, see Antonio Galli, *Apologia for Melanie*, Edizioni Segno, Trevagnacco (Ud.), 2001.

The facts of La Salette, which happened on September 19, 1846, also have as protagonists two children, Melanie and Maximin. Not only these aspects recall Fatima. La Salette seems to be part of that same prophetic cycle begun at Rue du Bac in 1830, concerning not a "private revelation" of the type one finds in traditional mysticism, but rather an apparition to shepherds with important public warnings the Holy Virgin gives to the Church and the world, in view of events absolutely unique and decisive in the history of humanity.[83]

Also, at La Salette the Madonna indeed speaks of a great modern apostasy, with the spreading of powerful anti-Christian forces; She speaks of great disasters which will weigh on humanity and of tremendous trials for the whole Church (revealing even the years in which will come the time of the Antichrist). In the details, the Virgin's words were reported in the two secrets confided to the two visionaries and sent by them to Pope Pius IX.

The two secrets were read attentively by Pope Mastai and then were "buried" (and unknown) for 150 years in the Pope's personal archives. By strange happenstance they were recovered and brought to light, thanks to the research of the Abbe Michel Corteville, on October 2, 1999, only a few months before the publication of the Third Secret of Fatima. In the text by Maximin Giraud, one reads among other things that "the Holy Father will be persecuted," and in the text by Melanie the Madonna says: "The Pope will be persecuted from every side, they will shoot at him, they will try to put him to death, but they will not be able to do anything. The Vicar of Christ will triumph yet again."[84]

Not only that. In the so-called "eschatological secret" of Melanie, one reads these words of the Madonna: "The Holy Father will suffer much. I will be with him until the end to receive his sacrifice. The evildoers will make many attempts on his life without being able to harm him in those days; but neither he nor his successor will see the triumph of the Church."

Antonio Galli calls attention to these words and those of Maximin in the letter to Pius IX, which speaks of a Pope that "no one is expecting." Then elsewhere the child "confided, among many inexactitudes, that that Pope would not be 'Roman,' perhaps

[83] See Donal Anthony Foley, *The Book of Marian Apparitions*, Gribaudi, Milan, 2004, and Livio Fanzaga (with Saverio Gaeta), *The Signature of Mary*, Sugarco, Milan, 2005.

[84] Antonio Galli, *Apologia for Melanie*, op. cit., pp. 406-408.

intending to say Italian, that he would reign for some 20 years and that he, Maximin, would not have wanted to be in his place, leaving one to understand that he would suffer a great deal. From these two documents and from other precisions by Melanie," writes Galli, "it is easy to deduce that this Pope is John Paul II." Indeed, "no one was expecting that he would be elected...his reign has already exceeded 20 years by a little. There were many attempts on his life, as Melanie predicted."[85] In fact, besides the attack on May 13, 1981, Pope Wojtyla suffered another on May 13, 1982.

It is easy to discern that the secret of La Salette (not the Third Secret of Fatima) corresponds perfectly to the events surrounding John Paul II. It is he who was subjected to attempts on his life, and it is he who, however, was saved by the protection of the Virgin. Then there is the other prophecy made at Fatima, that of a Pope who is killed. The same Galli—considering the text written by Lucia—asks: "Could this perhaps concern another Pope who will die a martyr?"[86] It appears evident that with these two great public prophecies, given by the Madonna in the two fundamental modern apparitions recognized by the Church, we find ourselves before a tragic *escalation* of Catholic history that culminates with a pope who is struck (but not killed), and with one of his successors who in his time is martyred. Probably the series of public apparitions of the Madonna in the Modern age—in an absolutely special way with respect to the previous history of the Church—should finally be evaluated together, as a prophetic cycle that has something to do with a particular moment in the history of Christianity.[87] And it should be interpreted as such in the Church. (In fact, for some years there has been attempted a joint reading of this celestial "lifesaving plan.")

My hypothesis of a double prophecy regarding two Popes

---

[85] Ibid., p. 410.

[86] Ibid., p. 411. After this happy intuition, Galli, not wishing to contradict the "official" version, concludes that "La Salette, like Fatima, points the headlights on the figure of John Paul II". Something that, however, seems to contradict what he himself has written.

[87] There is a singular passage in the book-length interview of Karol Wojtyla with Vittorio Messori, *Crossing the Threshold of Hope*, immediately before the Pope speaks of the assassination attempt. He says that "then I still knew little of Fatima. I had the sense, however, that there was a certain continuity, beginning with La Salette, through Lourdes, and finally to Fatima" (p. 243).

can perhaps also find a confirmation in an attentive reading of the three parts of the Secret of Fatima. In fact, in the second part, concomitantly with certain historical events, the Madonna speaks of a Pope who "will have much to suffer," and in the third part the vision shows a Pope who is martyred (together with a number of other Catholics) in the context of an apocalyptic trial of the Church at the end of which the Immaculate Heart of Mary would triumph.

This succession of events also reminds one—curiously—of a celebrated prophetic dream of St. John Bosco,[88] called "the dream of the two columns," which the saint of Turin recounted on May 30, 1862. To recall it:

> Imagine yourself to be with me on the seashore, or better, on an isolated rock and not to see any patch of land other than that under your feet. On the whole of that vast sheet of water you see an innumerable fleet of ships in battle array. The prows of the ships are formed into sharp, spear-like points so that wherever they are thrust they pierce and completely destroy. These ships are armed with cannons, with lots of rifles, with incendiary materials, with other firearms of all kinds, and also with books, and advance against a ship very much bigger and higher than themselves and try to dash against it with the prows or burn it or in some way to do it every possible harm. As escorts to that majestic fully equipped ship, there are many smaller ships, which receive commands by signal from it and carry out movements to defend themselves from the opposing fleet.
>
> In the midst of the immense expanse of sea, two mighty columns of great height arise a little distance the one from the other. On the top of one, there is the statue of the Immaculate Virgin, from whose feet hangs a large placard with this inscription: *Auxilium Christianorum* – *"Help of Christians"*; on the other, which is much higher and bigger, stands a Host of great size proportionate to the column and beneath is another placard with the words: *Salus Credentium* – *"Salvation of the Faithful (Believers)"*.
>
> The supreme commander of the big ship is the

---

[88] It is well-known that the saint of Turin had certain very particular supernatural charisms, one of which was precisely that of a prevision of coming historical events. (See Antonio Socci, *The Anti-Catholic Dictatorship*, Sugarco, Milan, 2004.)

Sovereign Pontiff. He, seeing the fury of the enemies and the evils among which his faithful find themselves, determines to summon around himself the captains of the smaller ships to hold a council and decide what is to be done.

All the captains come aboard and gather around the Pope. They hold a meeting, but meantime the wind and the waves gather in storm, so they are sent back to control their own ships. There comes a short lull; for a second time the Pope gathers the captains around him, while the flag-ship goes on its course. But the frightful storm returns. The Pope stands at the helm and all his energies are directed to steering the ship towards those two columns from whose summits hang many anchors and strong hooks linked to chains.

All the enemy ships move to attack it, and they try in every way to stop it and to sink it: some with books and writings or inflammable materials, of which they are full; others with firearms, with rifles and with rams. The battle rages ever more relentlessly. The enemy prows thrust violently, but their efforts and impact prove useless. They make attempts in vain and waste all their labor and ammunition; the big ship goes safely and smoothly on its way. Sometimes it happens that, struck by formidable blows, it gets large, deep gaps in its sides; but no sooner is the harm done that a gentle breeze blows from the two columns and the cracks close up and the gaps are stopped immediately.

Meanwhile, the guns of the assailants are blown up, the rifles and other arms and prows are broken; many ships are shattered and sink into the sea. Then, the frenzied enemies strive to fight hand to hand, with fists, with blows, with blasphemy and with curses.

Suddenly the Pope falls gravely wounded. Immediately, those who are with him run to help him and they lift him up. A second time the Pope is struck, he falls again and dies. A shout of victory and joy rings out amongst the enemies; from their ships an unspeakable mockery arises.

But hardly is the Pontiff dead than another takes his place. The pilots, having met together, have elected the

Pope so promptly that the news of the death of the Pope coincides with the news of the election of the successor. The adversaries begin to lose courage.

The new Pope, putting the enemy to rout and overcoming every obstacle, guides the ship right up to the two columns and comes to rest between them; he makes it fast with a light chain that hangs from the bow to an anchor of the column on which stands the Host; and with another light chain which hangs from the stern, he fastens it at the opposite end to another anchor hanging from the column on which stands the Immaculate Virgin.

At this point, a great convulsion takes place. All the ships that until then had fought against the Pope's ship are scattered; they flee away, collide and break to pieces one against another. Some sink and try to sink others. Several small ships that had fought gallantly for the Pope race to be the first to bind themselves to those two columns. Many other ships, having retreated through fear of the battle, cautiously watch from far away; the wrecks of the broken ships having been scattered in the whirlpools of the sea, they in their turn sail in good earnest to those two columns, and having reached them, they make themselves fast to the hooks hanging down from them and there they remain safe, together with the principal ship, on which is the Pope. Over the sea reigns a great calm.[89]

In light of contemporary events, the dream is easy to decipher in its integrity.[90] Some of its particulars appear perfectly recognizable to

---

[89] G.B. Lemoine, *Biographical Memoirs of St. John Bosco*, Vol. VII, International Editorial Society, Turin, 1909, pp. 169-171. After having recounted this dream, Don Bosco requested an interpretation from Don Rua, who said: "It seems to me that the Pope's ship is the Church, the boats are men, the sea is the world. Those who defend the large boat are the good, beloved of the Church; the others are her enemies. The two columns of salvation seem to me to be devotion to Mary Most Holy and to the Blessed Sacrament of the Eucharist."

[90] The servant of God, Cardinal Idelfonso Shuster, Archbishop of Milan, "gave such importance to this vision that in 1953, when he was at Turin as the papal legate to the National Eucharistic Congress, on the night of September 13, during the solemn pontifical closing rite at Piazza Vittorio, packed with people, he made this dream a prominent part of his homily." (Piero Manero and Valentina Ben, *Fatima: the Prophecy Revealed*, Edizioni Segno, Tavagnacco (Ud), 2000, p. 66). But Shuster tried to apply that prophecy to events that had transpired until then, when instead today it is evident that many of these events have yet to occur.

us, and their precise chronological place in the succession of events is truly striking, and greatly confirms its prophetic value. Most impressive are the two gatherings of pilots around the supreme commander: a clear prophecy of two Councils (Vatican I and Vatican II), convoked to confront an attack by the world, the first of which—Vatican I— was in fact interrupted (as foreseen in the "dream") by the fury of the tempest. Rome was indeed invaded on September 20, 1870, putting an end to the temporal power of the papacy, after centuries, with the Pope becoming a recluse in the Vatican.[91]

The image of the contemporary Church as buffeted by a tempest that seems about to cause her to capsize is the same identical image that Cardinal Ratzinger employed in that dramatic Way of the Cross on Good Friday 2005, which he wrote for a Pope who was by then gravely ill. This impressive text—certainly approved by John Paul II— represents in a sense a joint appeal by these two great Popes and— in hindsight—the first providential episode that would soon bring Ratzinger to succeed Pope Wojtyla. Almost an official investiture. Thus in the prayer at the Ninth Station of the Cross, the Cardinal wrote these dramatic words: "Lord, often your Church seems like a boat about to capsize, a boat taking in water on every side. And in your field we see more weeds than wheat."[92]

It is also evident that, after the two Councils, the other two events prophesied by the dream are the wounding of the Pope and then his martyrdom, which seems to give the impression that the forces of evil have prevailed. Finally, in the midst of a very particular situation, the arrival of a Pope who anchors the Church to the Immaculate Heart of Mary and to the Eucharist, which will permit the triumph to occur. Today—in light of Fatima—we can say that this involves not only a call to devotion, but a turning point, a "conversion" of the modern Church in the way she conceives of herself before the world and before God. It involves, for example, a reconsideration of that solemn act of the consecration of Russia (done collectively by all the Church, the Pope, bishops and faithful) to Her Immaculate Heart, requested in vain by Mary at Fatima, together with other disregarded things. (It is precisely on account of this deafness that Lucia, in successive interior locutions, has received extremely grave words from Jesus.)

It concerns a return to the Eucharist, an anchorage that signifies also a clear "conversion" to doctrinal orthodoxy after the frightening

---

[91] For the persecutions, generally little known, which the Church endured in that circumstance, see Antonio Socci, *The Anti-Catholic Dictatorship*, op. cit.

[92] *Way of the Cross*, Vatican Editions, 2005, p. 65 (Italian version).

deviations following the Council and, I hold, a return as well to adoration, therefore to the bimillennial liturgy of the Church that was liquidated in a post-conciliar coup. (I note in passing that these "conversions" are exactly the line of Pope Benedict XVI.)[93]

Two "columns," an anchorage to which would truly give a different face to the Church of today: more adoring than worldly; more a supplicant of God for grace and salvation than occupied with its own plans and projects; more devotions than debates. A Church that expects everything from Christ, and not from political acumen, from activism and from the mania for aggiornamento; a Church no longer suffocated by the "filth" and "weeds" denounced by Cardinal Ratzinger. There is foreseen, in sum, a "metanoia." It is after this return, and this anchorage to Jesus and to Mary,[94] that there is prophesied the triumph of Their two Hearts in present human history, which is also the final promise of Fatima: "My Immaculate Heart will triumph."

---

[93] Naturally, the abolition of the liturgy in different spoken languages is unimaginable, but already there has been manifested by Cardinal Ratzinger the necessity of repairing the tie with the millennial tradition, of retouching the modern rite in the traditional sense, and above all, of restoring liberty to all the faithful. Cardinal Ratzinger himself some time ago denounced "the attitude of smugness" that is manifested against the faithful who prefer the ancient liturgy. "Whoever today supports the continuation of this liturgy or participates directly in celebrations of this nature," said the current pontiff, "is put on the Index; all tolerance in this regard is vanquished. Nothing of the kind has ever happened in history; thus, the Church's entire past comes to be despised. How can one trust in her present if things stand this way? I don't understand in the least, to be frank, why there is such subjection to this intolerance on the part of many of my fellow bishops, which seems to be an obligatory tribute to the spirit of the times, and which appears to counteract, without any comprehensible reason, the necessary process of internal reconciliation in the Church." (Joseph Ratzinger, *God in the World*, San Paolo, Cinisello Balsamo (Mi.), 2001, p. 380.)

[94] What the angel says to Lucia in the first vision is "the Hearts of Jesus and Mary are attentive to the voice of your supplications." (From the Fourth Memoir in *Lucia Recounts Fatima*, Queriniana: Brescia, 1999, p. 92.)

3. Detective story in the Vatican

Is there a "secret" not revealed?

At this point the prophetic framework of Fatima places us before an event that is yet to happen: the martyrdom of a Pope and with him many pastors and Catholics, in the context of a frightening devastation. There is preannounced, therefore, a tragic situation for the world and for the Church. But what is the sense of this vision that is so enigmatic, and of these prefigured events? How can they be explained? Is it possible that the Madonna would appear so sensationally at Fatima to give a message-warning of such importance that nevertheless remains incomprehensible, confused or susceptible of differing and opposing interpretations; that the vision published by the Vatican in 2000 was not explained by the Holy Virgin?

Father Gerard Mura, Professor of Philosophy at the Seminary of the Sacred Heart in Zaitzkofen, Germany, has observed: "We cannot shake the impression of something missing [...]. We come to know simply of an enormous and unprecedented punishment of the Church, faithful and hierarchy. There is not given to us any indication of why this punishment should be visited upon us now, or how we can avoid it with conversion: divine prophecy normally has the character of a warning [...]. Thus, there are certain points which lead us to suspect and to doubt that the text that we possess is complete."[95]

One traditionalist study[96] affirms that according to the structure

---

[95] In *Catholic*, March 2002; in Marco Tosatti, *The Secret Not Revealed*, op. cit., pp. 119-120.

[96] Father Paul Kramer, *The Devil's Final Battle*, op. cit., pp. 186-188.

65

of the message of Fatima, or rather of the contents of the apparitions of June 13 and July 13, 1917 as they were set forth in Lucia's Fourth Memoir, the vision of "the bishop dressed in white" (the Third Secret) lacks the Virgin's explanation in Her own words. That is, it would lack a part that the Vatican decided not to reveal.[97]

I must recognize that in support of this hypothesis, according to which the Third Secret also has a part where the words of the Virgin would be found, there has emerged a very strong argument that must be considered a formidable point in favor of the "Fatimist" hypothesis.

It is the "detective story" of a little phrase. Sister Lucia wrote the Third Memoir (dated August 31, 1941) where she reveals the first two parts of the Secret, in which, we have seen, she makes known that there is also a "third part" that for now will not be revealed. A few months later she wrote the Fourth Memoir (dated December 8,

---

[97] The assumption of the "Fatimists" is as follows: The Madonna always explains the visions that She shows to the children. In the apparition of June 13 the Virgin speaks of the destiny of Jacinta, Francisco and Lucia and immediately after there is had the corresponding vision ("we saw ourselves in this light…"). Also, on July 13 "we see that the Madonna gives a vision to the shepherds and then explains to them its significance." In fact, Sister Lucia describes the terrible images of Hell and immediately after reports the words of the Virgin: "You have seen Hell where the souls of poor sinners go…" As Father Kramer notes: "In order that the shepherds would understand what they had seen, the Madonna had given them an explanation: 'You have seen Hell.' Yet again, we see that when the Madonna gives a vision to the shepherds, She explains its significance to them." But where the Third Secret is concerned we have only the vision, which is, moreover, very mysterious. Father Kramer asks: "Why would the Madonna have explained something so obvious as the vision of Hell, while failing to provide a single word to explain something as obscure as the passage published by the Vatican?" The answer could be the following: Because that vision does nothing besides explain the words just pronounced by the Madonna, those concerning the persecutions, which constitute the Second Secret. Father Kramer replies, however, that there are particulars of the vision that are highly symbolic that have not been explained and which remain mysterious. For example, that relative to the angel, and above all the assassination of the Pope and the others in the narration. Therefore, the vision cannot be a representation of that which is predicted in the Second Secret.

However, it is also true that Sister Lucia herself, in the Memoir of August 31, 1941, revealing the first two parts of the message of Our Lady, begins with a very important phrase: "The secret consists of three distinct parts, two of which I am going to reveal." In fact, she reveals the vision of Hell and the prophetic words of the Virgin concerning the twentieth century. There remained only one thing hidden, the so-called Third Secret, or the vision of "the bishop dressed in white." If one adds to this the explanation of the Madonna, we would have four parts. The reply of the "traditionalists," however, proposes to consider as one part the vision and the explanation of it given by the Madonna.

1941) in which the preceding memoir is copied exactly, but when it arrives at the end of the Second Secret ("and a period of peace will be granted to the world") she adds a new phrase that was not in the text from the summer: "In Portugal, the dogma of the faith will always be preserved etc."

A truly explosive little phrase. Above all, because the "etc" is within the quotation marks—that is, Lucia is referring to the words of the Madonna Herself. In the second place because that "etc" signifies that the discourse of the Virgin continues. "Is it possible that the words of the Madonna, given by the Mother of God in person, can end with an 'etc'? Obviously, it is not so. There is indubitably additional text after the 'etc'. What happened to this text?"[98]

In fact in the Third Secret published on June 26, 2000 there is not a single word from the Holy Virgin. It is therefore reasonable to ask oneself what has happened to the continuation of Her words. The "detective story" was made even more "explosive" by the Vatican's choice not to explain or attempt an interpretation of that little phrase, objectively of enormous importance. In fact, in the documents that accompanied the revelation of the Third Secret in 2000 it was chosen to insert not the Fourth Memoir, but the Third. And this phrase is relegated to a footnote where the words concerning Portugal are reported, but not the other phrase of the Virgin which Lucia wrote immediately after in the Fourth Memoir, and which states: "Tell this to no one. Yes, you can tell Francisco."

Besides, in the "Introduction" by which Monsignor Bertone closes the proceedings, these two phrases of the Madonna are disposed of thus: "In the Fourth Memoir of December 8, 1941, [Sister Lucia] added some annotations."[99] Some annotations? How can one elude that explosive beginning by the Virgin as if it were a marginal "annotation" by Lucia? There are two possible explanations.

First explanation: Bertone, writing thus, considers those phrases a reflection by Lucia and not words of the Virgin, thus implicitly discrediting the key witness of Fatima (who had quoted those words, attributing them to Mary) and therefore all of her testimony and all of the message of Fatima. Holding perhaps—without explaining why—that there is a part which is of supernatural origin and a part which is not. But, obviously, if it is admitted that Lucia

---

[98] Ibid., p. 174.

[99] *TMF*, p. 4.

could have invented that phrase of the Madonna, then everything can be put in doubt. Yet in the Fourth Memoir itself, Sister Lucia— by a providential inspiration—begins by stressing: "After a humble prayer at the foot of the tabernacle and of the Immaculate Heart of Mary, our most dear mother from Heaven, where I asked for the grace that I not be permitted to write even a single letter that is not for Her glory." And a little further on, emphasizing yet again: "I do not say and I do not write in such cases anything that comes only from me."[100]

Second explanation: Monsignor Bertone could be referring to other annotations that Lucia added in the Fourth Memoir, but in this case he would be resoundingly evading the existence of these crucial expressions with a frankly inexplicable silence. In either case, when (on June 26, 2000) from the official seat there is attempted to give an exhaustive explanation of the message of Fatima, one receives the clear impression of a great embarrassment before a phrase of the Madonna which they cannot explain [away] and there is attempted to remove this phrase silently (without drawing attention to this attempt). A very bad choice of communication. Because, naturally, it has furnished critics a formidable polemical argument.

Here, indeed, Father Kramer writes: "Why did they choose the Third Memoir (of Sister Lucia) when the Fourth Memoir offers a more complete text of the message of Fatima? The answer is obvious: They chose the Third Memoir to avoid any discussion whatever regarding the phrase 'In Portugal the dogma of the faith will always be preserved etc.' Through this expedient they succeeded in evading the obvious indication that the message of Fatima includes other words of the Virgin which follow the 'etc', and that these missing words must necessarily regard the Third Secret. If it were not so [...] they would not have evinced such an open aversion to this phrase."[101]

It is necessary to recognize that here there is an unresolved "detective story" (and this is one of the clarifications that I would have requested from Cardinal Bertone). Moreover, it is not only the phrase on Portugal and that significant "etc." After that "etc" the Madonna says to Lucia: "Tell this to no one. Yes, you may tell it to Francisco." It is an important phrase that can be explained. As

[100] *Lucia Recounts Fatima*, op. cit., pp. 88-89.

[101] Father Paul Kramer, *The Devil's Final Battle*, op. cit., p. 172.

noted, one of the shepherds, Francisco, saw the Holy Virgin, but did not hear Her voice.[102] It is easy to draw the conclusion: If the Third Secret consisted only of the vision revealed by the Vatican in 2000, Francisco would have seen it, as had Lucia and Jacinta. If there is a part that the Madonna says to relate to Francisco, it is because the Secret comprises also the words of the Madonna which he did not hear, evidently the continuation of that "phrase," the explanation of the vision. This is the thesis of diverse "Fatimists." Here, however, if we wish to be objective, there are grave doubts.[103]

It is clear that our investigation moves onto a minefield where it is necessary to proceed with caution, serenity, and objectivity. Attitudes of which, unfortunately, are not found a trace in a great part of the "Fatimist" journalism. Laurent Morlier, heavily critical of the Vatican, even arrives at the contention that the Third Secret contains *only* these words of the Virgin and that the vision revealed on June 26, 2000 is a fake. But it does not seem to me that he exhibits irresistible proofs or that he expounds decisive arguments to demonstrate such a grave accusation.[104] Also, because it is Lucia herself who authenticated the part of the Secret published in 2000,

---

[102] Sister Lucia speaks of this at the beginning of the Fourth Memoir (see *Lucia Recounts Fatima*, op. cit., p. 95). Morlier observes: "Now one can better comprehend why Francisco was deprived of the grace of hearing the Holy Virgin. The reason had remained mysterious until today. That 'handicap' serves today to reveal an enormous imposture." (*The Third Secret of Fatima…*, op. cit., pp. 54-55.)

[103] In reality it seems that the Madonna refers to that which was revealed on the 13th of July as the Secret in its entirety. Therefore, the phrase concerning Francisco could regard the words pronounced in the second part. However, it is true that the permission to "tell" Francisco does not appear in the Third Memoir, that containing only the First and Second Secrets, but rather in the Fourth Memoir immediately after the phrase on Portugal and immediately after the "etc," which have come to be considered the beginning of the Third Secret. Therefore, if the Madonna says to Lucia that she can relate Her words to Francisco, this could also be a reference to those words in the third part of the Secret, words (for now) hidden by the "etc" and still unknown.

[104] The evidence of the presumed "inauthenticity" of the text published in 2000 is set forth in the third chapter of his book. And the ninth chapter presents expert graphologists, according to whom the hand that wrote that text is not the same that wrote "the presumed authentic writings of Sister Lucia." There are interesting analyses, but they should be taken with care and counterbalanced with other studies and experts. (Besides the same American expert expresses his opinion "with reservations," because he had not been able to compare the original documents.) The linguistic expertise of Professor Russo, which I publish in the appendix, for example, traces a profile of the author of that text that coincides with that of Sister Lucia.

even identifying her own handwriting and the paper.[105] Hence the vision surely forms a part of the Third Secret. But Morlier comes to doubt even that the Sister, who is prominent or seen in celebrations in recent years, is the real Sister Lucia. He even hypothesizes that she could have been "substituted," and here everything becomes uncontrollable political fiction that I do not view as even worthy to discuss.[106]

Those mysterious words of the Madonna

Therefore the phrase on Portugal leads to suspicion that there is also a part not revealed, contained in the words of the Virgin which explain the vision. If, as we have seen, John Paul II declared in 1994 that "the words" of Mary spoken at Fatima to the three shepherds "seem to be moving toward their fulfillment,[107] and thus are not yet accomplished, it is sensible to hold that this refers to the words, still unknown, pronouncing the third part of the Secret, because the words pronounced in the second part have already been realized. This is evident in the past century (the October Revolution, the spread of Communism, the persecutions of the Church, the Second World War), and John Paul II has himself underlined this, even in the pages of the same book.[108] Therefore, it is the Pope himself who sets us to sleuthing for traces of a Third Secret that comprises "words" pronounced by the Madonna (and not revealed in 2000) which have yet to be realized.[109] Morlier brings forth other elements that

---

[105] *TMF*, p. 28.

[106] It is in the eighth chapter of his volume that Morlier asks if they "have put in place of the real, a false Lucia," expressing his doubts for several pages.

[107] Karol Wojtyla and Vittorio Messori, *Crossing the Threshold of Hope*, op. cit., p. 243.

[108] "And what does one say of the three Portuguese shepherds of Fatima who suddenly, in 1917, on the eve of the outbreak of the October Revolution, heard: 'Russia will be converted' and 'In the end My Immaculate Heart will triumph…'? It could not have been they who invented such predictions. They did not know history and geography and even less, in fact, were they oriented to social movements and development of ideologies. And yet exactly what they had announced happened." (Ibid., p. 145.)

[109] One could object that the Pope could have been referring to the words "In the end My Immaculate Heart will triumph." It is a plausible interpretation, but in what sense could the Pope in 1994 have held the triumph of the Immaculate Heart to be proximate? It cannot be affirmed that it coincides with the collapse of Communism, because in 1994 this had already occurred, and because the Pope himself was in these years denouncing the secularization of countries that had just escaped from communism,

prompt reflection. He cites for example Canon Barthas, who writes "in the documents of the canonical process (for the beatification of Jacinta and Francisco) that the Secret is discussed for the first time in the interrogation of Lucia, during the period of the investigation of 1924. Recalling the apparition of July 13, she declares: 'Then the Lady told us some brief words (palavrinhas) commanding us not to tell them to anyone, except to Francisco alone.'"[110]

If Sister Lucia's phrase refers precisely to the third part of the Secret, it is truly very significant because she speaks of "words" of the Madonna of which there are none in the text revealed in 2000. Furthermore, the same Barthas interrogated Sister Lucia on the Third Secret on October 17 and 18, 1946, and confirmed: "The text of the words of Our Lady written by Sister Lucia are enclosed in a sealed envelope."[111] Morlier also cites Cardinal Ottaviani, Prefect of the Holy Office under John XXIII, one of the few who have read the Third Secret, who said during a famous conference that "(Sister Lucia) wrote on a sheet of paper that which the Virgin told her to convey to the Holy Father."[112]

There have been many hypotheses on that phrase of the Madonna and on that "etc" held to be the beginning of the Third Secret. Is

such as Poland. Besides, if it is evident that that collapse was due to supernatural intervention by Providence and by Mary, nevertheless the Pope was the first to affirm that "it would be simplistic to say that it was Divine Providence that caused communism to fall. Communism as a system was in a certain sense fallen from the beginning. It fell in consequence of its own errors and abuses." (*Crossing the Threshold of Hope*, p. 146). Finally, the "triumph of the Immaculate Heart of Mary" is quite evidently a prophecy that concerns the faith, the prophecy of a great and planetary conversion of the world to Christ. It is difficult to discern in the "end of the century" signs of this general conversion, especially because the Pope in those years was denouncing the contrary: planetary apostasy. Hence there remains at least the mystery of this reference by the Pope: Which words of the Madonna seem to him to be near realization in 1994?

[110] Father Casimir Barthas, *Fatima, Marvel of the XXth Century*, op. cit., p. 81, in Laurent Morlier, *The Third Secret of Fatima*, op. cit., p. 55. This citation by Morlier has been contested by Fra Francesco in *Critical documents of Fatima*, p. 2, Sanctuary of Fatima Editions: 1999, pp. 128, 141. In essence, Morlier is accused of having extrapolated the citation. Morlier responds (pp. 195-197) by relating that passage, and actually appears convincing.

[111] Laurent Morlier, *The Third Secret of Fatima*, op. cit., p. 196.

[112] Ibid., pp. 55-56. However, elsewhere the exact words of Ottaviani are reported differently: "Lucia wrote on a sheet of paper, in Portuguese, what the Holy Virgin had asked her to tell the Holy Father." (FM, v. III, p. 725). Is this a strained interpretation on Morlier's part? Perhaps in both cases one could conclude that Ottaviani was speaking of words of the Madonna present in the Third Secret?

it reasonable to think that this is what it really is? Decidedly yes, at least in the absence of a convincing explanation of that phrase, which remains in suspense. At any rate, even Sister Lucia leads us to understand it that way.[113]

But perhaps a clearer testimony is that of Father Schweigl, an Austrian Jesuit (1894-1964), Professor at the Gregorian and at the Russicum, who was sent to Fatima to investigate with extreme care the affair of the apparitions, and was charged by Pius XII with interrogating Sister Lucia precisely concerning the Third Secret. The Jesuit met the sister on September 2, 1952, and the text of their meeting was then kept secret by the Holy Office. However, upon his return he confided with one of his own who, some years later, wrote a letter-testimony to Frère Michel. The Jesuit reportedly said: "I cannot reveal anything of what I learned at Fatima concerning the Third Secret, but I can say that it has two parts: one concerns the Pope. The other, logically—although I must say nothing—would have to be the continuation of the words: 'In Portugal the dogma of the faith will always be preserved [...].' Regarding the part that concerns the Pope, I had asked [our witness continues]: 'The present Pope or the next?' To this question Father Schweigl made no reply."[114]

It is clear that this declaration by the Jesuit would be absolutely dispositive, but it is not direct. It is not given by the interested party, firsthand, and is revealed 20 years after the death of Father Schweigl, moreover by a witness whom Frère Michel, quoting, leaves anonymous. Recognizing the scrupulousness of the work of Frère Michel, I believe that this is credible testimony, but it is also true that—offered in this manner—the testimony loses much of its weight. However, it is also necessary to observe that Frère Michel's book, in which this letter was published, appeared in 1985, a full 15 years before the Third Secret was revealed by the Church. And the description by Father Schweigl conforms exactly to the text of the vision (the part that "regards the Pope") and confirms those words of the Virgin ("In Portugal..."). Therefore, the thesis according to which the Third Secret would have two parts—the vision and the words of the Madonna—finds reliable confirmation.

For a long time this beginning of the Third Secret has led to the

---

[113] See Father Paul Kramer, *The Devil's Final Battle*, op. cit., p. 172.

[114] FM, v. III, p. 710.

conviction that the natural sequel is something catastrophic for the Church, and also for the world. Father Joaquin Alonso, the official archivist of Fatima, considered the greatest expert on the subject (who died in 1981) commented thus on the opening words of the Madonna: "This phrase clearly implies a critical state of the faith, from which other nations will suffer, and thus a crisis of the faith. Therefore, in the period that precedes the triumph of the Immaculate Heart of Mary there will occur terrible things which are the object of the Third Secret. Which things? If 'in Portugal the dogma of the faith will always be preserved' it can clearly be deduced that in other parts of the Church these dogmas will be obscured or even lost [...]. It is therefore probable that the text refers concretely to the crisis of faith in the Church and to the negligence of the Pastors themselves." Some years later Father Alonso will even write that the Secret speaks of "internal struggles in the womb of the Church and of grave pastoral negligence by the upper hierarchy," and "deficiencies of the upper hierarchy of the Church."

Frère Michel, reporting this thesis of Father Alonso,[115] adds two important observations. First of all, he shows that at the beginning, when he had begun to occupy himself with Fatima, Father Alonso had thought differently and then "totally changed his mind."[116] Therefore, he adds (as if to give an explanation of this about-face): "We are certain that in the meantime he (Father Alonso) had often met with Sister Lucia; we know that during his work on the critical edition of the documents on Fatima, he had opportunities to question her on several occasions. As the official expert appointed by Bishop Venancio, would he have adopted this new position on such a burning question without being certain of at least the tacit agreement of the seer?"[117]

Then Frère Michel reports another page by Father Alonso where he himself lets it be known that things stood this way. He speaks of *defaillances*[118] of the upper hierarchy, and he concludes: "For that matter, none of this is foreign to other communications Sister Lucia has had on this subject." Frère Michel comments:

---

[115] Ibid., pp. 687, 704-705.

[116] Ibid., p. 705.

[117] Ibid.

[118] It is interesting to note that *defaillance* can be translated with these terms: fainting, collapse, lack, failure, deficiency, weakness, crises.

"This phrase is doubly precious to us. Because beyond the solid induction by Father Alonso, established from numerous clues—'I have the texts,' he declared—this phrase reveals to us indirectly the thought of the visionary herself [...]. Indeed, if Father Alonso were mistaken on the contents of the final secret, we can be certain that Sister Lucia—who had not feared to deny imaginative hypotheses on many occasions—would have found a way to correct him."[119]

Thus, the words (still unpublished) of the Madonna would preannounce an apocalyptic crisis of faith in the Church herself beginning at its heights. Probably, however, there is also an explanation of the vision (that is revealed on June 26, 2000) in which the martyred pope, bishops, and faithful appear, after having traversed a city in ruins. Some doubt about Father Alonso's thesis arises, however, where he draws this certain conclusion: "the content of the unpublished part of the Secret does not refer to new wars or political upheavels, but to happenings of a religious and intra-church character, which of their nature are still more grave."[120]

The doubt derives from the vision revealed on June 26, 2000. If Father Alonso knew (the entirety of) the Third Secret, he would have known that this part—as we can well see—does not at all seem bloodless. Rather, it leads one to think that the context is that of a great and tragic war:[121] (from the angel of divine punishment, whose flashes of fire directed toward the world and are stopped by the Virgin, to the city in ruins, to the heaps of bodies, and finally to the soldiers who kill the pope and with him many bishops and faithful.

Different opinions on the "disasters"

Father Paul Kramer and Solideo Paolini—to give two examples from the traditionalist realm, but rather different from each other—are convinced of the "chastisements" of the world. The first, accusing

---

[119] FM, vol. III, p. 706.

[120] FM, vol. III, p. 687.

[121] Paolini speaks of the "affirmation attributed to Sister Lucia (1991) that the Third Secret will be revealed during a great war." (*Fatima*, op. cit., p. 249). It is evident that the "revelation" of 2000 did not come during a great war. However, there is no certainty on this declaration, neither was it verified in the official meetings with Monsignor Bertone.

the Vatican in his book of having hidden the Third Secret from the Church and the world, comes down extremely hard with words that are frankly unacceptable: "A grave crime has been committed against the Catholic Church and the world in general. The perpetrators of this crime are men who occupy high offices in the Catholic hierarchy. The victims of this crime are you and those you love. The consequences of this crime have already been catastrophic, and if those responsible are not stopped as soon as possible, the final result cannot but be apocalyptic in its proportions."[122]

Curiously, however, further on[123] the author of the book seems to make his own (thus contradicting himself) the words of the Bishop of Fatima, Alberto Cosme do Amaral, who declared during a press conference on September 10, 1984 that "The Secret of Fatima speaks neither of atomic bombs, nor nuclear warheads, nor Pershing Missiles nor SS-20s [...]. Its content concerns only our faith. To identify the Secret with catastrophic announcements or with a nuclear holocaust is to deform the meaning of the message. The loss of faith of a continent is worse than the annihilation of a nation; and it is true that faith is continually diminishing in Europe."[124]

However, we face some questions. First: The words of the bishop seem to contradict the initial assumption of Father Kramer's book, according to which the Third Secret would also contain an announcement of disaster for the world that the Vatican has hidden. The second question is whether and how the words of Archbishop do Amaral fit the text of the Secret revealed in 2000. Frankly, they do not seem to refer to that vision. Besides, Father Kondor, the secretary-translator, added as well that "the Pope has serious reasons for not publishing the Secret."[125] And I would not say that such "serious reasons" would have existed in 1984, if the Third Secret were the prophecy of an assassination attempt which had already occurred in 1981. At any rate, the text of the vision of the

---

[122] Father Paul Kramer, *The Devil's Final Battle*, op. cit., p. XXV.

[123] Ibid., pp. 193-194.

[124] FM, v. III, pp. 675-676. The bishop was in a certain way "constrained" to back off by the tacit ecclesiastical prohibition on speaking of the Third Secret. But in an interview in 1995 he reconfirmed the first declaration, furnishing further information that is almost a scoop: "Before affirming at Vienna (in 1984) that the Third Secret regards only the faith and its loss, I had consulted in person with Sister Lucia in advance and had obtained her approval."

[125] FM, vol. III, p. 676.

"attempt" was revealed in 2000. Had these "serious reasons" become less serious? And why? What had happened in the meantime? More probably the "serious reasons" regard another part of the Secret not yet revealed, and today those "serious reasons" still motivate the silence.

But let us return to the traditionalist literature. Even Solideo Paolini embraces the thesis according to which the Third Secret also contains a prophecy of grave disasters for humanity. Indeed, compiling various indiscretions that have come out in the course of the years, Paolini proposes a possible text of the Secret, that is, of the discourse of the Madonna which begins with the words concerning Portugal.[126] This reconstructed text speaks of natural catastrophes, of a "world convulsed by terror," of a "great war," of "fire and smoke that fall from heaven," of "waters of the oceans which inundate parts of the earth," and "millions of men who will perish suddenly."

Two of the sources from which Paolini draws (among many others) are the so-called "diplomatic version" of the Secret and the presumed declarations of John Paul II at Fulda.

The first is the famous "scoop" by the German magazine *Neues Europa*, which on October 3, 1963 "revealed" that Paul VI supposedly caused an extract of the Third Secret to reach the leaders of the two blocs, Kennedy and Khrushchev, and that this "diplomatic version" of the Secret had a decisive weight in the signing of the accord between the superpowers to halt the proliferation of nuclear weapons. This text speaks precisely of war and of immense catastrophes, and of Satan dominating the world even to the point of arriving at the summit of the Church.

Frère Michel criticizes the Vatican's silence which, by not denying the "scoop" in 1963 nor even afterwards, "permitted millions of Catholics to be tricked by this deception." Then he cites Father Alonso, who categorically refutes the German journal: "Nothing in this text is either true or authentic: the staggering claim that the text was communicated by the Pope to the heads of state; the historical errors it contains; the literary structure, so different from that employed in Lucia's writings, or the very ideas expressed, so absolutely foreign to those of Sister Lucia."[127] Then Frère Michel

---

[126] Solideo Paolini, *Fatima*, op. cit., pp. 266-268.

[127] FM, vol. III, p. 650.

proceeds to demolish point by point[128] the crude reportage of *Neues Europa*, which is littered with historical blunders (with certain parts, those concerning the Church, being more credible, however).[129]

Another "source" of Paolini is represented by the sensational declarations John Paul II is said to have made during his trip to Germany in November 1980, and which were published by a small German magazine, *Stimme des Glaubens*.[130] The Pope, questioned on the Secret and its non-publication in 1960, is said to have evoked the same images as *Neues Europa* (therefore accrediting them), and then to have indicated the prospect of martyrdom (one year before the assassination attempt) and great trials on the horizon.

Marco Tosatti notes: "One cannot see why the magazine would have invented out of whole cloth the pontifical declaration on such a delicate and controversial theme with the risk of denial."[131] However, between inventing a text "out of whole cloth" and reporting it with total fidelity, there are many middle ways. Father Alonso expressed "the most serious reserve" concerning this "scoop" and, like Frère Michel, holds that knowing the style of the Pope the story is not

---

[128] Ibid., pp. 650-659.

[129] Frère Michel affirms that "it really expressed certain themes of the true Secret"— those concerning the Church— whether by "fortuitous coincidence" or through some "Roman indiscretions" (vol. III, p. 655).

[130] "Given the gravity of its contents, and to avoid encouraging the world power of communism to make certain moves, my predecessors in the ministry of Peter have preferred for diplomatic reasons to avoid publication. On the other hand, all Christians should be content with this: If there is a message in which it is said that oceans will completely inundate certain parts of the world, that from one moment to the next millions of men will perish, truly the publication of such a message is no longer something to be desired. Many wish to know only for curiosity and a taste for the sensational, but they forget that knowledge implies responsibility. It is dangerous to wish only to satisfy one's own curiosity if one is not ready at the same time to do something, or if one is convinced that one can do nothing against evil announced."

The Pope at this point took out his Rosary saying: "Here is the remedy against this evil. Pray! Pray!—and ask nothing more. Entrust all the rest to the Mother of God." And then, when questioned on the Church, he answered: "We have to be prepared to suffer, before long, great trials which will require of us the disposition to sacrifice even our life, and a total submission to Christ and for Christ. Through your prayers and mine, it is still possible to diminish this trial, but it is no longer possible to avert it, because only in this manner can the Church be effectively renewed. How many times has the renewal of the Church been brought about in blood! It will not be different this time. We have to be strong, to prepare ourselves, to entrust ourselves to Christ and to His Most Holy Mother, to be assiduous, very assiduous in praying the Rosary." (In FM, vol. III, pp. 659-660.)

[131] Marco Tosatti, *The Secret Not Revealed*, op. cit., p. 88.

worthy of belief.[132] Frankly, in this recounting there are many aspects which call to mind the thought and attitude of Pope Wojtyla. On the other hand—as Monsignor Bertone would reveal in his own time—on that date (1980) John Paul II had not yet read the Third Secret, which, according to the official version, he will consult in the hospital in July 1981, immediately after the attack. As to the moment at which the Pope learned of the Third Secret, and "which" Secret he knew in 1981, however, there is an extremely delicate controversy which we will examine further on. It is almost certain that he read the secret discourse of the Madonna in 1978.

Therefore, the presumed declaration at Fulda, however denied by the Vatican,[133] is held to be probable (not word for word, but in its basic contents) by Paolini, who deduces from it many other indications that in the part of the Third Secret yet to be published there is a prophecy of cataclysms and disasters for the world. One has the impression that Father Alonso and Frère Michel were led to deny the hypothesis of a material chastisement because they feared that the emphasis placed on prophecies of disaster would overshadow the core of the prophecy—the darkness that descends upon the Church—which would be the cause of these tragedies. However, in other pages, as we will see, not even they exclude "punishments" for the world.

What all these authorities share, however, is the persuasion that the Third Secret begins with the words on Portugal and develops the prophecy of a grave crisis in the Church.[134] Paolini, like nearly all traditionalists, affirms in his attempt at a reconstruction of the (unpublished) Third Secret that it would speak also of the Antichrist, accrediting the idea that these are his times and that

---

[132] FM, vol. III, p. 660.

[133] It should be stated, however, that when Vittorio Messori, addressing Cardinal Ratzinger, hinted at the apocalyptic contents of the "diplomatic version," stating that "John Paul II himself in his pastoral visit in Germany, seemed to confirm (although with prudent paraphrases, privately, with a group of special invitees) the certainly discomforting contents of that text," he did not receive from the prelate a direct denial of the fact that the Pope had made these declarations (*Report on the Faith*, San Paolo, Cinisello Balsamo (Mi), 1985, p. 110). But when questioned on this during the press conference on June 26, 2000, during which the vision of the Third Secret was published, Cardinal Ratzinger issued a decisive denial: "On the basis of my information, this encounter [at Fulda] did not take place and the Pope did not say those things." (In Aura Miguel, *Totus Tuus*, op. cit., p. 143)

[134] FM, vol. III, pp. 841-849.

the Madonna came to Fatima to assist the Church in battle at this unique moment in history, prophesied even in the New Testament. And before Paolini, Frère Michel developed precisely this idea with considerations that are truly impressive.[135]

Moreover, the pontiffs themselves, from Paul VI—with his "the smoke of Satan has entered into the temple of God"—up to Benedict XVI, have recognized and denounced the present moment with words of exceptional gravity.

Paul VI arrived at evoking the end times: "There is a great disturbance in this moment in the world of the Church, and thus it is the faith that is in question. What is happening today reminds me of the obscure phrase of Jesus in the Gospel of St. Luke: 'When the Son of Man returns, will He still find faith on the earth?' Books are being published in which the faith is denied in important points, yet the bishops remain silent, as if they do not find anything strange in these books. This, in my opinion, is bizarre. I sometimes read the Gospel of the end times and discern that in this moment there are emerging some signs of this end. Are we near the end? This we will never know. It is necessary to hold oneself always ready, but things can go on for a very long time. What strikes me, when I consider the Catholic world, is that within the heart of Catholicism there sometimes appears to predominate a type of non-Catholic thought, and it could happen that this non-Catholic thought in the heart of the Church will tomorrow become the stronger. But it has never represented the thought of the Church."[136]

The same Cardinal Ratzinger, in the Fourth Station of the Way of the Cross written for Pope Wojtyla (Good Friday 2005) on the

---

[135] FM, vol. III, pp. 772ff.

[136] In Jean Guitton, *The Secret Paul VI*, op. cit., pp. 152-153. Pope Montini also pronounced publicly these terrible words: "We believe that something preternatural has come into the world precisely to disturb it, to suffocate the fruits of the ecumenical council and to prevent the Church from bursting out into hymns of joy... I have the sensation that from some fissure the smoke of Satan has also entered into the temple of God." (Paul VI, June 29, 1972). John Paul II expressed analogous judgments: "We must admit realistically and with profound suffering that Christians today feel lost, confused, perplexed and also disappointed; there are diffused ideas in contrast with the truth as revealed and always taught; there are diffused true and proper heresies in the field of dogma and morals [...] the liturgy has been altered; immersed in intellectual and moral relativism and therefore in permissiveness, Christians are tempted by atheism, by agnostics, by agnosticism, by a vaguely preached illuminism and by a sociological Christianity, deprived of definite dogmas and moral objectivity. It is necessary to begin all over again." (*L'Osservatore Romano*, February 7, 1981.)

eve of his succession, evoked the same disquieting evangelical phrase—certainly not by chance—but also gave the answer, the one truth, Jesus possessed at the moment of His execution: the answer is Mary. Here are the words of Cardinal Ratzinger:

> The disciples have fled, Mary did not flee. She stayed there, with a mother's courage, with the fidelity of a mother, with the goodness of a mother, and with Her faith, which resists in the darkness: "And blessed is She who believed" (Luke 1:45). "But the Son of Man, when He returns, will He find faith on the earth?" (Luke 18:8). Yes, in this moment He knows it: He will find faith. This, in that hour, is His great consolation.

In the darkest moment of history, when it seems that the seed of faith in Jesus the Savior is eradicated and extinguished, always the faith of the Madonna perseveres. The Madonna does not abandon the Church and the human race to evil, and She illuminates them. It is natural to interpret the words of the Cardinal in reference to this historic moment, and to see in Fatima the sign of the presence of Mary in the hour of darkness. For this reason the prophetic message pronounced by the Madonna is infinitely important—those words which remain unknown and are hidden away by that "etc."

We return therefore to our investigation. We return, that is, to the "detective story" of the phrase of the Madonna reported by Sister Lucia in the Fourth Memoir: "In Portugal the dogma of the faith will always be preserved etc."—the beginning of a discourse of an evidently prophetic nature, but never completed. A discourse which has fed for so many years (it seems to me with good reason) suppositions concerning a great apocalyptic crisis that would assail the Church (and the world).

Thus, it would have been of utmost importance that in the presentation of the Third Secret along with an entire apparatus of documents, comments and notes, the Vatican would provide, or at least attempt, a plausible explanation of that phrase of the Virgin concerning Portugal and of that "etc." At the very least in order to dissolve the doubts and extremist suppositions of some who arrive at counterpoising the Madonna of Fatima to the Second Vatican Council, judged *in toto* to be the cause of a planetary apostasy and of a general apocalyptic betrayal by the highest hierarchs.[137] Also,

---

[137] An almost equally harsh judgment also by Gianni Baget Bosso: "There was not

80

to respond to those who advance this thesis, it would have been very important to clarify that phrase left in suspense. In the press conference of 2000, to someone who posed a question on that opening phrase of the Madonna, Monsignor Bertone responded almost distractedly: "It is difficult to say if it refers to the second or the third part of the secret…It seems to me that it pertains to the second."[138]

To us it seems, frankly, difficult to believe that such a response can be viewed as exhaustive. It is obvious that it was not a response, but rather an embarrassing evasion. It is obvious that there was no desire to get to the root of the problem. And if one wished, it would be easy to ascertain whether the phrase pertains to the second or the third part of the Secret. It would suffice to ask this of the one who wrote it. Monsignor Bertone could have asked Sister Lucia in person to clarify the phrase during the meeting that he had with her in April of 2000, concerning the text of the vision. Or in the second meeting (of which we will speak), which took place on November 17, 2001, for which the same prelate was sent to the Portuguese sister in an absolutely surprising initiative for the Church—which had never wished to deny anything from *Neues Europa* to Fulda—precisely to have her negate certain critical suppositions concerning the text published in 2000. Can one really accept that a phrase of such capital importance, pronounced by the Madonna, was distractedly forgotten? What better occasion to clarify the meaning of those dramatic words remaining in suspense? But unfortunately, Monsignor Bertone did not want to ask Sister Lucia anything on this subject. (Was it because he was afraid of the response?)

Neither was it possible to obtain clarifications from Monsignor Bertone, because he had refused to provide any. A choice that perhaps bears out the idea of an insurmountable "embarrassment" concerning that phrase of the Madonna, and worse the suspicion

---

a crisis in the Church before the Council: it is the Council that has determined the crisis." (*The Anti-Christ*, Mondadori: Milan, 2001, p. 11.) In reality it seems debatable that there were not already signs of a crisis before the Council. (Even the Fatima event itself demonstrates this.) We feel more or less in agreement with Ratzinger, who sees in certain errors made during the Council, in the erroneous reception of the Council, and in the subsequent degenerations—not in the Council *in toto*—the phenomenon that has devastated the Council. At any rate, Baget Bosso arrives at drastic conclusions: "The Council has destroyed a Catholic order that it did not wish to destroy and has produced a doctrinal crisis that never existed before."

[138] Aura Miguel, *Totus Tuus*, op. cit., p. 141.

that one has something grave to hide, and what is more, something that is known not to have been hidden very well. Therefore, being unwilling to accept such a scenario—also because it would be fatally self-wounding for the Vatican—and in the absence of any attempt at self-defense by the ecclesiastical party, I tried to understand what reasons the Vatican could have for adopting such a posture. And I found myself before a surprising hypothesis.

Apocalypse now?

My hypothesis—which is based also on some private disclosures—is this: in the highly confidential discussion that took place in the Sacred Palaces between 1999 and 2000 concerning the Pope's wish to reveal the Third Secret of Fatima, a compromise solution was probably reached. In the Curia opposition to publication of the Third Secret had always been prevalent, above all because of the part concerning the Church, or because the prophetic words of the Madonna, which—according to the dominant opinion in the Vatican—would be used against the Vatican and would create great alarm among the people if made available to public opinion and the media.

Probably during these meetings around the Pope a point of agreement was reached, according to which it was decided that on May 13, 2000, at the end of the Mass for the beatification of the two shepherds of Fatima, publication of the text of the vision (with an interpretation that would link it to events in the past) would be announced, and then the essential contents of the message of the Madonna would also be published—implicitly but not explicitly— in the homily that John Paul II gave during that Mass. This would permit them to say in conscience that all of the Third Secret had been revealed, but without an integral explicit publication so as to avoid (in their opinion) a great shock to the Christian people, sensationalistic broadcasts and a reaction of panic.[139]

This decision probably also would have been made on the

---

[139] Solideo Paolini has observed acutely the lexical choice of the ecclesiastic hierarchy who from 2000 have assured that all had been "revealed" ("the so-called Third Secret has been entirely revealed," declared Cardinal Bertone to *Il Giornale*, August 29, 2006). To say "revealed" rather than "published" could eventually permit, in the future, the position that the part "not published" has also been "revealed" in an indirect manner, through the words of the Pope.

strength of an authoritative precedent (which in the Church is always important). Because it can be held that Paul VI, while deciding not to publish the Third Secret, wished in his surprising homily during the pilgrimage to Fatima in 1967—for the quite significant intention of peace in the Church and preservation of the faith—to reveal implicitly to the Christian people the essential secret message of the Virgin. He did so by touching precisely on three points which have always been imagined to be the contents of the Secret: the fidelity of the Church (at risk because of the possible victory of heresy and apostasy), the unity of the Church (at risk because of schisms and persecutions), and finally the peace of the world (threatened even to the extent that the world would not survive). Here are the three fundamental passages of that amazing homily of Paul VI:

The first intention is the Church: the one, holy, Catholic and apostolic Church. We wish to pray for her interior peace. The ecumenical council has reawakened many energies in the bosom of the Church, has opened more ample visions in the field of her doctrine, has called all of her children to a clearer conscience, and more intimate collaboration, a more lively apostolate. It pushes us so that this benefit and renewal will be conserved and will grow. What an evil it would be if an arbitrary interpretation, not authorized by the Magisterium of the Church, were to transform this spiritual renewal into a restlessness which dissolves the Church's traditional structure and constitution, substituting the theology of true and great teachings with new and partisan ideologies which depart from the norm of faith, that which modern thought, often lacking the light of reason, neither comprehends nor accepts, finally transforming the apostolic anxiety of redemptive charity into an acquiescence in the negative forms of the profane mentality of worldly customs. What disenchantment, then, would be caused by our effort at a universal approach!

This thought carries our memory at this moment to those countries in which religious liberty is practically suppressed and where the denial of God is promoted... We declare: the world is in danger. Therefore we have come by foot to the feet of the Queen of Peace to ask for the gift that only God can give: peace.... Men, think of the gravity and the greatness of this hour, which could be decisive for the history of the present and future generation. The picture of the world and of its destiny presented here is immense and dramatic. It is the scene that the Madonna opens before us, the scene that we contemplate with horrified eyes.[140]

And further:

And then a message of supreme utility seems today to reach the faithful from Her who is the Immaculate, the holiest of all the saints, the cooperator of the Son in the work of restoration of supernatural life in souls. In fact, in devoutly contemplating Mary they draw from Her a stimulus for trusting prayer, a spur to the practice of penance and to the holy fear of God. Likewise, it is in this Marian elevation that they more often hear echoing the words with which Jesus Christ announced the advent of the Kingdom of Heaven: "Repent and believe in the Gospel"; and His severe admonition: "Unless you repent you will all perish in the same manner."[141]

Most significant is this insistence on "penance" (which we have seen to be the beginning of the vision of the Third Secret) and that evangelical warning: "If you do not do penance, you will all perish in the same way." This makes us think seriously of a prophecy of grave trials for humanity. As we will see, it is exactly the same evangelical phrase (Luke 13:13) that Cardinal Ratzinger will cite when speaking of the Third Secret.[142] Frère Michel—as does Vittorio Messori—notes that in this homily Paul VI "has alluded to apocalyptic themes of the Secret," and he says it citing precisely the words of Messori which, addressed to Cardinal Ratzinger, were not denied.[143] But, curiously, no one has thought that this was exactly the road chosen by the hierarchy to reveal the contents of a secret which in its literal integrity appears too terrible to utter, because of planetary catastrophes it preannounces or because it speaks of Satan, who for

---

[140] In www.vatican.va

[141] Apostolic exhortation *Signum Magnum*, 4, 20 (written on the occasion of the pilgrimage by Paul VI to Fatima for the fiftieth anniversary of the apparitions).

[142] Vittorio Messori and Joseph Ratzinger, *Report on the Faith*, op. cit., p. 111.

[143] After having hinted at the presumed declarations of John Paul II at Fulda, Messori said: "Before him Paul VI, in his pilgrimage to Fatima, seemed also to have hinted at apocalyptic themes of the 'Secret.'" Ibid., p. 110.

some time conquers the heights of the Church (as *Neues Europa* had written), or because it identifies our historical moment even with that page of the Apocalypse in which the decisive conflict between Mary Most Holy and Satan is spoken of. Paul VI is referring precisely to this in the cited Apostolic Exhortation, *Signum Magnum*, given at Fatima that 13th of May in 1967.[144] Indeed, with the sensational "Miracle of the Sun" of the last apparition on October 13, 1917, the Madonna Herself seems to have evoked before the whole world the page from the Apocalypse concerning the "Woman clothed with the sun" (Apoc. 12:1).

Thirty-three years after Paul VI, John Paul II, at the same plaza in Fatima, shortly before the announcement of the publication of the text of the vision, preached a homily (which even Father Kramer pronounced "exceptional") with the same contents as that of Paul VI, the same recollection of that page from the Apocalypse,[145] yet revealing even more dramatically and explicitly what the mysterious words of the Madonna on July 13, 1917 herald for us:

> According to the divine plan, "a Woman clothed with the sun" (Apoc. 12:1) came down from Heaven to this earth to visit the privileged children of the Father. She speaks to them with a mother's voice and heart: She asks them to offer themselves as victims of reparation, saying that She was ready to lead them safely to God.... Later Francisco, one of the three privileged children, exclaimed: "We were burning in that light which is God and we were not consumed. What is God like? It is impossible to say. In fact we will never be able to tell people." God: a light that burns without consuming. Moses had the same experience when he saw God in the burning bush... "Another portent appeared in Heaven; behold, a great red dragon" (Apoc.

---

[144] There one reads: "The great sign that the Apostle John sees in the sky 'a woman clothed with the sun,' is interpreted by the Sacred Liturgy, and not without foundation, as a reference to the Blessed Virgin Mary. Mother of all men by the grace of Christ the Redeemer [...] On the occasion of the religious ceremonies which are taking place today in honor of the Virgin Mother of God at Fatima in Portugal, where She is venerated by innumerable faithful because of Her maternal and charitable heart, we wish to recall the attention of all the faithful of the Church yet again to the indissoluble link between the spiritual motherhood of Mary [...] and the duties of redeemed men toward Her, the Mother of the Church."

[145] Further, in the letter to the Bishop of Fatima-Leiria of May 12, 1997, John Paul II evoked those passages from the Apocalypse in order to explain the apparitions of 1917.

12:3). These words from the first reading of the Mass make us think of the great struggle between good and evil, showing how, when man puts God aside, he cannot achieve happiness, but ends up destroying himself. How many victims there have been throughout the last century of the second millennium! We remember the horrors of the First and Second World Wars... The message of Fatima is a call to conversion, alerting humanity to have nothing to do with the "dragon" whose "tail swept down a third of the stars of Heaven, and cast them to the earth" (Apoc. 12:4)...

Even Father Kramer asks whether—with those citations to the Apocalypse—the Pope had not "given the world a glimpse into the contents of the Third Secret."[146] To me this seems evident also because, by following in the footsteps of Paul VI but with a more accentuated revelation of the Secret, it is reasonable to suppose that this was the compromise on the basis of which the Vatican can today maintain that it has revealed "all" of the Secret of Fatima.[147]

The same Father Kramer recognizes this truth. In fact, he recalls the discourse of John Paul II at the Portuguese sanctuary in 1982: "'Can the Mother who, with all the force of the love that She fosters in the Holy Spirit and desires everyone's salvation, remain silent when She sees the very bases of Her children's salvation *undermined*?' The Pope then answered his own question: 'No, She cannot remain silent.'"[148] The Pope was referring to the message of Fatima. Father Kramer comments: "Therefore, it seems perfectly clear that Pope John Paul II was trying to tell us that the Third Secret relates to the great apostasy foretold in Sacred Scripture. Why did the Pope not

---

[146] Father Paul Kramer, *The Devil's Final Battle*, op. cit., p. 113.

[147] Moreover, every intervention of the Pope at Fatima during his multiple visits contains these same elements. For example, during the pilgrimage he wished to make on May 13, 1982, in order to give thanks for the protection from the assassination attempt the previous year, the Pope confirmed that the Madonna was profoundly "preoccupied by the threats of apostasy and of moral degradation which bring with them the collapse of society." And further on: "the evangelical invitation to penance and conversion, expressed by the words of the Madonna, is always current. More current than 75 years ago. And even more urgent.... The successor of Peter presents himself here as a witness to the immense suffering of man, as a witness to the almost apocalyptic threats which hang over nations and over humanity" (at www.vatican.va). A "veiled" revelation of the Third Secret could be contained also in the famous Way of the Cross of Cardinal Ratzinger (Good Friday 2005), in the Ninth Station.

[148] Father Paul Kramer, *The Devil's Final Battle*, op. cit., p. 170.

say these things directly and explicitly, but rather in a somewhat hidden manner, in language only the more learned would grasp? *It seems likely that he was sending a signal to the more astute about what he thought was going to be revealed very soon—namely, the whole of the Third Secret.*"[148a]

In my view, the message given by John Paul II is not at all obscure; it is a dramatic appeal to conversion. And if he has not made a formal, official, and literal revelation of the entire Secret, this could signify that because of serious and dramatic concerns (for the Church and public opinion) they have induced him (like his predecessors) to avoid that integral publication, nonetheless revealing substantially the Virgin's appeal.

But is it plausible that the Pope would have wanted to make the unknown part of the Third Secret known implicitly? Yes, because in the preceding years he had done exactly the same thing regarding that part of the Secret which is the vision, at least insofar as the interpretation which views it as having been realized with the assassination attempt in 1981. Hence Vittorio Messori—after having spoken of Fatima in his book-interview of Cardinal Ratzinger—observes: "It is the same John Paul II who, wounded by his would-be assassin on May 13—the anniversary of the first apparition in Portugal—made a pilgrimage to Fatima in thanksgiving to Mary 'whose hand (he said) miraculously guided the bullet,' and seemed to make reference to prophecies which, through a group of children, had been transmitted to humanity and concerned also the person of the pontiff."[149]

Messori wrote these things in 1985. This signified—for whoever wanted to understand—that the Pope had already recognized the vision of the Third Secret as a prophecy of the 1981 attack (at least according to the interpretation provided by the Vatican). Indeed, in the third volume of his work published in 1986, Frère Michel, commenting on this passage from Messori, wrote as follows:

> We have so many indications that the Third Secret "refers also to the person of the Pontiffs", that for us it is a certainty. But does this mean that the assassination attempt and the protection the Holy Father benefitted from are announced in the Third Secret? The text suggests it. But it

---

[148a] Ibid., p. 171.
[149] Vittorio Messori and Joseph Ratzinger, *Report on the Faith*, op. cit., pp. 111-112.

is not the Cardinal who proposes this interpretation, and Messori himself stays on the hypothetical tone.[150]

Then, in passing, there was a declaration by Ali Ağca during his trial, and reported by *Le Figaro* on May 29, 1985: "I wish to say one thing to the court: the attack against the Pope is linked to the Third Secret of the Madonna of Fatima." How did Ağca come to know this fifteen years before the Secret was revealed in 2000? In an interview by Marco Nese in *Corriere della Sera* published on May 14, 2000, the Turk explained: "I spoke of it many times during the trial. And the presiding judge of the Court of Santiapichi, a little annoyed by my insistence on this, asked me: 'But you really believe that the Third Secret is connected to his person?' And I responded: 'Certainly. Before I did not at all know that it was, but then the Vatican said that it was connected to me.'" "And it is true," comments the journalist for *Corriere*. "In 1985, while the trial on the so-called 'Bulgarian trail' was unfolding, from the Holy See it came to be understood for the first time that the Third Secret prophesied an attack on the Pope."[151] How the Vatican made this understood is not recorded, but the declarations by Ağca and those of *Corriere* are unequivocal.

And these declarations during the Ağca trial arise fifteen years before revelation of the Secret.[152] Therefore, the Secret officially revealed in 2000 would have been known implicitly for years—not in its literal formulation and contents, but in the official interpretation which links the prophecy to the attack in 1981.

One could therefore hypothesize that the same system was also followed with the other part of the Secret, comprised of the words

---

[150] FM, v. III, p. 836.

[151] *Corriere della Sera*, May 14, 2000. Also in *Crossing the Threshold of Hope*, published in 1994, Karol Wojtyla says to Messori, who had questioned him concerning the three shepherds, Russia, and the triumph of the Immaculate Heart of Mary: "Perhaps also for this reason is the Pope described as being from 'a faraway country,' and perhaps for this reason it was necessary that there be an attack in St. Peter's Square precisely on May 13, 1981, the anniversary of the first apparition at Fatima, so that everything could become more transparent and comprehensible, so that the voice of God who speaks in the history of man through the 'signs of the times' could be more easily heard and understood" (p. 146).

[152] There are even those who hold that Pius XII himself anticipated the contents of the vision in his discourse of March 19, 1958, where the last phrase is almost a literal reference to the text of the vision: "The time will come, dear children, when there will be rich and abundant harvests; the earth, bathed in tears, will smile with pearls of love and, watered by the blood of martyrs, will bring forth Christians."

of Mary. If it is not a mere coincidence that two Popes, Paul VI and John Paul II, had both spoken of Fatima by evoking that same passage of the Apocalypse in solemn discourses delivered at the Portuguese sanctuary, one can conclude that there is a strict linkage between the prophecy of the Apostle John and the Third Secret. At any rate, the confirmation arrives from a most authoritative source, because Sister Lucia herself, in her extremely rare (authentic) public declarations, explicitly linked the third part of the Secret to the Apocalypse: "It is all in the Book of the Apocalypse—read it!" She also indicated precisely Chapters 8 and 13 of the Apocalypse.[153] And this is truly disquieting, because the eighth chapter regards the plague that will rain down upon the earth and other things regarding the times of the Antichrist.[154] This reference to the Gospel seems even more disquieting because one's thoughts go immediately to the prophecy on the last times contained therein.[155] But if Sister Lucia's reference to the Apocalypse is known and documented, it is not clear when, where, and to whom the visionary would have made this reference to the Gospel.

What is involved, finally, is understanding whether all of this could refer to the text of the vision revealed in 2000, read with reference to the attack of 1981. Frankly, it appears that the answer is no. At any rate, the "Fatimists" play two other cards—objectively very strong—to demonstrate their thesis. The first card has a rather sensational name: Joseph Ratzinger.

That interview of Cardinal Ratzinger...

An epic in the history of the post-conciliar Church began with the publication in 1984 of the book-interview by the Catholic writer Vittorio Messori with the man that Pope Wojtyla, at the beginning of his pontificate, called to be the guardian of the faith of the Church: Cardinal Joseph Ratzinger, who in 2005 became his successor, Pope

---

[153] FM, vol. III, p. 533.

[154] Ibid., pp. 533-552. In summary Frère Michel says: "If Sister Lucia was able to say that the Third Secret is found in the Apocalypse, does this not correspond precisely to the passages concerning apostasy among the pastors of the Church who are placed in the service of an impious political power? Chapter 13, verses 11 through 18? The fact that the first two parts of the Secret correspond, in an amazing way, to the preceding verses strongly encourages us to think so."

[155] Matt. 24 and Thess. 2:4.

Benedict XVI. As Prefect of the Congregation for the Doctrine of the Faith, Cardinal Ratzinger was the closest collaborator of John Paul II and had the merit of having firmly advised the Church on the rupture of orthodoxy after the doctrinal, ecclesial, and liturgical lunacy of the post-conciliar period. Ratzinger is also one of the few persons who in 1984 knew the text of the Third Secret, because as Prefect of the former Holy Office he was in fact the party in the Church responsible for what concerned Marian apparitions. That interview with Messori was anticipated with an excerpt in the Pauline monthly *Jesus* of November 11, 1984, with the title "Here is Why the Faith Is in Danger." The excerpt carried precisely the question concerning Fatima in its very significant headline: "The Madonna as Defender of the Faith. 'Why it is necessary to turn to Mary.'"

I recount in full the part composed of Messori's questions and Ratzinger's answers:

> Cardinal Ratzinger, have you read what is called the Third Secret of Fatima: i.e., the one that Sister Lucia had sent to Pope John XXIII,[156] which he did not wish to make known and ordered deposited in the Vatican archives?
>
> "Yes, I have read it."
>
> Why has it not been revealed?
>
> "Because, according to the judgment of the Popes, it adds nothing different to what a Christian must know concerning from Revelation: i.e., a radical call to conversion; the absolute importance of history; the dangers threatening the faith and the life of the Christian, and therefore of the world. And then the importance of the 'novissimi' (the last things). If it is not made public, at least for now, it is in order to prevent religious prophecy from being mistaken for sensationalism. But the things contained in this 'Third Secret' correspond to what has been announced in Scripture and has been said again and again in many other Marian apparitions, first of all that of Fatima itself in its well-known contents. Conversion and penitence are the essential conditions for salvation."

---

[156] This is an imprecision of the interviewer's. The text of the Secret was consigned by Sister Lucia to Bishop da Silva in 1944, and in 1957 it was requested by the Vatican. Pius XII was Pope.

These are sensational declarations, especially when reread today. In fact, if the Third Secret had been only the prophetic vision of the attack on the Pope, one does not see why Cardinal Ratzinger in 1984—that is, three years after the attack in 1981—should say that publication had been withheld "in order to avoid sensationalism." Once the attack had happened, revelation of the vision that prophesied it would not have been so dramatic. In fact, in 2000 it was revealed in that form without provoking trauma or sensationalism.

If in 1984 Ratzinger spoke of the Third Secret as something that would unleash "sensationalism" because of the "religious prophecy" it contains, one is led to think that it speaks of a Third Secret different from that revealed in 2000, which appears "innocuous." Indeed, in 2000 the same Cardinal Ratzinger began his theological commentary with words exactly the opposite of those he used in 1984: "Whoever reads with attention the text of the so-called 'Third Secret'... will presumably be surprised or disappointed... No great mystery is revealed; the veil of the future is not parted."

It is improbable that the same Cardinal Ratzinger would give two antithetical judgments concerning the same text. Besides, in 2000 he remembered quite well what he had said in that celebrated interview, in which for the first time an authority of the Church explained the Third Secret. Therefore, either the prelate has totally reversed his judgment (but it is not known on the basis of which events) or the two different judgments regard two different texts: that of the vision and that of the mysterious words of the Virgin. Moreover, it is true that only four years before the revelation of 2000, on October 13, 1996, Cardinal Ratzinger held a press conference at Fatima (rather little known) in which, in response to a question on the eventual future publication of the Third Secret, he answered thus: "The revelation of the Secret must be made only when it will not be able to create one-sidedness and disequilibrium, concentrating only on its details; the revelation should be made only when it can be understood as an aid to the progress of the faith."[157]

If the text in 2000, the vision of the "bishop dressed in white," is the entire Third Secret, where are the "details" that have impeded its publication for years, "details" so explosive, according to Cardinal Ratzinger, as to imperil even the "progress of the faith"? In the

---

[157] Aura Miguel, *Totus Tuus*, op. cit., p. 137.

theological comment the same Cardinal made on this "vision," no particular "detail" of this portent and danger is examined. (If it had been, certainly the prelate would have taken care to illustrate its correct interpretation and to refute any mistaken interpretation.) Instead, no, not only in the text of the vision are there found no explosive "details," but the prelate says that this text will seem most "disappointing." In fact—at least according to the interpretation given to it—it does not contain anything destabilizing for the faith, but on the contrary is the fresco of a moving martyrdom of Christians. It is anything but embarrassing for the Church that she there appears as the Church of martyrs. Neither can one say that it was embarrassing before 1996 and that something happened which rendered it innocuous by 2000.

Therefore, Ratzinger in 1996 could not have been referring to this text. But then, of which text was he really speaking? And what is the explosive "detail" that could monopolize the attention of public opinion at the risk of being disruptive for the Church? To which text does it pertain if it is not found in the vision divulged on June 26, 2000? All of this leads one to think that it is found in the part—not divulged—concerning the discourse of the Madonna, which the Fourth Memoir omits with the "etc." And what "detail" does this involve?

This is the true, great mystery we are seeking to resolve. But we will see this further on. Here I wish instead to underline that the substantial elements of the Secret have in a certain way been summed up precisely by Cardinal Ratzinger in the 1984 interview. The Cardinal custodian of the faith, right arm of the Pope, explained officially—for the first time in seventy years[158]—that the Third Secret of Fatima shows "the absolute importance of history, the dangers which threaten the faith and the life of the Christian and therefore of the world."

The "Fatimists" object that if apocalyptic dangers "threaten" in 1984—when the prelate responded to Messori—then the interpretation that was given in 2000, according to which the great martyrdom had already happened in the 20th century between the two wars and had culminated with the attack on the Pope in 1981,

---

[158] Probably a precedent was the conference of Cardinal Ottaviani (who exercised the same role as Ratzinger) conducted in 1967, certainly by agreement with Paul VI. But Ratzinger seems much more explicit.

is not correct. The observation seems pertinent.

Furthermore, the expression "the dangers which threaten the faith and the life of the Christian and therefore of the world" should be underlined because it seems to contain everything (apostasy, persecutions, and chastisements for the world). But then the "Fatimists" denounced the fact that the Cardinal supposedly "reneged" on the anticipation in *Jesus* when, a few months later, in 1985, the integral text of the interview was published in book form, entitled *Report on the Faith*.

Let us then see the new rendering of Messori's interview of Ratzinger in *Report on the Faith*:

> There are circulating in the world versions never denied which describe the contents of that "Secret" as disquieting, apocalyptic, prophetic of terrible sufferings. John Paul II himself, in his pastoral visit to Germany, seemed to confirm (yet with prudent paraphrases, privately, to a group of select invitees) the certainly discomforting contents of that text. Before him, Paul VI, in his pilgrimage to Fatima, seems to have also hinted himself at apocalyptic themes in the "Secret." Why has it never been decided to make it public, even to avoid hazardous suppositions?
>
> "If until now that decision has not been taken"— he answered—"it is not because the popes wish to hide something terrible."
>
> Therefore, I persisted, is there "something terrible" in that manuscript of Sister Lucia's?
>
> "Even if there were"—he replied, avoiding going too far—"this would only confirm the message of Fatima already made public. From that place was launched a stern message, which goes against the prevailing superficiality, a call to the seriousness of the faith and of history, of the dangers which threaten humanity. And of that which Jesus Himself recalls very often, not fearing to say, 'if you are not converted, you will all perish' (Luke 13:3). Conversion— and Fatima recalls it to the fullest—is a perennial demand of the Catholic life. We should already know this from everything that is in Scripture."
>
> Therefore, no publication, at least for now?

"The Holy Father judges that it would not add anything to what a Catholic should know from Revelation and, also from Marian apparitions approved by the Church in their published contents, which cannot but reconfirm the urgency of penance, of conversion, of pardon, of fasting. To publish the 'Third Secret' would mean to expose it to the danger of the sensationalistic use of the contents."

Perhaps also political implications, hazards, it seems that also here—as in the other two "secrets"—Russia is mentioned?[159]

At this point, however, the Cardinal announced himself unwilling to proceed further, refusing with firmness to enter into other particulars.

We have said that the "Fatimist" literature accuses Cardinal Ratzinger of having reneged in the book in 1985 on what he said in the preview given in *Jesus* in 1984. They say that a terrible censure by the Vatican had constrained the prelate to retreat[160] on at least three essential points. The first: *Jesus* magazine speaks of "dangers threatening the faith and the life of the Catholic and therefore of the world," while *Report on the Faith* speaks more generically of "dangers which threaten humanity." Say the critics: "There is thus eliminated the reference to the threatened faith and to the consequent dangers which weigh on the world."

This would be the first point removed from the text. It seems to me a well-founded observation that raises, without doubt, a question. However, it is also true that these "dangers threatening the faith and the life of the Catholic" (interpreted as external perils, that is, persecutions, or as internal peril, that is, apostasy) are implicitly contained in Cardinal Ratzinger's reference to other "Marian apparitions approved by the Church," among which is certainly included the famous apparition of La Salette which, as we have seen, is literally apocalyptic concerning the Church and the Christianity of our times, evoking a terrible internal crisis and even

---

[159] In reality Russia is mentioned only in the Second Secret.

[160] For example, Father Kramer writes: "The key elements of the interview regarding the contents of the Third Secret were mysteriously suppressed in the book." Then, however, the same Father Kramer, almost without being aware of the contradiction, adds: "While the revelations concerning the Third Secret have been censured, in the book it is admitted that the crisis of the faith, which Father Alonso tells us is predicted in the Third Secret, is already upon us and threatens the entire world" (p. 316).

the coming of Antichrist. Besides, the text of *Report on the Faith* deepens the theme of "dangers which threaten humanity," even bringing to the fore the terrible prophecy of Jesus: "If you do not convert, you will all perish." (A citation not coincidentally made at Fatima by Paul VI as well.)

Second point: The alleged disappearance of a reference to the "end times" and to the "events predicted in Sacred Scripture" can be contested. This criticism arises in reality from an error, inasmuch as in *Jesus* Ratzinger had not at all said that Fatima has to do with the "end times," but rather confirms the "importance of the *Novissimi*." The *Novissimi*, in Catholic doctrine, are not the end times, but rather the "last things" that is, death, judgment, Heaven, and hell. Besides, in the Pauline monthly the prelate did not at all link the Third Secret to "events predicted in Sacred Scripture," but to the "prophecy of Scripture" which has an entirely different significance. He said in fact: "The contents of that 'Third Secret' correspond to what is announced in Scripture and what has been repeated many times in Marian apparitions." Then he explained, "Conversion, penance, are essential conditions for salvation."

This gross misunderstanding was already found in the study by Frère Michel,[161] where the text in *Jesus* is reported in French, and the translation of these two points is erroneous. It is probably from there that the other "Fatimists" arrived at the error, having taken the translated text as accurate. This considerable error could have been discovered quickly because the original page from *Jesus* was photographically reproduced and published in millions of copies by *The Fatima Crusader* no. 37, Summer 1991. The same photo was published in another volume of "Fatimist" orientation, the book by Father Kramer, at page 275, where one can check in Italian the Cardinal's authentic text.[162] The episode, at least on these two points, demonstrates that a more or less theological polemic against the Vatican is based on an error of translation and imprecision.

In conclusion, the "case" that an anticipation (of the contents of the Third Secret) was "retracted" by the Cardinal (or that he would have been made to retract it) is not well-founded. Yet it should

---

[161] FM, v. III, pp. 818-824.

[162] I do not know if the French translation by Frère Michel is due to a French edition of *Jesus*. In any case, it seems to me that the error of translation on these two points is very serious.

be emphasized that this interview wherein Cardinal Ratzinger speaks about the Third Secret is important news. Here the news is presented by an authority of the Church (number two after the Pope, from the doctrinal point of view) who, having recently arrived at the Holy Office, finally speaks of the Third Secret after years of Vatican silence. Here we are before a detailed revelation, made in an explicit manner and probably with the agreement of the reigning Pope. And it is understood with certainty that the Third Secret contains a "religious prophecy" which, if known, would provoke "sensationalism," and an alarming prophecy on "dangers threatening humanity" which make current the words of Jesus: "If you do not convert, you will all perish."

These two points are certain. Hence the explanation of the failure to publish—that is, "to publish the 'Third Secret' would also signify exposing ourselves to the danger of the sensationalistic utilization of its contents"—leads one to believe that, in fact, there is something unspeakable that has never been revealed. I reasonably conclude that it is above all related to the "dangers which threaten humanity" and to something grave concerning the Church. Some "Fatimists" are instead certain that it concerns only the Second Vatican Council, and that for this reason it would be unspeakable. As Frère Michel writes: "Yes, it is certain: it is because the great prophecy of Fatima announces not only a crisis of the faith, which has come since 1960, but also the *negligence* of the highest representatives of the hierarchy. And it is because it denounces in a more or less explicit way, but sufficiently clearly, the 'great conciliar orientations' that opened the Church to apostasy; that the Popes, for so long as they continued to govern the Church according to the spirit of the Council—exalting religious liberty, this abominable heresy, ecumenism, the ideals of 1789, and the cult of man—will never be able to make known to the world the words of the Queen of Heaven that condemn them."[163]

The "certainty" of Frère Michel, according to which the Third Secret predicts a Council that would have substantially consigned the Church to heresy, is stupefying. Would it not have been better to propose his idea as a hypothesis as opposed to a certain truth? Has he not been guilty of at least a temerarious judgment?

We return to the interview by Messori. Beyond the vision,

---

[163] FM, v. III, p. 826.

the Church has made known important aspects of the Secret, (intending to reveal the part relative to the words of the Madonna still unpublished): First of all, through these words by the Prefect of the former Holy Office, but also, as we have seen, through the words of John Paul II and Paul VI. Is it sufficient to have decided to reveal what is possible (above all during the pontificate of Pope Wojtyla), but with the concern of not disturbing the faithful and causing panic to spread rapidly among the people?

The second card of the "Fatimists" bears the name of Father Fuentes. This involves only determining whether the words reported by him are truly the words of Sister Lucia.

Thus spoke Sister Lucia

Father Augustin Fuentes was the postulator of the cause for the beatification of the Fatima visionaries, Francisco and Jacinta. For this reason he had free access to interview Sister Lucia. In his visit of December 26, 1957, very delicate subjects were touched upon. This extraordinary dialogue was published—with the approval of ecclesiastical authority—in the United States in 1958 in *Fatima Findings*, Father Ryan's magazine, and on June 22, 1959, in the Portuguese daily *A Voz*.

It is necessary to recall first of all the historical moment connected to this dialogue. In the springtime of 1957 the Holy Office had taken the Third Secret to itself, causing it to be brought to Rome, with every indication of impeding its disclosure. It is in this climate of growing closure toward Fatima, with other signals that indicate the same direction (such as the failure to consecrate Russia), that Sister Lucia, in December '57, speaks with Father Fuentes.

Here is the account:

> Sister Lucia was very sad, very pale and emaciated. She said to me: "Father, the Most Holy Virgin is very sad because no one has paid any attention to Her message, neither the good nor the bad. The good continue on their way, but without giving any importance to Her message. The bad, not seeing the punishment of God actually falling upon them, continue their life of sin without caring anything about the message. But ... the punishment from

Heaven is imminent …. I am not able to give any other details because it is still a secret. According to the will of the Most Holy Virgin, only the Holy Father and the Bishop of Fatima are permitted to know the secret,[164] but they have chosen to not know it in order not to be influenced. This is the third part of the message of Our Lady, which will remain a secret until 1960."

A comment on these first words of Sister Lucia: The Church which is showing herself to be deaf to the words of the Madonna of Fatima is the pre-conciliar Church (and so it was, as we shall see). We take up again the reading of the words of Lucia concerning the Third Secret:

Tell them Father that many times the Most Holy Virgin told my cousins Francisco and Jacinta, as well as myself, that many nations will disappear from the face of the earth. She said that Russia will be the instrument of chastisement chosen by Heaven to punish the whole world if we do not beforehand obtain the conversion of that poor nation.

Based on these words alone, the still-unknown part of the Third Secret would speak again of Russia, as Messori hypothesized in 1984, and as one is led to think by another declaration, already cited, by Sister Lucia.

Father, the devil is in the mood for engaging in a decisive battle against the Blessed Virgin. And the devil knows what it is that most offends God and which in a short space of time will gain for him the greatest number of souls. Thus, the devil does everything to overcome souls consecrated to God, because in this way the devil will succeed in leaving the souls of the faithful abandoned by their leaders, thereby the more easily will he seize them. That which afflicts the Immaculate Heart of Mary and the Sacred Heart of Jesus is the fall of religious and priestly souls. The devil knows that religious and priests who fall away from their beautiful vocation drag numerous souls to Hell.

Are these considerations of the crisis of the priesthood only a thought of Sister Lucia's or do they form a part of the Third Secret?

---

[164] This interview is from 1957. It is in 1960 that, according to Sister Lucia, everyone should have known it.

It is difficult to believe that in 1957 one could imagine this scenario (revealing itself, in fact, after the Council) and above all that a cloistered Portuguese nun would be able to discern it. Therefore, it is possible that this is an element of the "religious prophecy" contained in the Third Secret relative to a great crisis in the Church and of the Faith. There is also the news of a "decisive battle" that Satan was about to launch against the Virgin—a concept that clearly recalls the chapter of the Apocalypse, which will be cited at Fatima by Paul VI and John Paul II and which Sister Lucia will later repeat. This seems to be one of the keystones of the Third Secret, and it is evident at this point that the two pontiffs, in those two solemn homilies, wished implicitly to reveal the Secret's central point. In substance, the secret of Mary, still unknown, seems to be of an apocalyptic type.

> Tell them also, Father, that my cousins Francisco and Jacinta sacrificed themselves because in all the apparitions of the Most Holy Virgin, they always saw Her very sad. She never smiled at us. This sadness, this anguish which we noted in Her, penetrated our souls. This sadness is caused by the offenses against God and the punishments which menace sinners. And so, we children did not know what to think except to invent various means of praying and making sacrifices. The other thing which sanctified my cousins was to see the vision of Hell. Father, that is why my mission is not to indicate to the world the material punishments which are certain to come if the world does not pray and do penance beforehand. No! My mission is to indicate to each one of us the imminent danger we are in of losing our immortal souls for all eternity if we remain obstinate in sin.

Here Sister Lucia affirms that "certainly" a terrible "punishment" hangs over the world; and this must concern what the Third Secret, among other things, preannounces. In this case, therefore, Father Alonso and Frère Michel stand refuted. On the one hand they maintain the authenticity of these words of Sister Lucia, but on the other they limit the Third Secret to a "religious prophecy," denying the prophecy of punishments which burden the world. Probably the understandable desire to stress the importance of the religious prophecy led them to devalue the prophecy relative to the world, which obviously lends itself more to sensationalism and is easily confused with various other eccentric and false prophecies of misfortune. At any rate, it is strange that one would wish to deny something that is known to exist in the Third Secret.

Father, we should not wait for an appeal to the world to come from Rome on the part of the Holy Father, to do penance. Nor should we wait for the call to penance to come from our bishops in our diocese, nor from the religious congregations. No! Our Lord has already very often used these means, and the world has not paid attention. That is why now it is necessary for each one of us to begin to reform himself spiritually. Each person must not only save his own soul but also help all the souls that God has placed on our path.

Here, then, we arrive at an impressive declaration by the visionary:

Father, the Most Holy Virgin did not tell me that we are in the last times of the world, but She made me understand this for three reasons. The first reason is because She told me that the devil is in the mood for engaging in a decisive battle against the Virgin. And a decisive battle is the final battle where one side will be victorious and the other side will suffer defeat. Also from now on we must choose sides. Either we are for God or we are for the devil. There is no other possibility. The second reason is because She said to my cousins as well as to myself that God is giving two last remedies to the world. These are the Holy Rosary and devotion to the Immaculate Heart of Mary. These are the last two remedies, which signify that there will not be others. The third reason is because in the plans of Divine Providence God always, before He is about to punish the world, exhausts all other remedies.

Now, when He sees that the world pays no attention whatsoever, then, as we say in our imperfect manner of speaking, He offers us "with a certain fear" the last means of salvation, His Most Holy Mother. It is "with a certain fear" because if you despise and repulse this ultimate means we will not have any more forgiveness from Heaven because we will have committed a sin which the Gospel calls the sin against the Holy Spirit. ... Let us remember that Jesus Christ is a very good Son and that He does not permit that we offend and despise His Most Holy Mother.

In these considerations by Sister Lucia are expressions characteristic of her mentality and personal thoughts (relative to the last times),[165] and fragments of what she must have known through Revelation. It is worth the trouble to underline the ultimate reason for entering into the Fatima affair itself. Sister Lucia invites us—as does St. Paul—to "not despise prophecies." And she warns that contempt or indifference toward the message and to the final assistance that the Virgin came to Fatima to provide, involves that "sin against the Holy Spirit" which cannot be pardoned and will consign humanity to chastisement. It is natural to think that this warning has a special gravity for the pastors of the Church. Further on we will see, in fact, what their attitude towards Fatima has been.

> The two means to save the world are prayer and sacrifice. Look, Father, the Most Holy Virgin, in these last times in which we live, has given a new efficacy to the recitation of the Holy Rosary. She has given this efficacy to such an extent that there is no problem, no matter how difficult it is, whether temporal or above all, spiritual, in the private life of each one of us, of our families, of the families of the world, of the religious communities or even of the life of peoples and nations, that cannot be resolved through the prayer of the Rosary. There is no problem, I tell you, no matter how difficult it is, that we cannot resolve through the recitation of the Holy Rosary. Through the Holy Rosary we will save ourselves. We will sanctify ourselves. We will console Our Lord and obtain the salvation of many souls. Finally, devotion to the Immaculate Heart of Mary, Our Most Holy Mother, consists in considering Her as the seat of mercy, of goodness and of pardon and as the sure door through which we are to enter Heaven.

A point to be stressed: In the interview with Father Fuentes there is again proposed a nexus between the crisis in the Church and terrible trials for the world as contained in the Third Secret. But concerning this interview there was launched the first great censure, and the first true ecclesiastical polemic.[166] In fact, on July

---

[165] Not necessarily the epoch of Antichrist, that is, the "decisive battle" between Satan and Mary, signifying that history has reached an end (see Father Livio Fanzaga, *The Woman and the Dragon*, Sugarco, Milan, 2002).

[166] This is reconstructed in FM, vol. III, pp. 549-554.

2, 1959 the Curia of Coimbra—even though the interview had been published with ecclesiastical approval—issued an extremely harsh note condemning Father Fuentes who, being the postulator of the cause of the two shepherds and having spoken with Sister Lucia, "has been permitted to make sensational declarations of an apocalyptic, eschatological and prophetic character, which he claims to have heard from the lips of Sister Lucia herself."

Because of the "seriousness" of the matter, Father Fuentes was removed from his position and the curia published a declaration by Sister Lucia that categorically denied everything. When Father Alonso was called to edit the critical edition of the documents of Fatima, he was convinced by this official version. However, with time, studying the immense mountain of documents and above all having been able to speak at length with Sister Lucia, he developed an entirely different view. And in 1976, in *The Truth on the Secret of Fatima*, he substantially rehabilitated Father Fuentes, declaring that his text "certainly corresponds in its essentials to what has already been heard from Sister Lucia." Moreover, he made a significant observation: "This text does not contain anything that Sister Lucia has not already said in numerous known published writings."

Therefore, one comes to ask oneself: If that is how things stand, then where is the scandal? Why did the Curia of Coimbra intervene in such a heavy-handed way? According to Father Alonso, what provoked that reaction was the "enormous documentation" that the Portuguese journal published together with the interview—documentation of a prophetic-apocalyptic type. Indeed, rereading the note from the Curia of Coimbra, reference is made to this literature, but the choice not to distinguish it from the authentic text of Father Fuentes in connection with his removal from the position of postulator leads us to believe that there is something more. This "something," on the basis of which the Archbishop of Coimbra launched his fulmination, is indicated by Frère Michel: "The order came without doubt from Rome."

What in fact happened between the first publication of the interview and the note from the Curia of Coimbra? What happened was that at Rome a new Pope had been installed, John XXIII. And it was precisely in those months that the drastic decisions on Fatima were taken. First of all, the decision not to publish the Secret in 1960, as the Madonna and the Sister had requested, a decision that has tied the hands of all of his successors on the Chair of Peter. (Only painfully and with a thousand problems was John Paul II able, and only in part, to "liberate" Fatima.) Furthermore, it was precisely in these months that the decision was taken to silence Sister Lucia definitively, imposing that silence upon her by obedience.

All of this raises many question marks concerning the dry words of denial from the Curia of Coimbra attributed to Sister Lucia. Because there are only two possibilities: Either Sister Lucia, her arm twisted, had to say things that were not true and which were imposed upon her through obedience by ecclesiastical authority, or that harsh denial by Sister Lucia is not authentic. In either case, all of the subsequent declarations attributed to the Sister by ecclesiastical authority in support of their decisions become very dubious. Or, in any event, they are declarations which should have been documented by the handwriting of the visionary and video or audiotapes of the Sister herself.

With the Fuentes case, however, began one of the most incomprehensible paradoxes of Fatima: Everyone will be able to speak of the apparitions and of the message, except for the only living witness, who endures an inexplicable gagging. After 1960 Sister Lucia could receive, in fact, only family members and those who came authorized by the Vatican. A very bad decision—made moreover, by high-ranking ecclesiastics who promote the Council in a polemic against the Church of anathemas (that of Pius XII). In his famous discourse at the opening of the Council, John XXIII, implicitly rendering a heavy judgment against his predecessors, affirmed: "She (the Church) prefers today to use the medicine of mercy instead of the arms of severity" and proposed "teachings rather than condemnations." Therefore, there is no longer censure or excommunication for anyone—except that in the meantime here began a shameful persecution of Padre Pio[167] (who under Pius

---

[167] Under the pontificate of the "good Pope" there was recommended the persecution of Padre Pio which had already been launched in the last years of the 1930s under the pontificate of Pius XI. Besides humiliations and false accusations, the Capuchin saint had to endure almost a total prohibition on the conduct of his ministry and therefore doing good and assisting the conversion of thousands and thousands of people who came to him, often with the most extreme illnesses, who through him were able to find relief and the grace of healing. The unjust judgment and responsibility of the hierarchy is shown by one particular episode. One day in May, 1931, with the arrival of the news of new punishments and prohibitions from the Holy Office, Padre Pio remained serene and imperturbable. Later in his cell he was found crying. When someone tried to

XII had been left in peace) and the gagging and isolation of Sister Lucia.[168]

This was also a very bad choice of communication because it gave credit to the idea that the Vatican was hiding something terrible which compromised the Vatican. And it was accompanied, unfortunately, by a series of other inexplicable censures and "secretizations." We have seen the embargo that was imposed by the Holy Office in 1952 on the publication of the interview by Father Schweigl with Sister Lucia. The embargo remains in effect, which is strange after the revelation of the Third Secret in 2000. But weightiest of all is the veto imposed on the publication of the documents contained in the official Fatima archives: Father Alonso had been entrusted with the work of their publication, work that began in 1965 and ended in 1976—a monumental undertaking. But by the will of his superiors these 24 volumes, with more than 5,000 documents, have never seen the light of day.

There are, finally, the seals on the papers and letters of Sister Lucia. There have been voiced to Rome many insistent appeals by the Portuguese visionary to the Popes which, however, have never been made public. Of some of these we have certain evidence. For example, on September 27, 1967, "Monsignor Joao Venancio, during an audience granted by Pope Montini to the Portuguese, delivered to the pontiff a letter from Sister Lucia; but its contents are still secret, and nothing is known of Paul VI's reaction."[169]

Furthermore, on May 13, 1982, during the first pilgrimage by John Paul II, we know that the Pope met Sister Lucia who "delivered

---

console him, he replied rather brusquely: "But don't you understand, my brother, that you should not cry for me. I will have less work and more merit. Cry for all of those souls who will be deprived of my witness precisely by those who should defend it." (In Mauricio Ternavasio, *Padre Pio*, Lindau: 2006, p. 96.)

[168] On November 15, 1966, Pope Paul VI repealed Articles 1399 and 2318 of the Code of Canon Law which prohibited the publication without ecclesiastical imprimatur of writings which have as their object apparitions, miracles, prophecies. (Doc. Cat. N. 1483, p. 327). In essence, after the Council everyone was permitted to speak freely of supernatural events and apparitions such as Fatima, something that remained prohibited only for Sister Lucia, the only living witness to the supernatural event. What is even more lamentable is that one can speak freely of Fatima even by way of discrediting Sister Lucia, as has been done with articles and books. The poor sister did not even have the right to defend herself.

[169] Marco Tosatti, *The Secret Not Revealed*, op. cit., p. 75.

to him a letter written by herself."[170] According to Aura Miguel, this was the same letter a few lines of which would come to be cited by Monsignor Bertone in the "Introduction" of the *Message of Fatima* in 2000—a letter concerning the Third Secret which however would have been interesting to publish and know in its entirety. (We have already seen how that citation of a few lines from the letter contains many mysteries surrounding its contents and addressee.) Then there is another episode, which happened on May 13, 2000, when at Fatima the disclosure of the Secret was announced. Something happened of which there remained traces in the chronicle by Luigi Accattoli in *Corriere della Sera*: "Yesterday morning the television showed her (Lucia)—unsteady on her feet, but tranquil in her gaze—delivering to the Pope an envelope while greeting him. And who knows if there are not, in that envelope, other messages."[171]

What was written in that umpteenth letter of Lucia's? And why in that moment, when everything seemed already to have been revealed? It is difficult to think that it could involve simple greetings or other normal subjects, which she also could have conveyed to him orally. On the other hand, the writings of Sister Lucia which have been "buried" in the Vatican archives are even more significant, there having recently been discovered, as we will see, even a book.

A worse patch for the hole

On June 26, 2000, when the Secret was revealed, an editor of *Il Giornale* interviewed Father Rene Laurentin, the great Mariologist and student of apparitions. Asked if everything was now clear, Father Laurentin was heard to respond: "Not at all. There are some things that do not convince me." The cracks which were opening in the official interpretation of the Fatima *affair* after 2000 were becoming noisier and more numerous. The official version, according to which everything predicted at Fatima was already accomplished, was leaking water from every part. At any rate, the triumph of the Immaculate Heart of Mary is not seen in the world—far from it—much less the promised peace and the "conversion of Russia." Above all, after September 11, 2001, it appeared clear that the maternal warnings of the Madonna concerning imminent chastisements

---

[170] Aura Miguel, *Totus Tuus*, op. cit., p. 74.
[171] *Corriere della Sera*, May 14, 2000.

were not consigned to the past. In sum, not everything was revealed on June 26, 2000. And perhaps the mystery had been made even more impenetrable.

In fact, on October 26, 2001 the Catholic journal *Inside the Vatican*, very well received in the Sacred Palaces, along with other Italian journals, published an article entitled "Secret of Fatima: Is There Something Else?" There it is said: "News has arrived that Sister Lucia dos Santos, the last surviving visionary of Fatima, sent to the Pope a few weeks ago a letter in which she warns him clearly that his life is in danger. According to Vatican sources, the letter affirms that the events described in the Third Secret of Fatima have yet to occur, and it (the letter) was delivered shortly after September 11 to John Paul II by the bishop emeritus of Fatima-Leiria, Alberto Cosme do Amaral."

When questioned concerning this, the titular bishop, Serafim de Sousa Ferreira e Silva, "did not deny that Sister Lucia sent the letter to the Pope, but said (with a typically Jesuitical distinction) that 'there are not letters from the visionary which express danger to the life of the Pope.'" In the magazine article one also reads: "Sources have suggested that the letter from Sister Lucia encouraged the Pope to reveal the entire Third Secret." In addition: "It has been said that it contains the warning: 'Soon there will be great upheavals and chastisements.'"[172]

A joinder of hypotheses and indiscretions which, as one can see, are difficult to evaluate and verify. The nub of the question seems to be the history of the letter to the Pope from Sister Lucia. Yet, that there *is* a letter of this sort is certain. I do not know what to say concerning the letter which is held to have been carried to the Vatican by the bishop emeritus of Fatima. But it is certain that a letter was delivered to the Pope at Fatima by Sister Lucia herself, because the delivery was captured by television cameras on May 13, 2000. A letter of which, curiously, only the journalist for *Corriere della Sera* seems to have taken note,[173] yet—so it seems—without grasping the importance of the fact, which is enormous.

In any case there must have been something; something must have happened after the revelation of the Secret in 2000. Because in

---

[172] In Father Paul Kramer, *The Devil's Final Battle*, op. cit., pp. 222-223.

[173] Luigi Accattoli, "The Pope greets Sister Lucia and then asks her, 'Sister, how many years left do you have now?'", in *Corriere della Sera*, May 14, 2000, p. 3.

the fall of 2001, twenty days after publication of the news by *Inside the Vatican* and elsewhere, something entirely unusual took place. Archbishop Tarcisio Bertone—he who, as we have seen, was in charge of the Fatima *affair* in 2000, no less than "number two" at the Congregation for the Doctrine of the Faith—returned to Coimbra to interview Sister Lucia in order to have her deny everything that had begun to circulate. Marco Tosatti, the Vaticanist for *La Stampa*, defined it as "an unusual, not to say unprecedented, event in the bimillennial history of the Church."[174] It is even more strange if one considers that throughout the Fatima affair, for decades, the Vatican had allowed news, conjectures, hypotheses and theories to be published without denying any of them. Strange also, considering that—for some reason which remains unknown—the account of this interview was not published in *Osservatore Romano* until a month later, on December 21, 2001.

In substance, this interview and the publication of this account were intended to demonstrate definitively before the world that all of the Third Secret had been revealed, that the consecration of Russia has been done, and that there do not exist other revelations or messages from Sister Lucia. Instead, the mode of the interview, what was published and what was omitted from the interview, ended by reinforcing opposing theses, and represented—in the judgment of this writer—another disastrous "error of communication" in the Fatima affair on the part of the men of the Vatican.

It would have been better to continue to adopt the decades-old line of not reacting to revelations, objections, and polemics. Because once it was decided to do the interview—a unique case of exposing the Holy See in such a sensational manner—then it was necessary to respond totally and seriously to objections and questions, not evading them, pretending to ignore them, or furnishing clearly inconsistent responses. And it was necessary to do it in a way that was convincing, incontestable, verifiable by everyone, and above all suspicion. Otherwise, the result obtained would be the opposite of that desired: the furnishing of definitive proof that something serious is being hidden, and that this is being done with a mean and self-indicting expediency. The Vatican, if it had wished, could have declined to reveal the Secret of Fatima and could have decided not to respond to criticisms and polemics, standing above and beyond

---

[174] Marco Tosatti, *The Secret Not Revealed*, op. cit., p. 6.

the discussions of the world. But the offices of the Vatican could not permit themselves the luxury—especially today—of saying things or assuming attitudes that the mass media, public opinion, and the faithful themselves would not find credible. Because the Holy See and the Church would thereby be damaged.

We read therefore this unusual account published in *L'Osservatore Romano*:

> Meeting of His Excellency Msgr. Tarcisio Bertone with Sr. Maria Lucia of Jesus of the Immaculate Heart.
>
> On November 17 2001, His Excellency Monsignor Tarcisio Bertone, Secretary of the Congregation for the Doctrine of the Faith, met Sister Lucia in the Convent of Coimbra (Portugal) to clarify some aspects concerning the publication of the document *The Message of Fatima* (June 2000).
>
> The account of the conversation, which we report here as follows, bears the joint signature of Monsignor Bertone and of Sister Lucia.
>
> In recent months, especially after the sad event of the terrorist attack last 11 September, articles on alleged new revelations by Sr. Lucia, announcements of letters of warning to the Pope and apocalyptic reinterpretations of the Fatima message have appeared in the Italian and foreign press.
>
> The suspicion that the Holy See did not publish the whole text of the third part of the "secret" is being reaffirmed and certain "Fatimist" movements have repeated their accusation that the Holy Father has not yet consecrated Russia to the Immaculate Heart of Mary.
>
> It was therefore considered necessary, with the agreement of Cardinal Joseph Ratzinger and the Bishops of both Leiria-Fatima and Coimbra, that I meet Sr. Lucia in the presence of Rev. Luis Kondor, SVD, Vice-Postulator of the cause of Bl. Francisco and Bl. Jacinta, and of the Prioress of the Carmelite Convent of St. Teresa, to obtain explanations and information directly from the only surviving visionary.
>
> The conversation that lasted for more than two hours took place on Saturday afternoon, 17 November. Sr.

Lucia, who will be 95 this coming March 22nd, seemed in excellent form, lucid and vivacious. During the conversation, she professed her love for and devotion to the Holy Father, for whom, along with the whole Church, she very much prays. She was delighted with the distribution of her book, *Os apelos da mensagem de Fátima* ("The Appeals of the Fatima Message"), now translated into six languages (Italian, Spanish, German, Hungarian, Polish and English), and for which she is receiving many letters of thanks.

Going on to discuss the problem of the third part of the secret of Fatima, she says that she has read attentively and meditated upon the booklet published by the Congregation for the Doctrine of the Faith, and confirms everything it says.

She answers those who have voiced a doubt that some part of the 'third secret' might not have been revealed: "Everything has been published, there are no more secrets." To those who are talking and writing about new revelations, she says: "There is not a grain of truth in them. If I had had new revelations, I would not have spoken of them to anyone, but would have told them directly to the Holy Father!"

She then gladly recalled her youth and the difficulties she had encountered, first in becoming a sister; but even in gestures of kindliness, as when she remembers the "holidays" in Braga in the years 1921-24, with Mrs. Filomena Miranda, her Confirmation sponsor.

When asked: "What effect did the vision of 13 July have on your life before it was written down and presented to the Church?", she replied:

"I felt safe under the protection of Our Lady, who would watch carefully over the Church and the Pope", and she adds a new detail to her account of the famous prophetic vision:

"During the vision, Our Lady, shining bright, held a heart in her left hand, and in her right, a Rosary".

"What does the heart in Our Lady's hand mean?"

"It is a symbol of love that protects and saves. It is the

Mother who sees her children suffering and suffers with them, even with those who do not love her. For she wants to save them all and not to lose any of those the Lord has entrusted to her. Her Heart is a safe refuge. The devotion to the Immaculate Heart of Mary is the means of salvation for these difficult times in the Church and in the world. Cardinal Ratzinger's reflection at the end of his comment on the third part of the 'secret' is very relevant: 'My Immaculate Heart will triumph'. What does this mean? The heart open to God, purified by contemplation of God, is stronger than guns and weapons of every kind. The fiat of Mary, the word of her heart, has changed the history of the world, because it brought the Saviour into the world— because, thanks to her 'Yes', God could become man in our world and remains so for all time. The Evil One has power in this world, as we see and experience continually; he has power because our freedom continually lets itself be led away from God. But since God himself took a human heart and has thus steered man's freedom towards the good, towards God, the freedom to choose evil no longer has the last word. From that time, the words of Our Lord are well-founded: 'In the world you will have trouble, but take courage, I have overcome the world.' (Jn 16:33) The message of Fatima invites us to trust in this promise".

I asked her three more questions:

"Is it true that speaking to Rev. Luigi Bianchi and Rev. José dos Santos Valinho, you cast doubt on the interpretation of the third part of the secret?"

Sr. Lucia answered: "That is not true. I fully confirm the interpretation made in the Jubilee Year."

"What have you to say about the stubborn assertions of Fr. Gruner, who has been collecting signatures so that the Pope will finally do the consecration of Russia to the Immaculate Heart of Mary, which has never been done?"

Sr. Lucia replies: "The Carmelite community has rejected the forms for the collection of signatures. I have already said that the consecration desired by Our Lady was made in 1984, and has been accepted in Heaven."

"Is it true that Sr. Lucia is deeply upset by recent

events, that she can no longer sleep and is praying night and day?"

Sr. Lucia answers: "It is not true. How could I pray during the day if I did not rest at night? How many things they are putting in my mouth! How many things they make me seem to do! Let them read my book: in it are all the recommendations and appeals that correspond with Our Lady's wishes. Prayer and penance, together with great faith in God's power, will save the world."

Archbishop Tarcisio Bertone, SDB

Sister Maria Lucia of Jesus and of the Immaculate Heart

The "Fatimist" press issued many objections to this text. The most detailed critique is that found in Father Kramer.[175] Let us summarize them. It was said that the conversation lasted for "more than two hours," but there was not—so it seems—any audio or video recording for posterity of an "interview so crucial, with the only living witness of the Fatima apparitions, at the age of 94 years" (therefore naturally near to death). And there is not even a stenographic transcription. From this historic dialogue there does not exist (there not having been produced) even a list of questions and answers, as would have been required in any respectable interview-interrogation, above all on such an extraordinary subject; above all of a witness who was almost a hundred years old and therefore would not have other occasions to speak the truth. Especially because in this case the interviewee was consulted in order to dispel all doubts and polemics.

Although the interview lasted "more than two hours," Monsignor Bertone instead provided only his personal terse account with very few quoted words from the visionary. Father Kramer has calculated that from these two hours the prelate succeeded in extracting only 42 important words—42—attributed between quotation marks to the sister.[176] Evidently for this reason, in order to augment this scanty content, it was thought to attribute to the visionary an extremely lengthy citation from a passage by Ratzinger that the 94-year-old sister surely could not have recited from memory, but which was read or added subsequently by others. All in all, it makes for a very

---

[175] Father Paul Kramer, *The Devil's Final Battle*, op. cit., pp. 225-244.
[176] Ibid., p. 234.

bad impression. Because then there remain only a few actual words which would require only two minutes to pronounce. And what did the visionary say during the rest of the time? Why was there such fear of recording all of the authentic words of Sister Lucia? Why was it thought to be so risky to record the meeting with a video camera or a tape recorder or even a simple stenographer?

It is clear that if there were nothing to hide, the obvious and simple solution would have been to let Sister Lucia speak freely, seeing that to the prelate she "appeared to be in excellent form, lucid, and vivacious." If there had not been anything to hide or to fear, what could have been done, and what should have been done, was to let her say everything, videotaping it in a way that would dispel every doubt. Better still would have been to put the questions to her through *impartial* subjects, or at least with *impartial* witnesses, because Monsignor Bertone, say the critics, gives every sign of being involved in this matter in order to "defend his own credibility" before a series of well-founded objections.[177]

It is added that, in fact, no civil tribunal would accept as reliable testimony not given in person, but rather presented and filtered by one of the parties to the case, testimony that strangely enough confirms *in toto* [entirely] the position of that party. Besides, the sister belongs to a cloistered religious order, therefore is isolated from the world, feels intimately and rigorously held to obedience, has been under an order of silence since 1960, has not received anyone without the authorization of Rome (therefore can neither speak, nor confirm, nor deny), and the prelate is one of her hierarchical superiors. To have chosen this procedure already, objectively, stretches the credibility of the few words attributed to the visionary, especially because those words contradict what she has previously declared.

For example, based on this account, the sister said that she never put in doubt, during two meetings with friendly priests, the interpretation of the Third Secret given in 2000 ("I fully confirm the interpretation given in the Jubilee Year"). Yet—as Paolini reveals it—precisely Monsignor Bertone himself, in an interview that took

---

[177] With some excess Father Kramer writes: "Objectively speaking, Monsignor Bertone was the last person who should have conducted the interview. The Church and the world are entitled to hear from this vital witness directly, rather than receiving reports from a partisan interrogator with an axe to grind." Ibid., p. 201.

place a year before (the account of which is attached to the Vatican's Fatima dossier), Sister Lucia had said that she did not intend to advance any interpretation of the Secret. ("I have written what I saw, and the interpretation is not left to me, but to the Pope.")[178] Why then would she now eat her own words and state the contrary? And why did she come to reverse herself on such a question, seeing that—as Cardinal Ratzinger has repeated—"there is no intention by the Church to impose an interpretation" and thus "there does not exist an official interpretation of this vision by the Church"?[179]

It is unacceptable and unjust to say, as Father Kramer does in his book from 2002, that this is "the usual attempt to manipulate and exploit a captive witness, who is still prevented from coming forward and speaking freely."[180] But it is certain that if one wished to dispel all doubts, one would not act this way. In this document, which is not an interview on the memories of Sister Lucia but an extremely important and definitive clarification concerning doubts which have arisen for millions of Catholics, Monsignor Bertone even devotes lines to Sister Lucia's recollection of past vacations, when she was a child, "to Braga with Mrs. Filomena Miranda, her confirmation sponsor." But no space was found to report the questions which prompted the interview and the answers that only Sister Lucia was able to give once and for all. That is: the question concerning what follows the phrase on Portugal (the words of the Virgin substituted by the "etc."); the explicit and direct question regarding the previous statements on "the consecration of Russia," and that relative to the identification of the Pope killed with the assassination attempt of 1981. Further, the question concerning the letter recently delivered to the Pope. And finally, the question concerning the authenticity of the typewritten letter of 1989 (cited above) which, according to Father Gruner (in No. 64 of *The Fatima Crusader*), was a fake.[181] Seeing that the Cardinal had already asked Sister Lucia about Father Gruner's initiative concerning the consecration of Russia, it would have been obvious to ask her this as well.

It is attributed to Sister Lucia that the consecration of 1984 "was

---

[178] *TMF*, p. 29.

[179] *Il Giornale*, June 27, 2000, p. 3.

[180] Father Paul Kramer, *The Devil's Final Battle*, op. cit., p. 227.

[181] Ibid., p. 236.

accepted by Heaven,"[182] but as Paolini notes: "In itself this does not add anything new, because the act of 1942 [by Pius XII] also was said to have been 'accepted by Heaven,' but she also declared that it was not that which Heaven had requested."[183] In any event, adds Father Kramer: "It is rather significant that Bertone's Lucia does not tell us where, how, and when she had 'already said' that the consecration of 1984, which she previously considered unacceptable, had now become acceptable."[184]

Then there is a contradiction (the umpteenth) in Bertone's account that leaves us speechless. First, he has Sister Lucia say that she has not received new revelations, denying that she spoke of them ("That is not at all true. If I had had new revelations, I would not have spoken of them to anyone, but only directly to the Holy Father!"), and then a few lines later has her say: "The consecration desired by Our Lady was done in 1984, and has been accepted by Heaven." Father Kramer objects: "How would she know this, absent any new revelations?"[185]

The observation was a little too embarrassing to leave in suspense. Thus, four years later, the day after the death of Sister Lucia, Cardinal Bertone gave an interview to *La Repubblica* and revealed surprisingly: "Lucia had a vision in 1984, the last 'public' one, of which it has never been spoken, during which the Madonna thanked her for the consecration in Her name, which She had requested from the mystic."[186]

Now, apart from the fact that not even this time does the

---

[182] A strange formulation, given the good Italian in which Vatican documents are normally written. Even more strange, as Paolini reveals, is another passage from Bertone's account: "What do you say to the obstinate affirmations of Father Gruner that he collects signatures so that the Pope will finally do the consecration of Russia to the Immaculate Heart of Mary, which has never been done?" This last expression leaves us bewildered. As Paolini observes, one would expect that the prelate would say, "the consecration that *they assert* has not been done" or "that supposedly has not been done." (p. 142). In the terms in which it is reported, the phrase says exactly the opposite of what Bertone intended to affirm. It should also be remembered that the prelate, even in his previous writings, has never spoken of "the consecration of Russia," but always of a generic universal entrustment. Therefore, strictly speaking, Monsignor Bertone has never said that the consecration of Russia has been done.

[183] Solideo Paolini, *Fatima*, op. cit., p. 142.

[184] Father Paul Kramer, *The Devil's Final Battle*, op. cit., p. 205.

[185] Ibid., p. 203.

[186] *La Repubblica*, February 17, 2005. Title of the interview: "Bertone: Fatima, Mystery Clarified, but that prophecy is open to interpretation."

prelate speak of "the consecration of Russia," it being clear with this omission that he himself is denying that it ever took place, we are confronted with a disconcerting episode. It is obvious that in the interview of November 2001 the certainty with which Sister Lucia declared that the (1984) consecration was "accepted by Heaven" derived from a vision. And presumably, whether requested to or not, she told Bertone of it in order to substantiate her certainty. But then, why a few lines later is she made to say that she has not had any new revelations?

The motive appears quite clear. During that interview Monsignor Bertone had to extract from Sister Lucia both an approval of the consecration of 1984 and the declaration that there had not been new revelations in order to silence all of the rumors and polemics. And, heedless of the logical contradiction between the two declarations, the prelate had reported them consecutively. The critical eye caught the contradiction. And thus—strangely enough—after Sister Lucia's death there jumped out of the top hat the "unpublished news" of the apparition of 1984 (defined as the "last public" one; evidently there are other "secret" ones).

The "unpublished news" of the apparition of 1984, however, contradicts what Sister Lucia said in 2001. Should one deduce, then, that during that important meeting of November 2001 Sister Lucia uttered a falsehood, stating that she had not had new revelations? Or have words which are not hers been attributed to her? We want to imagine a third hypothesis that—at least in theory—would salvage things somewhat. Sister Lucia, adding the phrase "If I had had new revelations, I would not have told them to anyone, but would have told them directly to the Pope," could have been intending to say that there *had* been some new apparitions, but that she had revealed them only to the Pope. In any case, this would signify that during the meeting Sister Lucia had not exactly told the truth.[187]

But is it correct to attribute, on the basis of this text, lies or

---

[187] In any case, when and from whom would Monsignor Bertone have learned what he mentioned in 2005? It is natural to think that—if it was not from Sister Lucia—it came to his knowledge at the Vatican between November and December 2001 during those months of preparing the account, which transpired between the meeting in November and its publication in *L'Osservatore Romano*. Therefore, he knew that there had been new visions when he wrote the text for *L'Osservatore*. Otherwise, he could have and should have explained in the interview with *La Repubblica* in 2005 (also to protect the integrity of his own work), that in 2001 he had no knowledge of it because Sister Lucia had kept it from him.

half truths to the visionary? Let us reflect on this. In November-December 2001 Sister Lucia was a very elderly person, who lived isolated from the world with a prohibition against meeting anyone, who was held to silence and obedience, and who was not able to control the account of this meeting and the words that were attributed to her. In fact—and this is another enormous anomaly—the Italian communiqué appears to be signed by Monsignor Bertone and Sister Lucia jointly, but it does not appear that Sister Lucia spoke Italian, given that during the meeting in the preceding year—as Monsignor Bertone declared—"we spoke in Spanish and in Portuguese."[188] It can hardly be the case that in one year a nun in her nineties had acquired Italian, and therefore this text must have been produced in Portuguese. Why, then, does there not exist a Portuguese text? And if it exists, and if—as appears obvious—Sister Lucia would sign only that text, why was the Portuguese text not published? And why was the English version not signed by the sister?

These are more or less the questions posed by the critics[189] and which should be recognized as well-founded. They deserve clear answers.

The overall impression, now that Sister Lucia is dead, is that there was lost an immense occasion to leave to posterity her exhaustive and complete testimony on the most extraordinary Marian apparitions in the history of the Church, and that Sister Lucia had to live for 45 years of her life (from 1960 to her death) in a condition that is not imposed on anyone in the civilized world, not even the most dangerous prisoners. In the Vatican, starting from the time of Pope John XXIII, they had more than enough of hearing the testimony of Sister Lucia. So much so that they did not content themselves with simply impeding her from speaking and from meeting whoever would retain what she said, but from the ambient of the Vatican Curia—I have personal testimonies of what took place in the decade of the 1980s—they went so far as to discredit this little cloistered nun and made it impossible for her to defend herself. They defined her as a "graphomaniac" [a person obsessed with writing things down] and "obsessed with being the center of attention" because of the pressing appeals (never made

---

[188] Aura Miguel, *Totus Tuus*, op. cit., p. 147.

[189] See Father Paul Kramer, *The Devil's Final Battle*, op. cit., pp. 238-239.

public) that she had continued over the years to send to the Vatican.

Our generation has lived for years having the possibility of hearing the last living witness of Fatima, but has been deprived of her incomparable testimony. The few words attributed to her in the documents cited above are such as not to have objective credibility. Thus, concerning Sister Lucia, what have become significant above all are the silences. It is enough to consider the book she was permitted to publish in 2001, issued by the Vatican Library publishing house and which has obviously undergone an attentive editing "beyond the Tiber."[190]

Nevertheless, inexplicably, in 310 pages in which Sister Lucia could have amply expressed herself on the subjects cited above, while deepening and substantiating thoroughly the declarations attributed to her by Monsignor Bertone, there is not a single comment on this. Nothing at all on the Third Secret revealed in 2000, nor on the interpretation given of it (referring to the attack on the Pope), nor on the consecration of Russia (which was supposedly done in 1984), nor on the mystery of the phrase concerning Portugal, nor on the many polemics launched in the preceding years regarding her presumed interviews and letters, nor on the letter she delivered to the Pope. This is rather curious because this certainly would have been an exceptional occasion to set forth all of the truth, black and white. Instead, nothing. This all the more strange when one considers that at the beginning of the volume Sister Lucia informs us that she has written this book as an "answer and clarification of doubts and questions that have been addressed to me."[191]

Why, then, among all of the crucial subjects relative to Fatima, which have aroused such heart-rending questions among the

---

[190] In his preface the Bishop of Leiria-Fatima explains that Sister Lucia had requested permission from the Vatican to write this book because "she is submerged by incessant and repeated questions on the apparition and on the visionaries, on the message received, and on the raison d'être of certain requests contained in it." All of this shows how much hunger and thirst there is among the Catholic people to know and understand about Fatima and matters not yet clarified. The visionary had requested the authorization to "respond in a global manner, not being able to respond individually to everyone." (Sister Lucia, *The Appeals of the Message of Fatima*, op. cit., p. 3.) She received the authorization—curiously—between the first meeting with Monsignor Bertone (April 2000) and the second (November 2001). In the accounts of both meetings, strangely, this book is mentioned. It is almost as if the "collaboration" of the Sister in these meetings was the condition to obtain permission for that publication.

[191] Ibid., p. 17.

Catholic people, is *nothing at all* taken under consideration? How is this possible? How should one interpret this silence of hers? If the answers attributed to Sister Lucia in the accounts of the two interviews with Bertone are credible, why should she not have repeated and amplified them? This would have been in the Vatican's own interest. Instead—no, silence. She doesn't repeat them at all. She does not even *mention* these themes. It is inevitable to conclude that this heavy silence of hers is quite eloquent because it is a precise choice: She did not wish to confirm what has been attributed to her.[192]

The impression that one takes from this "management" of the

---

[192] One year after Sister Lucia's death a small book was published with the signature (posthumous) of the visionary: *The Message of Fatima*. The Carmelite provincial supposedly requested that Sister Lucia "write all of the particulars pertaining to the Message from beginning to end." To be precise it is from the preface we learn that Sister Lucia had already written a book on this in 1955, but "this work was sent to the Vatican by the order of Paul VI" and was never published. The Carmelite provincial said that "knowing the contents of the book," it was suggested that instead of publishing it, she write this other book "in a different style." This curious editorial operation has produced a booklet of memories interrupted by the death of the Sister. In the first part are repeated memories already fully recorded in her memoirs. In the second part are found certain things from the disputed interview with Carlos Evaristo. To begin with, the bizarre news that Gorbachev knelt before the Pope, which was denied categorically by Vatican spokesman Navarro-Valls on March 2, 1998. Curiously, the editors of the volume, published by the pastoral secretariat of the Carmel of Coimbra, mention the Vatican denial in a footnote, but add: "Nevertheless, Sister Lucia wrote of this because she had received it from a source that she considered worthy of belief" (page 55), almost as if she had wanted to attribute the lie to the Vatican. The book also attributes to Sister Lucia the bizarre idea that the prophecy of the Madonna that "Russia will be converted" should not be understood in the sense of a conversion to Christianity, but as a "transformation from evil to good, that is, a change" (pp. 55-56). In substance, the intention is to pass off a regime change in Russia as "the conversion" prophesied by the Virgin. This incredible interpretation obviously is in total contrast with everything Sister Lucia had always said, since she not only interpreted "conversion" as the return of the Russian people to the Christian faith from atheism, but precisely as a return to the Catholic faith. Father Alonso, with whom she spoke so many times, wrote in 1976: "We must affirm that Lucia has always thought that 'conversion' is not limited to the return of the Russian people to the Christian-Orthodox religion, rejecting the Marxist atheism of the Soviets, but rather refers purely, simply, and fully to the total, integral conversion of Russia to the one true Church of Christ, that being the Catholic Church." (In Marco Tosatti, *The Secret Not Revealed*, op. cit. p. 138). Another oddity is this: While being a draft that should have extended up to the last days of her life, in 2005, there is not a trace in these pages of the Third Secret, not even of the revelation that took place in 2000. This, together with the other circumstances, renders the publication—in the opinion of this writer—hardly worthy of belief. And the whole publication of this booklet is very strange.

last witness of Fatima, of this ecclesiastical diction and contradiction, is one of a certain cavalier attitude and of seasonal and colorful versions of the truth. Almost as if public opinion, the mass media, and the faithful do not know how to reason critically and to catch contradictions and elusive responses.

The interview of Cardinal Bertone in *La Repubblica* on February 17, 2005, upon his return from Fatima where the prelate had celebrated the funeral Mass of Sister Lucia in the name of the Pope, adds surprise after surprise. For the first time concerning the Third Secret revealed in 2000, Cardinal Bertone enunciates expressly what he has always implied ("the Madonna prophesied the assassination attempt"), but also adds "its interpretation is not definitive." In what sense? One does not know.

The prelate then formulated some surprising concepts: "prophecy must always be interpreted: It is enough to think of the Apocalypse, of the signs in heaven. Have these perhaps not already been seen with the airplanes that toppled the Twin Towers?" Let us reread this attentively, disentangling its laborious syntactical construction. It would appear that Cardinal Bertone, then the second in command of the Congregation for the Doctrine of the Faith and today Vatican Secretary of State—he who on behalf of the Holy See has "managed" relations with Sister Lucia and the revelation of the Third Secret—wishes to tell us that the attack of September 2001 has something to do with the Apocalypse and with Fatima. A veritable scoop. But, curiously, neither the interviewer nor the interviewee thought it necessary to develop such a sensational affirmation—of which, however, there is not a trace in the preceding interviews of Bertone (beginning with that of November-December 2001, where the intention is declared precisely to demolish the apocalyptic conjectures aroused by September 11). In fact, in a subsequent interview, one-and-a-half years later, having just become Secretary of State, he will declare the opposite: that is, that Sister Lucia had never connected Fatima with the attack on September 11.[193]

---

[193] The interviewer asked: "There is, then, something not said regarding Fatima?" The Cardinal answered: "Absolutely not. As confirmed officially, the Third Secret is that published in 2000 and Sister Lucia never predicted the election and the subsequent death of John Paul I; neither did she make a connection between Fatima and the attack of September 11." (*Thirty Days*, No. 7/8, 2006). The reference to Pope Luciani is probably due to the hypothesis, advanced by a number of parties, that the Pope "killed" in the prophecy could be him, given his mysterious meeting with the visionary which

But, turning to the interview published by *La Repubblica* after Sister Lucia's death, the surprises are not over. When Cardinal Bertone is questioned on the reasons the Pope had not revealed the Third Secret before, he responds elusively, speaking of Wojtyla as the "object-victim of the prophecy." And then he adds: "Certainly a Pope had already thought of breaking the silence: It was Paul VI who in 1967 went to Fatima to speak at length with Sister Lucia, to make her explain." Now, whoever has even a minimal knowledge of the Fatima affair would know quite well that in the course of Paul VI's visit to Fatima precisely the opposite happened. It was a sensational incident. The embarrassing scene has also been described by Aura Miguel in a book to which, among others, Monsignor Bertone has written the preface. Here is what happened: "When the Pope approached, the religious asked to speak with him, saying that she had a message to give him, but Paul VI made himself unavailable and sent Lucia to speak with her bishop."[194]

Here is the same scene described by Andrea Tornielli: Sister Lucia is on her knees, she is seen to say something to the Pope, but here "the attitude of the pontiff changes, it is perceived from his gestures that he has said no and has invited the religious not to insist. Lucia had wanted a face to face meeting, Montini invited her courteously but firmly to address herself to her bishop." In substance the pontiff "did not want to speak in private with her" and "the refusal of the Pope was fixed forever on the films of the cameramen."[195] Everyone can see the annoyed refusal of Pope Montini.

Thus, what took place is exactly the opposite of what is affirmed by Bertone. He then said a series of other things on which it would be well to linger. For example, the prelate declared (at Sister Lucia's funeral): "We will know whether there are other accounts and truths in her letters because they will be examined one by one in the process for beatification which will begin soon. And the letters are many because she loved to write." Here a question spontaneously arises: In the famous interview of November-December 2001 Bertone, referring "to whoever writes and speaks of new revelations," had Sister Lucia respond that "there is no truth to this."

How does it happen that two days after the death of the visionary,

---

took place before his election (see Tornielli, op. cit., pp. 62-63 and 95-104).

[194] Aura Miguel, *Totus Tuus*, op. cit., p. 61.

[195] Andrea Tornielli, *The Secret Revealed*, op. cit., pp. 93-94.

with a view to the opening of the process of beatification that will bring to light the sister's letters, the same prelate who had produced that account now holds it possible that there will be "other truths" in those letters (which have become "many") of Lucia? And why is it not explained what are these "many letters" which she "loved to write"? Were they letters to the Pope, such as that delivered on May 13, 2000 at Fatima, concerning which nothing is known? Were there other letters?

The curious thing is that the same Monsignor Bertone, interviewed by Andrea Tornielli in 2000, denied that there exist other documents of Sister Lucia's. Pressed by the journalist, he responded: "But what omissions, what 'whiteouts'! The faxes of the Congregation for the Doctrine of the Faith have been clogged. So many people have sent letters, requests, messages. Many traditionalist circles believe that there is something else, but there is nothing else."[196]

But, curiously, five years later, just after the death of Sister Lucia, the same prelate makes it known that "the letters (of the Sister) are many because she loved to write." Not only letters. As I have already written, in 2006, a year after the death of the visionary, we came to know—almost accidentally—that for almost four years there has even been a book by Sister Lucia in the Vatican which has to be added to the enormous quantity of documents on Fatima placed under lock and key. This was revealed, almost without giving any importance to it, by Father Jeremiah Vechina, the provincial of the Carmelites.[197] That work, which was requested of Lucia in 1955 by the head of the Carmelite order, "was sent to Rome by order of Paul VI, but remained forgotten in the Vatican archives."

Forgotten? An unpleasant euphemism for saying that its publication was blocked and—for the umpteenth time—that the book was secreted. The reason has never been made clear. It is strange that for years the existence of other documents by the visionary was officially denied, and that only after the death of the sister, in view of an approaching process of beatification, does everyone become aware of a quantity of her letters and writings and books delivered

---

[196] *Il Giornale*, June 28, 2000.

[197] The news is contained in the introduction that Fr. Vechina wrote for the booklet, published posthumously in 2006, which, as already noted, supposedly collects some (contradictory) thoughts of Sister Lucia. (*The Message of Fatima*, published by the Carmel of Coimbra, February 2006.)

to the Vatican years ago and strangely "forgotten" there. (Certainly they were all written before death—one hopes!—but it would have been better to give them context when she was still alive.)

Immediately after Sister Lucia's death, among others, even the rector of the sanctuary of Fatima, Monsignor Luciano Guerra, interviewed by *Avvenire* (February 17, 2005), made it known that "there exist many unpublished writings of Sister Lucia, perhaps even a diary."

In the interview of 2005 Cardinal Bertone also felt the need to add that the Sister "at the end even used the computer"—words that perhaps are meant to respond to all of those who have placed in dispute the authenticity of the letters of 1989. But these words also give rise to some perplexities: that "at the end," that is, at 98 years of age, the visionary would have learned to use the computer seems rather strange, but we cannot exclude it. However, it does not follow that she was already using it in 1989, especially since in 1989 the computer was not yet widely used in offices; hence there is reason to doubt that it would be found among 90-year-old sisters in cloistered Portuguese monasteries. In any case, we know that the visionary, very wisely, always wrote what was requested of her, even in recent years, with her distinctive handwriting and signature.

Whispers and shouts

There are various other personages from whose testimony the "Fatimist" press has deduced that the official version does not add up, that the truth has been hidden. I will cite only some of them. The most authoritative seems to be Cardinal Ciappi, theologian from the pontifical household from 1955 to 1989, from Pius XII to John Paul II. The prelate—in a letter sent to Professor Baumgartner, published in March 2002 but written by the Cardinal before 2000—reveals that "in the Third Secret it is predicted, among other things, that the great apostasy in the Church will begin at the top."[198] One supposes that a cardinal so important, serious and esteemed by so many Popes, would not play games, especially in matters so grave and delicate. Therefore, his words have to be seriously considered. However, we do not know how and when he learned of the Third Secret (probably at the time of John XXIII). Certainly, though, we can say that that

[198] In Solideo Paolini, *Fatima*, op. cit., p. 150.

phrase does not seem to refer to the text revealed in 2000.

Then there is the account published by *30 Days* (April 1991) of a meeting, lasting one hour, between Cardinal Oddi and Sister Lucia in 1985, when he went to preside over the celebrations of May 13 in Fatima. Oddi asked the visionary why the Secret had not been divulged. Sister Lucia, who for years had requested its publication, recounted that in a private meeting she had had with Pope Wojtyla in 1982, speaking of the problem, the Holy Father told her that it had not been divulged "because it could be badly interpreted."[199] The meeting between the Pope and visionary took place in 1982, thus a year after the attack by Ağca. If the vision concerned a prophecy of that shooting, one does not see how it could have been badly interpreted.

Cardinal Oddi, upon hearing the words of the Pope referred to by Sister Lucia, deduced that the Third Secret "preannounces some grave error committed involuntarily by the Church which, because of bad interpretations, is now going through difficult moments."[200] Evidently, Oddi was referring to the Council, or rather misinterpretations of the Council and the deterioration that followed. In fact, in another interview he explained: "In my opinion what is written, more or less, is that in 1960 the Pope would have convoked a council from which, contrary to his intentions, there would arise many difficulties for the Church."[201]

There is Father Jose dos Santos Valinho, a Salesian priest born at Fatima and, above all, the nephew of Sister Lucia, and thus one who had always had access to the visionary. He was interviewed shortly before revelation of the Secret in 2000 and said: "I have my own idea, which naturally could be totally mistaken. I hold that that part of the Secret concerns the Church, internally. Perhaps doctrinal difficulties, a crisis of unity, wounds, rebellions, divisions. The last phrase written by my aunt, which precedes the still-unknown

---

[199] See *La Stampa*, May 14, 2000. One inevitably recalls the declarations of Cardinal Sodano to journalists in May 2000, when he preannounced the publication of the Secret: "For some time the Pope had expressed the intention to do it. Also because it concerns symbolic visions which contain nothing mysterious." *Corriere della Sera*, May 14, 2000. If the vision were the entire Third Secret, given that it contains "nothing mysterious" and can calmly be made public, why—as Pope Wojtyla said in 1982—could it be "badly interpreted"?

[200] In Aura Miguel, *Totus Tuus*, op. cit., p. 133.

[201] *30 Days*, November 1990.

portion of the Secret says 'In Portugal the dogma of the faith will always be preserved.' Afterwards begins the passage which we do not know. However, that phrase makes clear that the theme of the missing part could be linked to the last published affirmation. Therefore, in other parts of the Church this dogma could waver. But we are in the area of suppositions."[202]

In the preface of the book in which Father Valinho's comment appears, the celebrated Mariologist Rene Laurentin adopts Father Valinho's thesis, according to which "the famous secret regards the Church," and adds: "as Cardinal Ratzinger also asserts"[203] (evidently referring to the published interview with Messori).

But the witness with more explosive declarations is Father Malachi Martin, former Jesuit, and a professor of the Pontifical Biblical Institute, who came to be a close collaborator of Cardinal Bea, the important prelate-protagonist of the Council (especially under John XXIII).

In 1998 Martin gave a sensational interview on the *Art Bell Show* in which he provided a behind-the-scenes account of the Vatican and of the "war to the death" between progressivists and traditionalists. At a certain point the interviewer asked him about the Third Secret of Fatima, and the ecclesiastic, who claims that he read it precisely because of his closeness with Cardinal Bea, explained that its publication would be devastating: "It could be a shock ... It could strike people in different ways. Some, if they came to know that this really was the Third Secret of Fatima, would be extremely angry." These words leave one to think of the preannouncement of a catastrophe, but when the interviewer recalled the horrible planetary cataclysms contained in the document from *Neues Europa* and asked if the Secret is that traumatic, the response by Martin is: "Worse." To the disconcerted journalist the ecclesiastic repeated: "Much worse. Look I am proceeding very cautiously. The central element of the Third Secret is terrifying and is not contained in that [in the passage that you have read me]."

The interviewer then asked: "Are you telling me that what is contained in the Third Secret is more terrible than what I have just read?" "Oh yes. It is. Because what you have just read is, essentially, the extermination by natural powers ... [I]t is as if nature is revolting

---

[202] Renzo and Roberto Allegri, *Reportage da Fatima*, op. cit., p. 128.

[203] Ibid., p. 9.

against the human race. It is substantially what happens by means of these terrible catastrophes and chastisements. And this is not the essence of the Third Secret, not that which is more terrifying."

Confronted by the astonished exclamation of the interviewer, Martin explained: "Yes. It goes beyond the imagination." Reveal it? "It should be revealed," "they were going to uncover it," but "there is the problem of shock, of scandal, of terrifying people and mankind in general ... I would like to be able to do it because a thing of this kind, so far as can humanly be foreseen, would give a shock, would terrify people, would fill confessionals on Saturday night, would fill the cathedrals, the basilicas, and the churches with believers on their knees, beating their breasts."[204]

It is obvious that such a description of the Third Secret does not concern the vision revealed in 2000, but another text. Also because Father Martin adds: "The Secret was intended [by Heaven] for the people, not for the Pope or the bishops. It was intended to be revealed in 1960, by the explicit order of Heaven .... The Pope decided that it would be better if the world did not know it, contrary to the order of the Queen of Heaven, the order She gave to the Pope by means of the children: to publish it. Therefore, the will of God has not been done." Father Martin was at pains to stress that it is not the Church which hides the prophecy, but "only the men of the Church, who are not faithful to their vocation." (The distinction between the Church and the men who are a part of it is theologically correct.) He then added: "Pope John XXIII did not think that the Secret should be published in 1960. It would have ruined the negotiations that were taking place at that moment with Nikita Khrushchev, head of the Soviet state at that time. And besides he had a rather different vision of life, a vision that would be revealed clearly two years later, with the opening of the Council, during his discourse of October 11, 1962 in St. Peter's before the assembled bishops .... He mocked, disdainfully, those whom he called 'prophets of doom.' And there was no doubt among any of us that he was speaking of the three prophets of Fatima, toward whom he was hostile."

This notwithstanding, "the Secret," Father Martin continued, "will one day be revealed and fulfilled. Only this time it will be painful... We cannot avoid it, it is too late. We can mitigate its effects somewhat if we know what it concerns .... Pray, receive

---

[204] In Solideo Paolini, *Fatima*, op. cit., pp. 150-151 and 203-208.

Holy Communion, recite the Rosary. But they will not be easy days, unfortunately." Finally, a terrifying "news flash." A listener intervenes on the precise content of the Secret: making reference to confidences received from a Jesuit, he speaks of having heard from him that it supposedly speaks of a Pope who "would be under the control of Satan. Pope John was reeling, thinking that it could have been him." Father Martin responds: "Yes, it seems that this person would have had a means of reading or would have been given the contents of the Secret." Then he got to the heart of the matter: "It is sufficiently vague to cause hesitation, but it seems to be that."

Thus spoke Father Malachi Martin. It is necessary, however, to ask oneself what credibility these declarations have. It is difficult to say. There is, however, one point that arouses concern. How and when would Martin have become cognizant of the Third Secret? "I was made to read it" he revealed "one morning early in February 1960 .... The Cardinal who showed it to me [Bea] had been present during a meeting held by Pope John XXIII in 1960, to inquire of a certain number of cardinals and bishops what they thought should be done with the Secret."

This information is surprising. The facts are not thus. We reconstruct them briefly. Father Laurentin explained that "John XXIII had extremely confidential consultations at Castelgandolfo in the summer of 1959. Then, without taking account of these preliminaries, he 'opened' the Secret officially, in the presence of only Cardinal Ottaviani, Prefect of the Holy Office ... The official opening in the presence of Cardinal Ottaviani would not have been the official conclusion of the private investigation conducted outside the Holy Office."[205]

Monsignor Capovilla claims that the consultation was expanded to include different collaborators: "The contents of the letter [sic!] were made known to all the leaders of the Holy Office and the Secretariat of State, and also other persons."[206] Frère Michel comments: "Does this mean perhaps that John XXIII had all these people read the exact and integral text of the Secret written by Sister Lucia? We have solid reasons to doubt it ... Without question the Pope limited himself to speaking of it to them: to some even in

[205] *Le Figaro*, May 4, 1981.

[206] In FM, v. III, p. 373.

1959; to most in 1960 or later, and in a rather vague manner."[207]

It is therefore rather difficult to think that a cardinal like Bea, in the Church of that time, could have extended to his collaborator the knowledge of an explosive document on which the Pope had imposed an absolute obligation of secrecy. But above all it is unimaginable that in February 1960 a cardinal could calmly dispose of the Secret as if it were an article in a newspaper, bringing it for fun to the Vatican and causing it to be read from left to right like a headline. Frankly, a thing of this kind does not correspond to the formidable "sanitary curtain" that we know has been imposed "beyond the Tiber" since the times of Pius XII, who—not by chance—kept the Third Secret to himself, in his bedroom. As we will see, even John XXIII retained personal custody of it next to his bed.[208]

It is still more improbable that the Cardinal would have allowed his collaborator to read, not the original, but a copy or a transcription of the Secret—both because Martin does not say so, but says rather "he showed *it* to me" and "he had me read *it*," and because the authorization of copies by the Pope would automatically have signified that he wished it to leak out.

In sum, there is something that does not add up in the "revelations" of Malachi Martin, who is in any event controversial enough. In the ample monograph that he dedicated to Cardinal Bea, *Agostino Bea: The Cardinal of Unity*,[209] Stjepan Schmidt, having been the Cardinal's special secretary, cites Martin only once as "an author more than any other in search of sensation," regarding a book on behind-the-scenes Vatican events[210] (written under a pseudonym)—a volume concerning which the Cardinal, smiling, said: "There is scarcely anything true in these constructions."[211] Yet it is true that this comment was obligatory on his part, and that it

---

[207] Ibid.

[208] The other noted "deployment" of the Third Secret (as we will see) is the archive of the Holy Office, which by definition is inaccessible.

[209] The book was published by Citta Nuova in 1987. It has to be said that even this book is not without its critics. According to Giancarlo Zizola, "besides a certain apologetic tone there are serious historical lacunae." For example, "that concerning the role of Bea in contacts with the USSR and the thaw on the question of communism." Giancarlo Zizola, *John XXIII: Faith and Politics* (La Terza: Bari-Rome, 2000), p. 217.

[210] Michael Serafian (pseudonym of Malachi Martin), *The Pilgrim: Pope Paul VI, The Church and the Council in a Time of Decision* (New York: Farrar, Straus and Co., 1964).

[211] Stjepan Schmidt, *Agostino Bea*, op. cit., p. 473.

was quoted in a book defensive of the Cardinal.

But even Gordon Thomas and Max Morgan-Witts, two investigative journalists who devoted a bulky study to the two conclaves in 1978,[212] filled with international behind-the-scenes events and espionage, speaking of the book by Martin, *The Last Conclave*, described it as "very novelistic," recognizing in it the quality (in their opinion) of "a sharp criticism of the tenure of Paul VI" (above all, in relation to Sindona). Precisely considering the character of Martin's journalistic activity—polemical toward the Vatican hierarchy—it is rather doubtful that if the loquacious ex-Jesuit had had direct knowledge of the Third Secret, he would not have made its contents known.[213] It is true that in making the Secret known to Martin, Cardinal Bea made him promise or swear silence, but—logically speaking—even the Cardinal himself should have sworn maximum secrecy when he was given knowledge of the Secret by the Pope; and to cause it to be read by his collaborator would have been a deviation from that solemn obligation. With this, one cannot exclude the possibility that Father Martin in fact came to a knowledge of the Secret, perhaps hearing it spoken of by the Cardinal (perhaps his words contain various truths). But it is difficult to believe that he saw it physically and read it with his own eyes.

---

[212] Gordon Thomas and Max Morgan-Witts, *Pontiff*, Pironti, Naples, 1989.

[213] David Yallop, in the book *Marcinkus: The Adventure of the Vatican Finances* (Pironti: Naples, 1988), even describes Malachi Martin as "a confidante of John XXIII" (p. 139). One may be permitted to harbor some doubt of this.

4. The Fourth Secret of Fatima

"Precisely so!"

On July 5, 2006, Solideo Paolini, a young Catholic intellectual, from the Marches, author of a book on Fatima which we have cited often, and who has dedicated himself for years to the study of the Portuguese apparitions, went to Sotto il Monte in the province of Bergamo.[214] After having been a bishop for a number of years and now spending his old age in the small village of Pope Roncalli, was he who had been the personal secretary of John XXIII—that is, Monsignor Loris Capovilla. The appointment between the two was for 7 p.m. at the prelate's residence.

After some reminiscing by Capovilla concerning the years he had spent in Loretto as bishop, Paolini advanced a question: "Excellency, the reason for my visit arises from the fact that I am a student of Fatima. Seeing that you are a primary source[215] of information, I would like to pose to you a few questions..."

---

[214] The written account of this meeting and of successive telephone calls was drafted by Dr. Paolini and sent as a personal testimony to this author on July 31, 2006. I would like to thank Paolini again for this precious unpublished "tile," which he permits me to insert into the mosaic.

[215] Monsignor Capovilla was not only present at the moment in which the Pope opened and read the Third Secret, but also materially assisted in carrying out the sentence (of "condemnation") emitted by John XXIII. [Translator's Note: In the inner circles of the Vatican it is widely believed that Msgr. Capovilla was the one who leaked the statement of February 8, 1960 to the press regarding suppression of the Third Secret. At that time he was identified only as an anonymous source within the Vatican.] He was besides, over the course of the years, an important witness for the reconstruction of certain particulars concerning the attitude of the Popes toward the Third Secret. In a certain way—on account of his personal link to John XXIII—he himself is a protagonist in this affair.

At first the bishop was guarded: "No, look. Seeing that it has been officially revealed and to avoid imprecisions, I am held to what has already been said. Even if I may know something more, it is necessary for one to hold to that which has been said in the official documents."

While smiling he added a promise: "Write me your questions and then I will respond to them; I will go and look at my papers—if I still have them, because I have donated everything to the museum—and I will send you something, perhaps a phrase… You write."

A phrase? In what sense will he send "a phrase"? What phrase was he referring to, the young scholar asked himself? Meanwhile, Monsignor Capovilla continued to express some of his thoughts. Paolini recounts: "The archbishop continued to speak, touching on various subjects: the risk of taking as supernatural manifestations those which are passing fantasies of the mind; the risk that in certain situations one can become monomaniacal [a person who gets fixated on one subject]; the risk also of getting a swelled head. I stayed silent, I listened. And within me," Paolini confides, "I was thinking of poor Sister Lucia… hardly 'inclined' to that type of phenomena: who for months, even after having received the order, was not able to write the text of the Third Secret, so much did it terrify her!"

Archbishop Capovilla continued to speak, and he began to criticize "the ease with which one can take for possessed persons those who could simply have mental illnesses, from which imprudence—which he of Loreto did not exhibit—one could launch immediately into exorcisms when (while not excluding exorcism as an ultimate possibility) that person could simply be suffering from a mental illness. There could instead have been a need for confession, Mass, Communion, and if one wishes, a good prayer such as the Rosary." There followed some other anecdotes and evaluations of the Popes.

Returning home on Saturday, July 8, Paolini sent the prelate his written questions according to the previous agreement. On July 18 an envelope arrived in the mail. "Just next to my written questions regarding the existence of an unpublished text of the Third Secret which had not yet been revealed, of which there were many indications, Monsignor Capovilla (who is well known to have read the Third Secret) had written literally: 'Nulla so' [which means 'Nothing I know']." "This answer" Paolini confides, "surprised me.

In fact, if the mysterious and never-revealed text were a fantasy, the prelate, one of the few who know the Secret, would have been able to and was obliged to reply to me that this is a completely unfounded idea and that everything had been revealed in 2000. Instead he answered: 'Nothing I know.' An expression that I imagine he wanted to invoke, ironically, a certain *omertá* [code of silence]..."

Perhaps that was the promised "phrase," but in reality there was something else. The envelope from Monsignor Capovilla also contained a curious little handwritten page, of the most normal appearance, which stated as follows:

14 July 2006 A.D.

I cordially greet Dr. Solideo Paolini. I transmit to him some pages from my files. I advise him to obtain a copy of *The Message of Fatima*, a publication of the Congregation for the Doctrine of the Faith, Vatican City Publishers, year 2000. Cordial blessings.

Loris F. Capovilla

It was curious that the archbishop had advised a Fatima scholar to obtain the Vatican's official publication on the Third Secret. It was obvious he already possessed it. Was this not, then, an invitation to read something in particular in that publication related to the documents sent by the same Capovilla? Such was Paolini's interpretation, and in fact he got the point—or, better yet, "the phrase."

"Comparing precisely that booklet with the pages the Secretary of John XXIII had sent me, what leaps into view," says Paolini, "is principally this contradiction: In his 'confidential note,' which bears a lot of seals, it is certified that Pope Paul VI read the Secret on the afternoon of Thursday, June 27, 1963; while the official Vatican document affirms: 'Paul VI read the contents with the Substitute Secretary of State, His Excellency Monsignor Angelo Dell'Acqua, on March 27, 1965, and sent the envelope back to the archives of the Holy Office with the decision not to publish the text.'[216] I asked myself therefore: June 27, 1963 or March 27, 1965?"

Could this perhaps involve a mistake? Or does the discrepancy hide the solution to the mystery we have thus far been investigating? With these same questions, Paolini picked up the telephone

---

[216] *TMF*, p. 4.

and on that same day, at 6:45 PM, called Monsignor Capovilla directly.

The scholar recounts that after some greetings "I brought to his attention the contrast between his 'confidential notes' and what is asserted in *The Message of Fatima*, to which he himself had directed me. He answered: 'Ah, but I have spoken the truth. Look, I am still lucid!' 'My goodness, Your Excellency, but how can one explain this evident discrepancy?' At this point he responded with considerations that seemed to refer to eventual lapses of memory, interpretations of what he had intended to say, to the fact that we are not speaking of Holy Scripture… I objected: 'Yes, Excellency, but my reference is to a clear written text [the official Vatican document, namely *The Message of Fatima*] which in turn is based on the notes in the Archive!' Monsignor Capovilla: 'But I am right; perhaps the Bertone envelope is not the same as the Capovilla envelope…' Immediately, I interrupted him: 'Therefore, both dates are correct because there are two texts of the Third Secret?' Here there was a brief silent pause. Then Monsignor Capovilla responded: 'Precisely so!'"

The Vatican mystery of the dates

Now the promise of the "phrase" finally becomes clear, and truly intriguing. More than a "phrase," what was sent to Paolini is a veritable bomb. That which we until now only suspected is openly affirmed by a key witness: There exists a Fourth Secret, or rather a part of the Third Secret (evidently what follows the words of the Virgin interrupted by the "etc.") not yet revealed and which has taken a different course in its meanderings through the Vatican offices. The Secretary of Pope John reveals it through the decisive particular of the dates and then by stating explicitly that there exist two different texts of the Third Secret. These are sensational revelations[217] also because of the central role that John XXIII's secretary had in secreting the third part of the message of Fatima.

But, one asks, what allows the prelate to know with such precision the date on which Paul VI read the "Capovilla envelope" at a time when he was no longer secretary of the (new) Pope?

---

[217] On the hypothesis of two texts of the Third Secret already elaborated, drawing upon many clues, see the article by Andrew Cesanek, presented in the book compiled by Father Kramer.

The answer is contained precisely in the precious document the Monsignor sent to Paolini. Let us read it. It is a folio, on paper impressed with the episcopal seal, characterized as a "Confidential Note of L. F. Capovilla." It is dated May 17, 1967. Here is the text:

Thursday the 27th of June 1963, I was on duty in the Antechamber [the outer office where the Pope meets various persons]. In the early morning Paul VI received, among others, Cardinal Fernando Cento [who had been Papal Nuncio to Portugal] and shortly afterwards the Bishop of Leiria Monsignor Joao [John] Pereira Venancio. Upon leaving, the Bishop asked for "a special blessing for Sister Lucia".

It is evident that during the audience they spoke about Fatima. In fact, in the afternoon the Substitute [acting Secretary of State] Monsignor Angelo Dell'Acqua telephoned me on Via Casilina (I was a temporary guest of the Sisters of the "Poverelle" [Saint Francis of Assisi]:

"They are looking for the Fatima envelope [*plico*]. Do you know where it is kept?"

"It was in the drawer on the right hand side of the desk, named 'Barbarigo,' in the [Papal] bedroom."

One hour later Dell'Acqua called me back: "Everything is okay. The envelope [*plico*] has been found."

Friday morning (28 June), between one meeting and another, Paul VI asked me: "How come on the envelope there is your [Capovilla's] name?"

"John XXIII asked me to write a note regarding how the envelope arrived in his hands with the names of all those to whom he felt he should make it known."

"Did he make any comment?"

"No, nothing except what I wrote on the outer file [*involucro*]: 'I leave it to others to comment or decide.'"[218]

---

[218] Here Monsignor Capovilla refers to the attached page of the agenda of John XXIII for the 10th of November, 1959, in which one reads: "Interesting conversations with C.S.S. (Cardinal Secretary of State) in preparation for the consistory and with young Bishop of Leiria—the Bishop of Fatima—Monsignor J. Pereira Venancio. We have spoken at length of the seer of Fatima, who is now a good religious at Coimbra. The Holy Office will take care of everything to a good end." One does not comprehend the connection between leaving it to others "to comment or decide" and that page of the Pope's

In truth, Capovilla had already, quite recently, recounted this request by Paul VI to retrieve the text of the Third Secret. But evidently the importance of the discrepancy of the dates with the official Vatican text of 2000 was not grasped.[219] Now, at any rate, this page from the "Confidential Note" of Capovilla is indisputable and demonstrates some things of exceptional importance.

First observation: Paul VI was elected Pope on Friday, June 21, 1963. He had not even been officially installed (the Mass was celebrated on June 29) when on June 27, only six days after his election, he met with the Bishop of Leiria (the recipient of the Third Secret) and the cardinal who was the Nuncio to Lisbon and who brought the Third Secret to Rome, in order to request a reading of that mysterious text. If one considers the days required for the closure of the celebrations of the conclave and those necessary for the formal installation of the Pope, it can be said that before anything, even before receiving his responsibilities over the various dicasteries and taking cognizance of all of their files, even those of the Vatican Council (which was still suspended), Paul VI met with the "emissaries" of Sister Lucia and proceeded to read the text of the Third Secret of Fatima (or rather the words of the Madonna which have yet to be published), and immediately decided to leave it buried, as had his predecessor.

Second observation: In the Vatican booklet *The Message of Fatima* one reads that before Paul VI "John XXIII decided to send the sealed envelope back to the Holy Office and not to reveal the third part of the 'Secret.'" We know, however, through the certain testimony of Monsignor Capovilla, that Paul VI found the Third Secret, as indicated by the same Monsignor, in the drawer of the writing desk in the bedroom of Pope John. This is in contradiction to the official reconstruction.[220] But considering instead, as Capovilla

diary, whose implication is that from that moment Sister Lucia, "managed" by the Holy Office, is peremptorily prohibited from either speaking or meeting people (outside of her immediate family).

[219] Tornielli thinks that it is an error of dictation on the part of Capovilla. (See Andrea Tornielli, *The Secret Revealed*, op. cit., pp. 60-61.)

[220] Concerning the custody of the Third Secret in the papal apartment, presented with this "umpteenth contradiction" of the official version, "Monsignor Bertone attempted to resolve the difficulty, saying that 'perhaps' Monsignor Capovilla was referring to a photocopy of the manuscript. (*Il Giornale*, June 27, 2000.) 'Perhaps.' But, Your Eminence, if the Pope had had in his residence a photocopy of the Secret, why would he have ever requested it from the Holy Office archive (as you have written in the official

has revealed to us, that there are two different texts which comprise the Third Secret, and considering that the chronology the Vatican furnishes us through the pen of Monsignor Bertone relates to the text of the vision (but not the text of the discourse of the Madonna), then everything adds up: both are speaking the truth. Evidently, John XXIII sent back the part relative to the vision, deciding to keep to himself, in his bedroom, the other part. He must have held it so "explosive" and shocking as to justify such an anomaly. But there is another reason: because Pius XII had done the same thing.

In the previously cited "Introduction" by Bertone of *The Message of Fatima*, one reads that John XXIII caused the Third Secret to be brought to him from the Holy Office.[221] But here the accounts also seem not to add up, because we know with certainty—there being also photographic documentation—that instead his predecessor, Pius XII, kept the text of the Secret of Fatima (the "explosive" one) in his own room, next to the bed.[222] All of the accounts, however, add up if one considers that there exist two different texts, one of which, that of the vision, Pope John caused to arrive from the Holy Office (as Bertone says) and the other which was retrieved

---

booklet, on page 5)?" (Solideo Paolini, *Fatima*, op. cit., p. 156.)

[221] "According to the records of the archive, with the agreement of His Excellency Cardinal Alfredo Ottaviani, on August 17, 1959 the Commissioner of the Holy Office, Father Pierre Paul Philippe, O.P., brought to John XXIII the envelope containing the third part of 'the secret of Fatima.'" (pp. 14-15.)

[222] The discovery of this fact was made by the French journalist, Robert Serrou, who went to the Vatican for a photographic feature on the papal apartments for a story in *Paris Match*. It was May 14, 1957, just a month after the arrival of the Third Secret in the Vatican. Obviously under the surveillance of Sister Pasqualina, the very faithful collaborator of Pius XII, the journalist visited the papal apartment where he encountered a little wooden safe placed on a table, on which was written: "Secret of the Holy Office." Serrou asked the sister to enlighten him ("Sister, what is in that little wooden safe?"), and she immediately explained: "The Third Secret of Fatima is there inside…" A year-and-a-half later *Paris Match*, as part of that photographic feature, published the photo of the safe (twice, on the occasion of the death of the pope, in No. 497, dated October 18, 1958, and in the special issue No. 2, Fourth Quarter of 1958). Much later Frère Michel, while working on his volumes on Fatima, contacted Serrou to ask him to confirm, because the words of the Sister had not appeared in the article but rather had reached his ears through Abbé Caillon. Then, on January 10, 1985, he received from the journalist this letter: "I can confirm that I was engaged in doing a story in the apartment of Pius XII on May 14, 1957 …. It is exactly so: Mother Pasqualina told me, indicating to me a little wooden safe bearing a label on which was written 'Secret of the Holy Office': 'In there is the Third Secret of Fatima.' I think that it can be said that there is no doubt of the veracity of the information provided to me by the religious." All of this is recounted in FM, vol. III, pp. 484-486.

from the little wooden safe of Pius XII kept in his own room. "This proves," according to Frère Michel, "that Pius XII attributed great importance to the Third Secret."[223] Or rather it proves that he thought it to be "explosive." Probably for the same reason, as we have already seen, John XXIII decided to do the same: restoring to the Holy Office the text of the vision, but retaining the other part in the papal apartment.

Third observation: Paul VI read a part of the Third Secret (the Capovilla envelope, that containing the words of the Madonna, that is, the explosive part of the Secret) on June 27, 1963, as noted by Monsignor Capovilla himself. And then he read the other part, that containing the vision (revealed in 2000)—that is, the Bertone envelope—on March 27, 1965, as mentioned in the official reconstruction by Bertone himself.[224] Thus we can say that, even in this case, both Capovilla and Bertone speak the truth. Again, all possible contradictions are resolved only if one considers that there exist two different texts of the Secret.

This is also the only possible explanation for a series of other presumed contradictions on the dates and locations of the document. In fact, also with John Paul II, as with Paul VI, there arise—strangely enough—two different dates which locate in different moments his reading of the Third Secret. Why should this strange split in dates repeat itself for both Popes if not because we are dealing with two different texts, kept in two different places, and read in different moments by both Popes?

Thus, concerning Pope Wojtyla, on July 1, 2000, it was the *Washington Post* that noted there was a problem with the dates, while being unable to grasp the import of this news. The American journal wrote: "On May 13 Vatican spokesman Joaquin Navarro-Valls said that John Paul II read the text of the Secret for the first time days after having assumed the papacy, in 1978. Monday, an assistant of Cardinal Ratzinger [Monsignor Bertone],[225] affirmed that the Pope saw it for the first time in the hospital, where he was recovering after the attack [therefore in 1981]."

The reconstruction by Monsignor Bertone in the Vatican publication *The Message of Fatima*, which naturally provides only

---

[223] Ibid.

[224] *TMF*, p. 4.

[225] *New York Times*, June 26, 2000.

the chronology for the "Bertone envelope," that is, the text of the vision, does not give the date of 1978, as does spokesman Navarro-Valls, but rather 1981: "John Paul II, for his part, requested the envelope containing the third part of the 'Secret' after the attempt on May 13, 1981." The envelope arrived from the Holy Office on July 18, 1981 (while the Pope was in the hospital precisely because of the assassination attempt) and on the following August 11 it was restored to the archive of the Holy Office.

But—as we have seen above—immediately after Monsignor Bertone writes something of a contradiction: "As noted, Pope John Paul II thought immediately of consecrating the world to the Immaculate Heart of Mary and he himself composed a prayer for this which set forth an 'act of entrustment' for celebration in the Basilica of Saint Mary Major on June 7, 1981."

Here one must ask how it is possible to connect ("immediately after he thought...") the reading of the text of the vision (which happened on July 18, 1981), with the decision of the Pope concerning the act of entrustment to Mary, which had already happened on June 7, 1981? That solemn act, clearly referring to the apparitions of Fatima, could not have been prompted by a reading of the Third Secret that took place a month-and-a-half later, but could only have come from knowledge the Pope had of the other part of the Secret, that containing the words of the Madonna—which, according to his spokesman, was read in 1978, immediately after his election, as with Paul VI.

Indeed, in the archives of the Holy Office, where the so-called "Bertone envelope" is found, there is not a trace of any consultation of the Secret by the Pope in 1978. Therefore, this reading could refer only to the so-called "Capovilla envelope," and evidently that document had already been lodged in the papal apartment, where it was placed by Pius XII and where it was also kept by John XXIII and Paul VI.

The fact that John Paul II had knowledge in 1978 of the secret words (still unpublished) of the Holy Virgin also explains his (presumed) declarations at Fulda, which happened in November 1980, some months before the attack by Ağca and the reading of the text of the vision, and the reference he made to martyrdom on that occasion. ("We must prepare ourselves to suffer in the not-too-distant future great trials, which will require on our part a willingness to lose life itself...") This leads one to think that the words of the Madonna also contain Her commentary on the vision of the "Pope who is killed," probably the explanation of the vision itself.

The different locations in the Vatican of two parts of the Third Secret perhaps explains also the extremely strange phrase of Cardinal Ottaviani in his famous discourse of February 11, 1967, when he was pro-Prefect of the Congregation for the Doctrine of the Faith: "The Pope [John XXIII] placed the 'Secret' in another envelope, sealed it, and sent it into one of those archives which are like a well, deep and dark, into which papers go, and no one ever sees anything more of them. Therefore, it is difficult to say where 'the Secret of Fatima' is."[226] Incredible statements. In fact everyone knew—it was official—that the Third Secret was being kept in the archives of the Holy Office; and yet, curiously, it is precisely he, the guardian of the Holy Office, who leads us to believe that "it is difficult to say where the 'Secret of Fatima' is."[227] This was a cryptic way of making it known that the truth is more complicated than the official version.

However, during the conference in 1967 the Cardinal said something else very strange. He retraced thus the trajectory of the Secret: "The Bishop of Leiria remitted it to the Papal Nuncio, who was Monsignor Cento, today Cardinal, present here, who transmitted it faithfully to the Congregation for the Doctrine of the Faith as he had been requested .... The Secret thus arrived at the Congregation for the Doctrine of the Faith; and, still sealed, it was transmitted to John XXIII."[228]

Frère Michel, who has documented the custody of the Secret in the personal apartment of the Pope, while catching the contradiction between his information and that furnished by Ottaviani (according to which the envelope had been kept in the Holy Office), judges it

---

[226] In Luigi Gonzaga da Fonseca, *The Miracle of Fatima*, op. cit., p. 214.

[227] Moreover, it is known (Solideo Paolini, *Fatima*, op. cit., p. 180) that the Cardinal, only a few days earlier, had retrieved the document from the archives and that it had been read by a collaborator (because of his blindness) to prepare for that same conference. Therefore, he knew well that a part of the Third Secret was in the Holy Office.

[228] FM, vol. III, p. 486. Frère Michel rightly notes that if the envelope was brought "still sealed" to John XXIII, this means that it had never been opened by Pius XII, who therefore did not read the Secret.

138

to be "an imprecision" of the Cardinal.[229] In reality, knowing today of the existence of two different texts which compose the Secret, we can recognize that he (Ottaviani) also spoke the truth. In fact, that part of the Secret (the text of the vision) really was brought to and conserved by the Holy Office, while the other part of the Secret was indeed kept by Pius XII in the papal apartment.

In 1977, however, Cardinal Ottaviani went further. Responding by letter to three questions, he wrote: "The true text of the 'Secret' was written by the visionary Lucia and sent to Pope John XXIII,[230] and it remained truly secret, because the Sovereign Pontiff himself had not revealed anything of it. He forgot completely where he had put the text that had been sent to him." All of this was written by the elderly prelate on July 7, 1977.[231] We can say that Ottaviani, by now very old, wanted to reveal explicitly that the "true text of the Secret" was not in the Holy Office, as the official version had maintained, but was found directly in the hands of the Pope (the Holy Office having kept instead the text of the vision).

But there is another clue that gives insight into the existence of two texts. Cardinal Ottaviani in fact asserts: "John XXIII opened the envelope himself. And although the text was written in Portuguese, he told me afterwards that he had understood it entirely." "Yet," Frère Michel objects, "we know that he had first requested the help of Monsignor Tavares to understand the meaning of certain Portuguese expressions."[232] In fact, Monsignor Capovilla also testified that since the text "contained expressions in Portuguese dialect ... he called for the priest, Monsignor Tavares, who was engaged in Portuguese affairs within the Secretary of State."[233]

These two opposing pieces of information can be explained if one holds that there are involved two readings of two different texts.[234] However, it is also the case that we must ask ourselves: are

---

[229] Ibid., p. 487.

[230] Here the prelate is imprecise insofar as the text of the Secret was sent by Sister Lucia to the Bishop of Leiria, da Silva. And the Vatican had it brought to itself during the reign of Pius XII.

[231] In *Mother of God*, November 1977; in FM, vol. III, p. 734.

[232] FM, vol. III, p. 557.

[233] In *World Perspectives*, VI, 1991.

[234] Frère Michel adheres to the idea of Father Laurentin, according to which the Pope first conducted a preliminary investigation, and when he opened the envelope before Cardinal Ottaviani, he had not read the text for the first time.

there really "dialectal expressions" in the text of the vision made public in 2000? I put the question to an expert, Professor Mariagrazia Russo, who, after having made an exacting linguistic analysis with surprising results (see Appendix, where the inexactitude with which the Vatican translated a document of such importance is shown), has revealed that in that text one does not encounter regionalisms, nor provincialisms. This means that the part of the Secret of which Capovilla speaks, that which had need of the aid of a translation by Monsignor Tavares of the presumed "dialectal expressions," is not the text that was revealed in 2000. Here, therefore, is further proof that there are two different parts of the Third Secret—one revealed (but of an uncertain interpretation), and one still hidden, whose very existence is denied, so explosive is it.

The "Fatimite" literature affirms that even the arrival in Rome of the two parts of the Secret happened on different dates which can be traced. In fact, Frère Michel writes in 1985, without ever having been contradicted, that the document "arrived at Rome on April 16, 1957," and even that "confirmation of delivery was received at Leiria."[235] And he writes this with reference to the indisputable authority of Father Alonso.[236]

But, in the official publication of 2000, *The Message of Fatima*, Monsignor Bertone, reconstructing the trajectory of the text of the vision, affirms that "the envelope was delivered on April 4, 1957, to the secret archives of the Holy Office."[237] Did it arrive, therefore, on April 4 or April 16? How is it possible to have at one and the same time two different dates for one and the same document? Either one of the two sources lies (but there would not have been any motive, neither for Father Alonso nor Frère Michel who wrote in 1982 and 1985, respectively, neither for Monsignor Bertone who writes in 2000). Or—as is more plausible—we are not dealing with the same document, and both sources speak the truth. Everything becomes explainable if one considers that Father Alonso and Frère Michel speak of the text containing the words of the Madonna (the so-called "Capovilla envelope"), while Monsignor Bertone speaks of the text of the vision made public in 2000.

But how is it possible that the two parts of the Secret were

---

[235] FM, vol. III, p. 321 (French edition).

[236] *De nuevo el Secreto de Fatima*, Ephermerides mariologicae, 1982, p. 86.

[237] *TMF*, p. 4.

delivered at different moments? For what reason would this have happened? It seems improbable, but if we proceed to examine what happened at Leiria when the request arrived from Rome for the writings of Lucia, we are able to account for how the sending of the documents really was staggered in time.

It falls as usual to Frère Michel[238] to reconstruct these days. Accordingly, in January 1957 there arrived at the Curia of Leiria from the Holy Office, through the Nuncio Monsignor Cento, the request to send all of Lucia's writings. Immediately, the execution of the order began. "When the work of photocopying was finished, Monsignor da Silva asked the Nuncio if he should also send the Third Secret. The Nuncio turned himself in the direction of Rome and answered: 'Naturally! Also the Secret! Above all the Secret!'"

The Third Secret, however—the part with the words of the Madonna—stayed in a sealed envelope and therefore had to be sent as such; it could not be photocopied if for no other reason than that only the addressee had the option of doing so. Knowing this, Monsignor Venancio, the Auxiliary Bishop of Leiria, went to see the titular Monsignor da Silva, who by now was 85 years old and was practically immobilized by blindness and illnesses. And he asked him: "But listen Monsignor, you have the Secret, and you can read it. Lucia has said that you have the power. Open it! Make me a photocopy of it. It is the last chance that we will have." But the Bishop responded: "No, it doesn't interest me. It is a secret; I don't want to read it." The next day Venancio tried again, but received the same refusal. So he himself, very sad, had to take it himself to the Nunciature at Lisbon to deliver the sealed envelope of the Third Secret to Monsignor Cento, who beamed when he received it in his hands. It was 12 noon on March 1, 1957.[239]

From this chronology it is easy to deduce that the delivery of the requested material happened in a temporal arc of two months, and therefore it is entirely possible that there first arrived at Rome (on April 4) the text of the vision and then (on April 16) the envelope with the part of the Secret concerning the words of the Madonna.

[238] FM, vol. III, pp. 479-481. It should be stressed that the author reconstructs these events in the 1980s, being in the dark as to the fact that the Third Secret is composed of two different parts and that they came to be sent at different times.

[239] The date and the hour were noted by Monsignor Venancio himself in a manuscript memoir conserved since 1982 by the Studies and Publications Service of the Sanctuary of Fatima (SESDI). See Aura Miguel, *Totus Tuus*, op. cit., p. 141.

But is there documentation which proves that the Third Secret was thus composed, that is, that Sister Lucia had written it in two parts? In fact, it is precisely her accounts of its drafting which confirm this. Sister Lucia, about to put pen to paper, explains: "I have been ordered to write it, be it in the notebooks where I have been ordered to write my spiritual journal, be it on a sheet of paper and to put it in an envelope sealed with wax."[240] Thus, the two texts were born. It seems strange to write the two parts of the Secret on different sheets of paper, one part in the notebook and the other part on a folio, but Sister Lucia so advised in the following communication to the Bishop of Leiria, which shows precisely what she had done: "I have written that which you have commanded of me; God has willed to try me a little, but finally that was His Will: [the text] is in a sealed envelope, and that is in the notebooks."[241]

Notice the dates. This communication to Monsignor da Silva is dated January 9, 1944. But we know that the text of the vision, made public in 2000 by the Vatican, bears the date January 3, 1944, as is confirmed officially by Monsignor Bertone.[242] In fact—after two months of extremely heavy anxiety which had made it impossible for her to write the text (so great was its drama)—to unblock the situation there was in aid of Sister Lucia the umpteenth apparition of the Madonna, which happened on Sunday, January 2, 1944, and which assured her that it was the will of God that she write the

---

[240] FM, vol. III, p. 44. To speak the truth, the same passage, reprised in the book by Father Alonso, *The Truth Concerning the Secret of Fatima* (p. 33), came to be translated differently in the Italian edition of the book by Aura Miguel: "They told me to write it either in the notebooks where I have been told to record my spiritual diary or, if I wish, on a sheet of paper and to then put it in a closed and sealed envelope." (*Totus Tuus*, op. cit., p. 129). It is evident that "and... and..." is the contrary of "either... or..." To resolve the controversy, it suffices to keep in mind that Sister Lucia, advising that she had written the Secret, will deliver both the folio (inside the envelope) and the notebooks. Evidently, she had used both.

[241] FM, vol. III, p. 47. An interesting explanation is that of Andrew M. Cesanek, contained in the book compiled by Father Kramer: "Why would she (Lucia) have delivered to the Bishop of Gurza, as she informed the Bishop of Fatima, both the envelope and the notebook? It is entirely plausible that this obscure vision—that which could be called the 'calmer' part of the Secret—was written in the notebook, while the explanation of the vision, with the words of the Virgin Herself—whose impact could be rather terrible—was sealed in the envelope that Sister Lucia had placed inside the notebook." (p. 183)

[242] "The third part of the 'secret' was written 'by order of His Excellency the Bishop of Leiria and by the Most Holy Mother' on January 3, 1944," in *TMF*, p. 4.

Secret. And immediately, evidently within the span of 24 hours, Lucia wrote the text of the vision that was indeed dated January 3. Why, then, would Sister Lucia have waited six days, until January 9, to communicate this to the Bishop?

The "Fatimite" thesis is simple: "This difference of dates demonstrates that there exist two documents: the document relevant to the vision, which was completed on January 3, 1944, and that containing the words with which the Madonna explained the vision, which was completed on January 9, 1944, or not much before."[243]

The same authors of this thesis recognize that it involves proof "of a circumstantial nature," and thus is a deduction, however plausible and well-founded it seems. On the contrary, to us it appears indisputable—at this point in our investigation—that the Third Secret is composed of two different texts, whose material characteristics are also revealed to be different. The first surprising clue arrives to us from Monsignor Venancio himself, who—with neck craned, and before delivering the sealed envelope to the Apostolic Nuncio—examined it carefully.

An explosive folio

Monsignor Venancio, who came into possession of the envelope containing the Third Secret before going to Lisbon to deliver it to the Apostolic Nuncio, on March 1, 1957, at 12 noon, carefully examined its precious contents under a light. Inside the large envelope the Bishop saw the smaller envelope of Sister Lucia, and inside of it, a normal sheet of paper. He discerned also the writing of Lucia which he calculated to be a few lines, around 20 to 25, but he was not able to read anything.

Here we have already an explosive piece of information: The Third Secret is written on a single sheet of paper [*unico foglio di carta*]. It is evident to everyone that that single folio is not the same Third Secret that was published in 2000, which is written on four pages, comprising 62 lines,[244] which evidently come from the

---

[243] Father Paul Kramer, *The Devil's Final Battle*, op. cit., p. 178.

[244] According to Frère Michel (p. 481) Monsignor Venancio even noted that the writing on the paper had ¾ centimeter margins, and Father Kramer (p. 185) calls attention to the discrepancy with the manuscript of 2000, which does not have margins. But the

notebook of which Sister Lucia speaks. Are there other sources which confirm the information according to which the Secret with the words of the Madonna is written on a single sheet of paper? To tell the truth there are very many. We begin with Sister Lucia herself.

"Lucia told us that she had written it on a sheet of paper." Thus writes the authoritative Father Alonso well before 2000, reporting scrupulously what he had heard from the visionary.[245] Certainly there are also the four pages of the notebook on which are transcribed the vision. But from the words of Sister Lucia one deduces that for her the "true" Third Secret is this message of the Madonna, while the text of the vision (as with the previous vision of Hell in the first and second part) is the departing point from which the Virgin begins to give Her explanation of Her message to all Christians and to humanity.

But we turn to the words of Lucia referred to by Father Alonso, according to which the Secret was on "a sheet of paper." Also reporting this information—never contested and given as certain— is Aura Miguel in his book[246] which, moreover—I repeat—has an introduction by Cardinal Bertone. In this book is also cited the corroborative testimony by Cardinal Ottaviani, who said during the famous conference of 1967: "She (Lucia) has written on a single sheet of paper that which the Virgin told her to convey to the Holy Father."

It is curious that these testimonies—according to which the Third Secret is written on a single sheet of paper and contains the words of the Virgin—are cited without noticing and or acknowledging the glaring difference with the text published in 2000 which is on four pages and does not contain even a single word from the Madonna. Aura Miguel cites these words of Lucia and of Ottaviani, considering them authentic, but curiously does

---

recently published document by Monsignor Venancio says something different. The prelate noted the dimensions of Lucia's envelope (12 x 18 centimeters) and observed that "the letter, also seen under the light, was a little smaller in dimension, 3 to 4 centimeters less above and on the right, while on the other sides it coincided with the internal envelope." (Aura Miguel, *Totus Tuus*, op. cit., p. 141.)

[245] This information was always confirmed by Father Alonso: "The document was written on 'una hoja' (that is, on a page)." *De Nuevo el Secreto de Fatima*, op. cit., in FM, vol. III, footnote 23, p. 55 (2001 edition).

[246] In Aura Miguel, *Totus Tuus*, op. cit., p. 136.

not draw out the obvious consequences: that is, that there exist two different documents, one of which is still secret.[247]

Therefore, the mystery remains locked away in this letter, of 20 to 25 lines, written on a single sheet of paper. In order to transcribe this brief message from the Madonna—after having received the order from the Bishop—Sister Lucia was tormented and blocked by anxiety for almost three months and, as has been noted, succeeded in overcoming her dramatic difficulty only thanks to the direct intervention of the Madonna, who appeared on January 2, 1944. She assured her of the fact of the duty to write the Secret and assisted her in recording its every word. But why that great anxiety of Lucia? Why that block? Did it arise from prophecies of terrifying catastrophes that could be contained there?

In reality there are already prophecies of terrible tragedies in the first and second parts of the Secret (there is preannounced all of the horrors of the 20th century which are truly chilling, not to mention Hell, whose literal description is contained in the first part). What,

---

[247] Monsignor Venancio, in the note deposited in the archives of the sanctuary of Fatima, speaks of this folio as a "letter." Therefore, the "Fatimites" have deduced from this that the Third Secret is written in the form of a letter addressed to Bishop da Silva. This would be a very important particular because the text of the vision published by the Vatican in 2000, on the contrary, does not at all have an epistolary form. But is this certain? In this case the witnesses who confirm the information furnished by Monsignor Venancio are also innumerable. Frère Michel lists a few (pp. 586 and 470-473). Father Jongen, for example, who met Sister Lucia on the 3rd and the 4th of February, 1946, questioned her on the third part of the Secret and heard the visionary respond: "I have already communicated the third part in a *letter* addressed to the Bishop of Fatima." However, one might ask if this could not involve simply a cover letter. There is also the testimony of Canon Galamba: "When the Bishop refused to open the *letter*, Lucia made him promise…" And there is also Cardinal Cerejeira, Patriarch of Lisbon, who on September 7, 1946, writes: "The third part of the Secret is written in a sealed *letter* which will be opened in 1960." And further: "Lucia has written the Secret in a letter." (p. 586) Even Monsignor Capovilla, one of the few who have been able to read the document, during a two-page interview in *World Perspectives* (VI, 1991) used the word "letter" no fewer than four times to describe the Third Secret, and always in the strict sense. However, the expression "letter" could also have a generic sense. In fact, the term was used by John Paul II himself even for the text of the vision revealed in 2000, which is not in letter form. Writing to Sister Lucia (*TMF*, p. 27), the Pope says: "your handwritten letter containing the third part of the 'secret'". And on the following page in the account concerning her meeting with Monsignor Bertone, one reads: "That which is in the letter contains the third part of the Secret." In this case "letter" is synonymous with "envelope." It is difficult, therefore, to know whether Lucia, when she speaks of "letter addressed to the Bishop of Fatima," intends to say that the Secret is in epistolary form.

therefore, could have provoked such a paralyzing terror in her?

Even Father Alonso—based on a profound personal acquaintance with Sister Lucia—maintained that if it were only the prophetic announcement of great cataclysms that certainly would have been painful, but "we are certain that Lucia would not have encountered such difficulty as to require the special intervention of Heaven to overcome." What is it, then, that could have paralyzed and terrorized a cloistered nun like Lucia, born and raised in obedience and in devotion to the Church? "If it concerned," explains Father Alonso, "internal struggles in the heart of the Church itself and great pastoral negligence by the highest members of the hierarchy, one can comprehend that Lucia would have had a repugnance all but impossible to overcome by natural means."[248] Internal conflicts and great negligence by the highest pastors? Is this enough to explain that paralyzing terror? Here is the thought of Frère Michel.

In fact, she leaves one to conclude with certainty that with these 20 brief lines was launched into the history of the Church, into the history of the world, an event of formidable portent. Because for Lucia, habituated in the school of the Holy Virgin to evaluate all things according to the light of God, war, cataclysms, and famine, the Bolshevik Gulag extended throughout the planet, many nations annihilated, all of this is infinitely less grave than the apostasy within the Church itself and the apostasy of her Pastors. Certainly, the Church possesses the promise of eternal life and the forces of Hell will not prevail against her. The infallibility of the Pope will never be induced to err. It is certain that no Pope will ever be able to teach error in the exercise of his infallible magisterium, ordinary or extraordinary.

This does not preclude that the malfeasances of the Pastors in areas outside of their infallibility can have consequences more disastrous. By their error, the faith can be lost among the faithful, thus determining—with terrifying injury to God from this collective apostasy— the eternal perdition of millions of souls. It is here that the Third Secret is reconnected to the first concerning the vision of Hell. It is in this, in its insistence on the responsibility of the heads of the Church, that the Third

---

[248] FM, vol. III, p. 707.

Secret seems without doubt to Sister Lucia more terrible and above all the most difficult to transmit. For a humble religious—habituated to see always in her superiors the authentic representatives of God—to find herself suddenly constrained by Heaven to communicate to them such severe warnings of rebuke and so directly related to their conduct was for her an extremely painful mission.[249]

Is the evaluation by Frère Michel correct? One has the sensation that not everything can be explained with these considerations of his. If it concerns only the negligence of the highest pastors, that would not explain Sister Lucia's paralyzing terror. Indeed, on other occasions the visionary had no problems offering—while with sorrow—severe reflections on the upper ecclesiastical hierarchy. (In the conversation with Father Fuentes, she began precisely thus: "The Holy Virgin is very sad because no one has paid attention to Her message, neither the good nor the bad".)[250]

But she did much more. There is a sensational precedent, that of the dramatic interior locution Sister Lucia received in August 1931 at Rianjo after the Vatican's refusal to adhere to the requests by the Madonna (above all that of the consecration of Russia to Her Immaculate Heart). Sister Lucia made known these precise words of Jesus: "Make it known to My ministers that, given they follow the example of the King of France in delaying the execution of My command, they will follow him into misfortune."[251]

How does the King of France come into play? The explicit reference is to the apparitions of Paray-le-Monial in 1689 (100 years exactly before the French Revolution). There Jesus gave to Margaret Mary Alacoque a message for the King of France, Louis XIV—a message which implied a grand design of Providence concerning France: Insert the Sacred Heart of Jesus into the coats of arms; construct a temple in His honor where the kings of France would

---

[249] Ibid., pp. 707-708.

[250] Lucia then continued: "What offends above all the Immaculate Heart of Mary and the Heart of Jesus is the fall of the souls of priests and religious. The devil knows that for every priest or religious who reneges on his ecclesiastical vocation many souls will be led to Hell."

[251] FM, vol. II, pp. 543-544. It is worth noting, even if *en passant* [in passing], a particular of enormous importance: Jesus says, "My request," whereas it had been the request of the Madonna. It is thus an expression filled with significance: the Heart of Jesus and the Heart of Mary are united.

venerate Him; make a consecration of France to the Sacred Heart; request from the pope—as sovereign of France—a Mass in honor of the Sacred Heart of Jesus.[252] Nothing was done. Thus, exactly 100 years later, the French Revolution exploded and the nephew of the Sun King, Louis XVI, remembered these requests only in 1792 while he was in prison. There, in desperation, he decided to fulfill them, but it was by then too late. He was guillotined on January 21, 1793. France had taken the opposite road.

Now, having communicated in 1931 these clear and terrible prophecies with the harsh judgment on the "ministers" of God, Sister Lucia had demonstrated that she was perfectly able to make public a message that involved a harsh judgment of Heaven on the pastors of the Church and a prophecy of a tremendous punishment. Therefore, why in 1944 would she have felt herself paralyzed and terrorized? Evidently things were even graver than supposed by Father Alonso and Frère Michel, and the contents of the Secret are more terrible than the prophecy of 1931. It seems that we are able to deduce that in these 20 lines, in these few words of the Madonna, are contained something more, something unimaginable and unspeakable, which after having "paralyzed" Sister Lucia for three months had "terrorized" even the Popes, inducing them not to reveal these words.

We will attempt to understand the nature of this tremendous mystery. But first we must turn to the contents of the prophecy of 1931 which evoke the fate of the King of France. It is inevitable, rereading it, to think of the resemblance of what is presented here to the vision of Lucia revealed in 2000, where she sees precisely the martyrdom of a Pope and, together with him, of many bishops. Would this tremendous massacre, therefore, have something to do with disobedience to the will of Heaven? Would it be a tragedy that could be avoided if one accepts the assistance of the Madonna?

---

[252] "The first apparition took place on December 27, 1673 [...]. Jesus allowed the Sister to rest her head on His breast for a time. Then He revealed to her "the inexplicable secrets of His Sacred Heart." He showed her the Heart on a throne of flame, brighter than the sun, with the open wound of the lance in His side, surrounded by thorns and surmounted by a cross. "My Divine Heart"—He told her—"is so inflamed by a love for all humanity, and for you in a special way, that, not being able to contain within Myself the flame of its ardent charity, it must spread forth by means of you." Jesus revealed to her that the devotion to His Heart will deliver men from the dominion of Satan, giving them the graces of salvation." Father Livio Fanzaga, *Pellegrino a quattro ruote* (Sugarco: Milan, 2005), pp. 71-73.

In 1936, reconstructing in detail for Father Gonçalves the apparition of Tuy in 1931, Sister Lucia referred more completely to the message received: "Our Lord told me, complaining of it: 'They did not want to heed My request! …. Like the King of France they will repent and do it, but it will be late. Russia will have already spread her errors throughout the world, causing wars and persecutions against the Church. The Holy Father will have much to suffer.'"[253]

It is difficult to hold that this prophecy has already been realized.[254] At any rate the same prophecy of Rianjo in 1931 (as with the vision of Jacinta) seems to make known that the consecration of Russia will be done when it is already "late," thus in circumstances analogous to those of the "repentance" of the King of France, who—in a situation dramatic and tragic because of his historic delay—will not be able to avoid an apocalyptic martyrdom of the pastors of the Church. In fact, the visions which the little Jacinta also had are scenes of sorrow: the Holy Father on his knees "with his face in his hands," while outside he is insulted and besieged by a violent crowd. While in her other analogous vision there appeared "the Holy Father in a church, before the Immaculate Heart of Mary, in prayer … and many people in prayer with him."[255]

---

[253] FM, vol. II, p. 544.

[254] According to Frère Michel, "The sufferings of the Holy Father to which the Secret makes reference cannot be identified—as many believe—with the trials of Pius XII during the Second World War. No, in 1945 Sister Lucia let it be understood that the great tribulations of the Pope are yet to come." In fact, the visionary wrote to Father Aparicio in 1945: "It is necessary to pray unceasingly for the Holy Father. Days of great affliction and torment still await him." (FM, vol. III, p. 709). There will be therefore another, the Pope who will have to endure that special trial. Is it possible that this alludes to John Paul II and the consecration done by him in 1984? It does not seem that one can recognize even in this pontificate the characteristics of Jacinta's vision: A Pope almost besieged, attacked, burdened by immense and special sufferings (even if all of the Popes have had and have their trials and their sufferings). The consecration of 1984 at any rate cannot be considered to be that requested by the Madonna, as has been shown.

[255] *Memoirs of Sister Lucia*, op. cit., pp. 111-112. In a note which was added to a comment on this vision of Jacinta, one reads: "The reason for this hypothesis is that Pius XII was a great devotee of the Immaculate Heart of Mary" (p. 112). But above all one does not understand which "hypotheses" are spoken of (it is a vision, not a hypothesis) and above all one does not see how Pius XII enters into the moment Jacinta (who died in 1920) had these visions when Benedict XV was Pope. Pius XII was not even on the horizon (there was first the pontificate of Pius XI). Besides, Pius XII had not made the requested consecration of Russia. This vision seems to relate to a pontiff who will

This seems to be the scene of the future consecration. It is not yet clear to which pope Jacinta's vision refers or if it is the same one who "will repent," as preannounced by the prophecy of Tuy. But it seems the "repentance" does not relate only to the unheeded requests of the Virgin of Fatima. It also refers to the situation in the Church, to something even more of the crisis within the Church, to those things which Father Alonso called "grave negligences of the upper hierarchy" and which—as was seen when analyzing the "terror" of Lucia—could be something even much more grave. Not by happenstance, the Pope who walks toward the cross and then comes to be killed in the vision revealed in 2000 is described in the text as *acabrunhado*, which the official version translated as "afflicted," but (see Appendix) could more precisely be translated as: "dejected, oppressed, humiliated, mortified"—adjectives which could express an immense sense of guilt and sorrowful repentance.

There are two illuminating episodes concerning two witnesses, among the few who have read the entire Third Secret. The first is Monsignor Capovilla. Father Alonso, interviewing him in 1978,[256] hypothesizes three probable reasons why the Third Secret was not revealed: "Some reasons perhaps were: a) because it names expressly certain nations or hierarchs of the Church (cardinals, bishops)?; b) because there were references to the religious crisis in the Church?; c) because there were references—yet again—to Russia and its influence on the world?"

The response by Capovilla is most significant: "It does not appear to me that what is involved is a motive to keep in reserve the names of persons and nations, or of references of a political nature." He thus denies hypotheses a) and c), but does not respond at all to hypothesis b). If even hypothesis b) were erroneous, as are the other two, the prelate would not have had any problem responding no, as with points a) and c). But if he were being exacting, Capovilla would not have been able to say that this was so, because of the

---

finally do the requested consecration. Twisted interpretations of this kind abound in the Fatima affair. It is enough to say that in the same book, in a footnote (p. 107), it is asserted that the disputed letter of November 8, 1989 attributed to Lucia (the one cited by Monsignor Bertone in the "Introduction" of *The Message of Fatima*, as confirmation that the consecration took place), was addressed to "the Holy Father," when nothing of the kind was said, even by Monsignor Bertone. On the contrary, it appears to have been addressed to a Mr. Walter Noelker (see Aura Miguel, *Totus Tuus*, op. cit., p. 100).

[256] In *Rosarium*, 4-5 a. XI, 1978.

Secret to which he is linked. Therefore, by not responding at all he leaves the clear impression that with this hypothesis—point b)—Father Alonso has hit the target. Thus, in the Third Secret there are "references to the religious crisis in the Church," and it is only for this reason that the Secret was sequestered.

An identical episode happened with Cardinal Ottaviani: questions and answers which appeared in the November 1977 review *Mother of God*.[257]

It should be said that this information (on the crisis in the Church being contained in the Secret) would be perfectly consistent with the discourse of the Madonna (which begins with the words: "In Portugal the dogma of the faith will always be preserved"). But it cannot at all be adapted to the text of the vision divulged in 2000 in which there is not a trace of a "religious crisis in the Church"—at least on the basis of the official interpretation.

In fact, there is even a hypothesis that one can discern precisely something of this kind in the strange phrase of Sister Lucia: "(and we saw) a bishop dressed in White 'we had the impression it was the Holy Father.'" Why—one could ask—does the visionary resort here to a complicated paraphrase (a bishop dressed in white) when, a few lines later, she expressly and directly identifies the Pope, calling him "the Holy Father"? Is the formula "bishop dressed in white" who "we had the impression was the Holy Father" in this part of the Secret only a somewhat convoluted way of designating the Pope, or could it be a reference to someone who will don the pontifical habit, but without being the Pope or without being him legitimately? In fact, such an expression cannot be accidental because in itself it is inexplicable, complicated, and illogical: it would have made sense

---

[257] No. 10, November 1977, p. 7. To tell the truth, there is recounted an identical episode even for Sister Lucia—not, however, involving the direct written testimony of the visionary, which we possess for the other two witnesses. We only hint at it, not at all holding it to be documented. The priest, Father Luigi Bianchi, concelebrated a Mass with Monsignor Hnilica on May 14, 1991 in the Carmelite monastery of Coimbra. Having just written the book *The Secret of Fatima*, he took advantage of the occasion to ask Sister Lucia if she agreed with his hypothesis. He holds in fact that the contents of the Third Secret are (1) a crisis in the Church (institutions, faith, contents, sects, etc.); and (2) the physical world (earthquakes, floods, and other cataclysms). "Sister Lucia, not wishing under obedience to speak of certain things, inclined her head in a sign of assent. In sum: a silent affirmation…" Thus comments Piero Mantero, who reports the confidence of Don Bianchi (*Fatima: The Prophecy Revealed*, op. cit., pp. 91-92). I note only that it seems to me a strained interpretation to deduce so much from a simple nod of the head, however unequivocal.

151

to say "a man dressed in white" because that is what the children saw. But how could Lucia have seen "a *bishop* dressed in white"? No one writes on his forehead that he is a bishop; to be a bishop is not a visible aspect like being blonde or brunette. The use of the word "bishop," but a "bishop *in white*," leads one to think that this could truly involve [a bishop who is] an illegitimate Pope, an antipope, a usurper.

Sister Lucia affirmed having written the Secret with the direct assistance of the Virgin "word for word."[258] Therefore the use of that formula was directly inspired from on high. What would such a simile signify? Is the "bishop dressed in white" a person different from the one who—called precisely "the Holy Father"— a little later traverses the city in ruins, agonized and humiliated, and comes to be barbarously massacred?

It is clear that such a hypothesis opens the road to an interpretation of the vision entirely different from that which was given in 2000. But it involves always and only a hypothesis, inasmuch as that expression could simply be due to the fact that the children had seen the Pope for the first time. To gain knowledge of the correct interpretation it would be necessary to read precisely the other part of the Third Secret, that in which the vision is explained by the Madonna Herself.[259] And it is this text on account of which

---

[258] Joaquin M. Alonso, *The Truth Concerning the Secret of Fatima*, op. cit.

[259] Frère Michel, at the conclusion of his work, summarizes what the data of the Third Secret, after an accurate investigation, should contain: "While 'in Portugal the dogma of the faith will always be preserved', in many nations, perhaps in almost the entire world, the faith will be lost. The pastors of the Church will fail gravely in the duties to their office. Because of their fault, consecrated souls and the faithful will allow themselves to be seduced in great numbers due to ruinous errors spread everywhere. This will be the time of the definitive combat between the Virgin and the demon. A wave of diabolical disorientation will sweep the world. Satan will infiltrate even the highest summits of the Church. Evil spirits will blind and harden the hearts of the Pastors. Then God will leave them abandoned to themselves in punishment for their refusal to obey the requests of the Immaculate Heart of Mary. This will be the great apostasy announced for the last times, the 'false lamb', 'false prophet', who betrays the Church for the benefit of the 'beast' according to the prophecy of the Apocalypse. Perhaps the Secret announces also one or another of the prophesied chastisements from Scripture pertaining to the 'last times'? Perhaps it evokes the persecution the Holy Father will have to suffer when he 'will return' in order to 'confirm his brethren' and finally obey Our Lady's requests." (vol. III, pp. 841-842.) This "reconstruction"—while made during the 1980s when the part of the Secret revealed in 2000 had not yet been made public—would indeed suggest an interesting and different interpretation of the vision in which the bishop dressed in white and the Holy Father appear to be slaughtered

Lucia was terrorized, the text which is hidden, and whose existence, on the contrary, is even denied. What is there that renders it so frightening and explosive?

Satanic verses?

In particular we are dealing with one or two phrases: "abstruse locutions," dismissed as such by John XXIII. It was a cunning way of not saying simply that to him these words of the Madonna were displeasing, that they annoyed him, probably frightened him, disturbing his magnificent sort of blissful and progressive optimism. Thus he cancelled them. He hid them, preventing all of the Church and all of humanity from hearing the distressed warning of the Mother of God who appeared at Fatima, and preventing a settling of accounts—laically speaking with the heart of the message of Fatima.

Those words of the Virgin in the Third Secret were so grave that that Pope, while denying and hiding them forever, held that they were probably not from the Madonna but could be "fantasies" of Sister Lucia—who from that moment, by order of the Vatican, began to be practically "mute" and unreachable.[260] So, in those same days in which Pope Roncalli announced the Council (thinking he himself would reform the Church), he assessed the Third Secret to be a message "not entirely supernatural," perhaps because it warned him to be on his guard against taking the Church in that direction.

This was recent news with which no one seemed to have been acquainted—and disconcerting news as well, because Pope Roncalli did not have the courage to give such a judgment solemnly and publicly, engaging his authority, inasmuch as that would have involved a great responsibility (which is what should have motivated him) because it would almost demolish the whole of Fatima. Thus

---

ferociously.

[260] It is appropriate to remember, yet again, in order to appreciate the chasm in which the Church then found herself, that in these same days in which the Third Secret was buried and Sister Lucia was "silenced" (together with the Madonna), there was also launched again the persecution of Padre Pio through whom there had been thousands of conversions. But Vatican Council II had been convoked, presenting itself as the beginning of the era of dialogue, of renewal, the dawn of new times. There would be revealed an *Aurora Borealis*.

he left his opinion, kept extremely confidential, to weigh like a boulder on his successors, who found themselves before a colossal difficulty.

The attitude of John XXIII, who should have made the Third Secret public in 1960 (by the will of the Madonna) yet did not do it, has never been clearly explained.[261] Now, instead, the judgment by John XXIII is leaking out. It is found explicated precisely in the recent declarations—to Marco Tosatti—of his secretary and collaborator Monsignor Capovilla, who reconstructs as follows the event of the opening (and of the closing) of the Third Secret:

> [John XXIII] after having spoken with everyone [the collaborators he had consulted] told me: "Write." And I wrote under his dictation: "The Holy Father has received from the hand of Monsignor Phillipe this writing. It was decided to read it on Friday with his confessor. There being abstruse locutions, he called for Monsignor Tavares, who translated. He allowed his most intimate collaborators to see it. It was finally decided to reseal the envelope with this phrase: "I do not give any judgment." Silence before something that could or could not be a manifestation of the divine.

So it seemed, therefore, to Monsignor Capovilla, who reports the words of the Pope transcribed in minutes that he himself drafted ("I wrote under his dictation"), while until now only the writing he had placed on the envelope was known: "I do not give any judgment." In the minutes there is certainly this extremely heavy judgment, like a boulder. In fact, the same Capovilla, testifying during the process for the canonization of Roncalli, said that "Pope John imposed the silence for two reasons: (1) it did not seem to him 'to consist entirely of things supernatural,' (2) he did not dare to risk an immediate interpretation, in the midst of the complex 'Fatima phenomenon,' prescinding from minute precisions, leaving them to the foreseen development of authentic religious piety."[262]

---

[261] Shortly thereafter Monsignor Capovilla affirmed: "Pope John XXIII did not pronounce himself on the contents of the Secret. He said he preferred to leave its evaluation to others." According to Father Alonso, John XXIII maintained more precisely: "This does not concern the years of my pontificate." (FM, v. III, p. 557.)

[262] In Enrico Galavotti, *Processo a Papa Giovanni. La Causa di canonizzazione di A.G. Roncalli* (1965-2000) [*The Process for Pope John: The Cause of the Canonization of A.G. Roncalli* (1965-2000)], p. 470.

If only these "minute precisions" were not the heart of the message of the Madonna. From these two points it is evident that John XXIII did not wish to believe that the Madonna had really pronounced these words. However, he did not intend to assume the responsibility of saying so publicly, because Fatima was a fact recognized by the Church and by the faith of the people. And he did not wish to declare it publicly also because it would have been evident that these words of the Madonna were not in contradiction to Catholic orthodoxy, but probably only with his personal opinions and certain of his choices.

If in fact the words of the Madonna contained in the Third Secret had had an heretical content, according to canonical norms it would have been clear that the Virgin did not appear at Fatima. Therefore, it would have been the precise duty of the Church to intervene publicly (in defense of the faith of the people); and one can be certain that the Holy Office, then guided by Cardinal Ottaviani, known as "the Carabinieri of the Church," would have placed an insuperable veto on Fatima, rejecting that apparition.

But nothing of the sort happened. John XXIII consulted a dozen Cardinals of the Curia, but not the only cardinal, the Patriarch of Lisbon, who should have been consulted obligatorily, being designated the depositary of the Secret by Sister Lucia, but who was first dispossessed and then excluded. Therefore, Roncalli decided that the Secret (which nonetheless was "addressed to every human being," as John Paul II said) would be buried silently and without any explanation or public judgment. To evade the great expectation of its publication in 1960, the Vatican chose the shameful road of throwing a rock at Fatima while hiding its hand. In fact it issued a communiqué by the agency A.N.I. on February 8, 1960, headlined: "It is probable that the Third Secret of Fatima will never be published." On the basis of anonymous Vatican sources it states verbatim: "It is very probable that the letter [sic!] in which Sister Lucia wrote the words of the Virgin Mary [sic!] addressed to the three shepherds at the Cova da Iria, will never be opened."

It is scarcely necessary to emphasize that the Third Secret of which we have been speaking, the Third Secret with "abstruse locutions" [they are not abstruse at all, they are explosive], by all evidence is not the text of the vision made public in 2000, but rather—it is stated explicitly—"a letter" where Lucia reports "the words of the Virgin Mary addressed to the little shepherds". (In the text of the vision there are no words of the Madonna.)

The communiqué, which the Vatican caused to be issued anonymously, proceeds to declare the reason the Pope had decided not to reveal the Secret: "While the Church recognizes the Fatima apparitions, she does not wish to take upon herself the responsibility of guaranteeing the veracity of the words that the three shepherds say the Virgin Mary revealed to them."[263]

Frère Michel defines what the agency tossed out as "a true bomb. In the history of the Church it has weighed more heavily, perhaps, than the five large volumes of the *Discourses, Messages and Colloquies* of His Holiness John XXIII wherein, evidently, it does not appear. At any rate, it is Pope John who bears the primary responsibility for it."

The choice of anonymity bespeaks objectively of the bad conscience of the ecclesiastics. Frère Michel maintains that "this bizarre and cunning procedure is unworthy of the Successor of Peter"[264] and he finds it scandalous that—apart from this anonymous text—"neither John XXIII nor Paul VI deigned to give to the Church even one sentence of explanation for their decision not to reveal the Third Secret." All of this while the same two Popes were placing extreme emphasis on "the spirit of the Council" and thus on the idea that the Church, with them, was finally open to men's questions, dialoguing with the world, available to receive the inquiries of reason, transparent and attentive to "the signs of the times."

The reality of the facts bespeaks a comportment diametrically opposed. First of all, according to the communiqué published by the A.N.I. newswire service, the hierarchy "does not wish to take upon itself the responsibility" of guaranteeing that the contents of the Third Secret are really the words of the Madonna. Thus the pastors fail to measure up to their duty to make a judgment on the supernatural character of an event.

In the second place, they also fail to measure up to their duty when, in the face of the asserted abstention from judgment, they in fact "sequester" a precious document, depriving the Catholic people and the world of a message that was addressed to them.

---

[263] FM, v. III, pp. 578-579.

[264] Ibid., p. 580.

In the third place, they fail to measure up to their duty when they do this without furnishing any doctrinal or pastoral reason, even cloaking themselves in anonymity, but leaving—like John XXIII—a "confidential" memo that insinuates the non-supernatural character of a part of the message, thus tying the hands of his successors.

Cardinal Ratzinger and John Paul II have comported themselves quite differently, first of all by setting forth the reasons for non-publication (I am thinking of the episode at Fulda and of other interventions by Pope Wojtyla, as well as the interviews of Ratzinger in 1984 and 1986). Then they have comported themselves differently by taking seriously the request for the "consecration" made by the Madonna (even while being unable to succeed in accomplishing it because of the opposition encountered). And finally, by publishing in 2000 that which was possible—that is, the text of the vision—but without in fact being able to remove the boulder represented by the "failure" of John XXIII concerning the words of the Madonna (with which Paul VI is associated).

The problem, therefore, is represented by that pair of phrases that Pope Roncalli characterizes as "abstruse locutions" and which elsewhere Monsignor Capovilla has called "dialectical expressions,"[265] which they attempted—vainly—to render less harsh with the aid of a translator whose mother tongue was Portuguese. And then it was decided to hide them, evidently also because Sister Lucia, who had been assisted in writing the Secret "word by word" by the Madonna, was not disposed to revisit them or "tame" them.

That the Vatican, in the succeeding decades, remained paralyzed by the "No" of Roncalli is also demonstrated by an episode in which John Paul II spoke openly of the Third Secret with journalists. It was just after the fall of the Berlin Wall (two months earlier) when the Eastern regimes were disintegrating. Pope Wojtyla was questioned on January 25, 1990,[266] during a trip by airplane, by the Portuguese

---

[265] Monsignor Capovilla has spoken of a Secret written in the "form of dialect" in the testimony for the process of the canonization of John XXIII. And he has spoken of "dialectical locutions" in the cited interview published in *Rosarium*. Finally, he spoke of "expressions of Portuguese dialect" in the cited interview in *Prospettivi nel mondo*.

[266] As it so happens, it was the same calendar day as the announcement of the Second Vatican Council, January 25, 1959. And January 25th in 1938 was the date of the Aurora Borealis that Sister Lucia considered to be the signal preannounced by the Virgin for the breaking out of the Second World War (which in fact erupted shortly thereafter)—another detail prophesied by the Madonna which has taken place.

Vaticanist Aura Miguel. The question was this: "Holy Father, many believe that the recent events in Eastern Europe and in Russia were predicted by Our Lady of Fatima. Do you, who know the whole Secret of Fatima, hold that the conviction of so many Portuguese is well founded?"

The Pope, speaking off the cuff, said this, among other things: "The problem is that which people know and that which they believe. Certainly this trust of people in the Madonna is theologically justified, because we know well that She is the Mother of men, of peoples. And thus what happened in Russia, in the Eastern part of Europe, we can attribute to Her motherly solicitude. In this sense, theologically, we can accept the conviction of the Portuguese and of so many others. Naturally, in this sense also the revelations of Fatima, the private revelations, are all in accord with the doctrine of the Faith. However, this accord with the doctrine of the faith does not enter into details, does not enter too much into details."[267]

In this case the Pope was speaking of a specific question, of a "detail" of the Fatima prophecies that seemed to have come true. But what precisely did he intend by these words? At first glance he seemed to wish to say that the orthodoxy of the Fatima apparitions cannot be put in question if some detail of the prophecies does not come true. But how can a prophecy by the Mother of God not come true? Or did he intend to say that some detail might not correspond entirely to the "doctrine of the faith"? Was he posing an historical or a doctrinal problem? Or perhaps both?

It is difficult to say. We know only that John Paul II himself, questioned by Sister Lucia on the publication of the Third Secret, replied to her that it was not opportune to make it public "because it could be wrongly interpreted." And we also know that Cardinal Ratzinger in 1996, at Fatima, made it understood that it had not yet been published because there were "details" that could be used against the Church.[268]

This seems to be a step forward with respect to John XXIII. Neither John Paul II nor Cardinal Ratzinger had caused the paralyzing doubt of Roncalli, according to which the words of

---

[267] Aura Miguel, *Totus Tuus*, op. cit., p. 111.

[268] "The revelation of the Secret should be done only when it will not be able to create one-sidedness and disequilibrium, concentrating only on its details. The revelation should be made only when this fact can be understood as an aid to the progress of the faith." (In Aura Miguel, *Totus Tuus*, op. cit., p. 137.)

the Secret would not really be entirely the words of the Madonna. However, after having revealed the text of the vision in 2000, they found themselves in the difficult circumstance of having to deny the existence of that other part of the Secret, which is like denying the obvious.

According to Solideo Paolini, "probably John Paul II in 1982, taking himself to Fatima on a pilgrimage of thanksgiving for surviving the attack, had intended to publish the entire Third Secret. In fact, the news leaked out that one day in the first months of 1982 he had a Portuguese prelate of the Curia, Monsignor Carreira, read the Secret because he asked him to translate it 'with all the nuances of the language.'"[269] It was the second time that recourse was had to a translator; John XXIII also had requested this of Monsignor Tavares. But not because there were "abstruse expressions" or "dialect expressions" which, once translated, would not require further re-translation. It is evident that he was trying to get around the obstacle of that pair of explosive phrases, trying to understand whether they could be translated differently and attenuated or given a different meaning.

Perhaps the problem is only a single particularly shattering expression. Suspicion is also aroused by the reasoning of Cardinal Ottaviani during his conference of 1967, where he insistently compared the Third Secret to the "prophecies of Sacred Scripture which are covered in a veil of mystery," "not generally expressed in manifest language, clear, comprehensible to everyone." "What, for example, is said in the prophecies contained in the Book of the Apocalypse?" (This reference seems anything but happenstance.) Yet, says the prelate, in the Third Secret "there is a sign which is as if it were veiled; it is not in language which is altogether manifest and clear."[270]

In reality, the "Secret of Fatima," Father Alonso gives us to understand, "has a clear, logical and definite content [...] it is not a mysterious, extravagant or nebulous text. Still less is it a cryptic text."[271] There arises, then, the well-founded suspicion that when it was subjected to censorship it was not because of supposed "abstruse locutions" or (non-existent) "dialect phrases" or

---

[269] FM, vol. III, p. 636 and Solideo Paolino, *Fatima*, op. cit., p. 180.

[270] In FM, vol. III, p. 665.

[271] Ibid., pp. 666-667.

"veiled prophecies." In reality, it was wished to hide the problem represented by a prophecy that is quite clear, but too strong and disturbing to be given. Could it be—by way of hypothesis—a reminder of the Antichrist (a typical Biblical prophecy, as Ottaviani would have it) that, for the Vatican, renders the Third Secret terrible and unspeakable?

It is obvious that in 1982, given the desire of Pope Wojtyla to make the Secret known, there was recourse to Sister Lucia to see if the phrases that sounded so terrifying could be sweetened. "In fact," explains Paolini, "it is possible that the letter of May 1982 by Sister Lucia, mis-cited by Monsignor Bertone in *The Message of Fatima*, was precisely the visionary's answer to this type of request."

Rereading everything according to this key, it becomes understandable that Sister Lucia wrote to the Pope stating that "the third part of the Secret, that you are so anxious to know," because it is not the text of the Secret that the Pope wished to know, but its exact significance—the how, the when and the who of its realization. Or its possible, more acceptable, "translation."

Based on this letter of Sister Lucia's, the "chilling" contents of the Secret relative to the noted "details," would seem not to have been realized in the year 1982. In fact the visionary writes: "If we have not yet seen the complete consummation of the final part of this prophecy, we see that we are moving toward it, little by little, in large steps .... And do not say that it is God who punishes us thus; on the contrary, it is men themselves who are preparing their own chastisement. God caringly warns us and calls us to the right path, respecting the liberty that He has given us: therefore, men are responsible."

But what does it concern precisely? What, finally, are the unspeakable "details" that she had so much terror in revealing? According to Paolini, "without excluding other specific possibilities, I note that there are two recurrent themes which are, moreover, plausibly connected: one of a great apostasy in the Church at its summit (the testimony of Cardinal Ciappi); the other— accompanied by an image—is that Satan will succeed in infiltrating even the summit of the Church (according to the formulation of the 'diplomatic version') or 'the Pope under the control of Satan' (according to Father Malachi Martin). At La Salette these two themes are joined ('Rome will lose the faith and become the seat of the Antichrist'); and I recall that Cardinal Ratzinger, in the interview mentioned, speaks of the Third Secret, indicating precisely contents of this kind, and stating that they are already present in other apparitions recognized by the Church. All of this—as Cardinal Ratzinger was still hinting—would be accompanied by planetary catastrophes."

Is Paolini very far from the truth when he supposes that in the Third Secret there are prophesied apocalyptic catastrophes? Is he not exaggerating? Is there not the risk of ending in millenarianism? To tell the truth, Sister Lucia herself, while she was always very measured and prudent, preannounces them in the cited letter to the Pope of 1982. And in the dialogue with Father Fuentes she makes a shocking declaration: "Father, the Most Holy Virgin did not tell me that we are in the last times of the world, but She made me understand this for three reasons" (we have already seen what these three reasons are).

Previously, on July 15, 1946, in response to a question by William T. Walsh ("Has Our Lady given you any revelations on the theme of the end of the world?"), Sister Lucia reacted in a way that was clear and significant: "I cannot answer that question."[272]

Naturally there is a need to avoid the always threatened confusion (into which perhaps Sister Lucia fell) between the "last times" and the "end of the world," which are two very different things. But is the hypothesis of a (devastating) Third World War thus precluded? This is precisely the risk that John Paul II indicated when, in 2000, he solemnly entrusted the Third Millennium to the Immaculate Heart: "Humanity possesses today instruments of unheard of power that can make this world a garden or reduce it to a mass of rubble [...]. Today, as never before in the past, the world is at a crossroads."

In effect, the Secret confided by the Madonna in the apparition of July 13, 1917 could possibly follow this sequence of events: She begins the first part by asking for the recitation of the Rosary because the war—World War I—will end soon. Then, in the second part, She explains that if Her appeal is not heeded and there is

[272] Ibid, p. 668. It could be added that the Polish mystic, Saint Maria Faustina Kowalska, who died in Krakow on October 5, 1938 and was canonized by John Paul II, heard during a vision of Jesus Christ in 1938: "I love Poland in a particular way and, if it is obedient to My will, I will exalt it in power and holiness. From her will come the flame that will prepare the world for My final coming." *Diary*, VI, p. 93.

not a turning toward God, "during the reign of Pius XI" there will commence "another worse" war. (That is exactly what happened: the Second World War.) Perhaps the third part of the Secret—among other things—foretells a Third World War into which humanity will plummet if it remains obstinate in its way of sin. In the end, the vision which forms a part of the Third Secret shows precisely a scene of ruin and destruction.

This involves a hypothesis, naturally. But that there is a part of the Secret not revealed and considered "unspeakable" is certain. And today, having decided to deny its existence, the Vatican exposes itself to very heavy pressure and even blackmail. A signal of this was received the day after Sister Lucia's death. The protagonist was Ali Ağca. We have already seen how he had publicly declared, in 1985, that he had been made aware by the Vatican that the Third Secret concerned the attack in 1981. He was pardoned and sent to Turkey (and there locked away in a jail) precisely between May 13 of 2000 (when publication of the Secret was announced) and the following June 26,[273] when it was published.

On February 15, 2005, two days after the death of Lucia, from the Istanbul jail in which he was incarcerated, Ağca kept in touch with an "Open Letter to the Vatican" sent to *La Repubblica*. In this missive, written in "perfect Italian," the Turk maintains—according to the summary of it provided by *La Repubblica*—that "the Third Secret should be revealed in its entirety, especially the part which perhaps makes reference to the Antichrist."

And here is the verbatim passage as reported by the journal: "I express my condolences for the death of Sister Lucia of Fatima ... The Third Secret of Fatima is also connected to the end of the world..." And he continues: "On December 31, 1992 or 1993, during the celebration of the *Te Deum*, the Pope said: Since many Antichrists have come, the end of the world is near. Now the Vatican should reveal to the world the name of the man it considers to be the 'final Antichrist.' So that humanity can amend its ways and better confront this period of the end of the world." The letter concludes thus: "I, Ali Ağca, am not afraid of being cursed by humanity. On

---

[273] To be precise, Ağca was freed on the 13th of June, which was the anniversary of the second Fatima apparition as well as the anniversary of the apparition of 1929 in which the Madonna asked Sr. Lucia for the consecration of Russia, and the Feast of Saint Anthony, the patron saint of Portugal and of the parish of Fatima.

the other hand, the Jews have been depicting Jesus of Nazareth as the Antichrist for two thousand years."

Delusions? Madness? The presiding judge—who was for twelve years the conductor of the inquest into the assassination attempt and knew the Turkish killer quite well—described Ağca as "one of the most intelligent people I have ever known." And he gave this probable interpretation of his letter: "In the document there is a novelty, and that is the words regarding the *Te Deum*, where Ağca invites the Vatican to reveal the name of the Antichrist. During the interrogations this element could perhaps be discerned, but the Turk had never stated it explicitly. Now it is as if Ağca were saying: the Vatican knows, the Vatican speaks." The judge continues: "I have the impression that this type of message consummates a sort of blackmail, an invitation to speak. Otherwise, it is implied, 'I will do it myself.' As if Ağca were issuing the invitation: 'Let's all agree on what to say: both you and I know, so let's say it.'" [274]

It has never been understood who was and is behind Ağca, from the moment of the attack until today. Through him, perhaps, others are threatening the Vatican that "they know," that concerning the Third Secret not everything is revealed and that they are ready to make it known so as to create a colossal scandal implicating the Vatican, both because the contents of that writing would—in this case, yes—be used in a scandalous way against the Church, and because the Vatican would be accused of having lied publicly regarding the entirety of the Third Secret. The reply to Ağca's letter, which arrived the day after from an important Curial cardinal, was stupefying: "The Antichrist does not exist." It is February 21, 2005. (We are a week removed from the death of Sister Lucia, and shortly thereafter Pope John Paul II will die.) The cardinal, José Saraiva Martins, a likable Portuguese prelate who knew and personally met with Sister Lucia, is Prefect of the Congregation for the Causes of the Saints. Reached by a journalist for *La Repubblica*, the Prefect "began to laugh when he heard mention of the Antichrist [...] 'I don't believe in it, and I have never believed in it,' he stated firmly, commenting on the recent explosive media coverage surrounding the Antichrist, provoked by Ali Ağca in the letter he sent to the Pope on the occasion of the death of Sister Lucia."

Here is the Cardinal's explanation: "I don't believe in it for the

---

[274] *La Repubblica*, February 20, 2005.

simple reason that there are no objective data to demonstrate the existence of such a figure [...]. It would perhaps be more correct to speak of an Anti-man, because there are people who with their plans and their actions operate, and have operated, against the dignity of human life. Such as dictators, especially those who are the bloodiest and most despotic. It is enough to look at the past century, exemplified by figures such as Hitler and Stalin, who, as we know unfortunately from recorded history, put to death millions and millions of men, women and children..."

The interviewer then asked if it were true, as Ağca wrote, that the Third Secret has not been revealed entirely, and that the part still secret would speak precisely of the Antichrist. The Cardinal dismissed the question: "In the writings of Sr. Lucia, there is not even a mention of the Antichrist." Does there exist a part of the Third Secret yet to be revealed? "I don't think so," said the Cardinal. "I am certain that everything there was to know was revealed on May 13, 2000, when, among other things, there was mentioned a bishop in white who falls as if dead under gunfire. I have heard that someone advances the hypothesis of other secrets. I am sure there is nothing else to reveal, much less the presumed name of the Antichrist. Concerning the Third Secret of Fatima, everything was revealed that 13th of May in Portugal, before the Holy Father. The rest is only fantasy. It is a fantasy, combined however with ignorance, to continue to speak of an Antichrist."

In reality, the text of the Secret was made public on June 26, 2000 at the Vatican, not at Fatima "that May 13th before the Holy Father." But obviously the declarations concerning the Antichrist were those of such a high prelate, and moreover a professor of theology, as to cause a sensation.

Sandro Magister, a Vaticanist for *L'Espresso*, pointed out vis-a-vis these surprising declarations that it is the New Testament which speaks of the Antichrist and that this is based upon the constant teaching of the Church: "The learned cardinal forgets the first letter of John, 4:3: 'Every spirit that does not recognize Jesus is not from God. This is the spirit of Antichrist who, as you have heard, is coming, and indeed is already is the world.' He forgets the second letter of John, 1:7: 'For many seducers are gone out into the world, who confess not that Jesus Christ is come in the flesh: this is a seducer and an Antichrist.' He forgets the second Epistle of Paul to the Thessalonians, 2:3-5: 'Let no man deceive you by any means, for unless there come a revolt first, and the man of sin be revealed, the son of perdition, who opposeth, and is lifted up above all that is called God, or that is worshipped, so that he sitteth in the temple of God, showing himself as if he were God. Remember you not, that when I was yet with you, I told you these things?'"[275]

One must add 1 John 2:18-21, and also the Apocalypse of St. John, the last book of the New Testament.[276] But above all one must add the eschatological discourse of Jesus reported by the Gospels (Mk. 13, Matt. 24, Lk. 21) in which for the first time the "false Christ" is prefigured.

The very next morning this letter from the prelate was published:

> Dear esteemed Dr. Magister,
>
> I read on your blog of yesterday, February 25, 2005, your comment on my interview by Orazio La Rocca, published in *La Repubblica* on February 21, 2005, and I was not a little amazed because it does not correspond to my thought. I wish therefore to make some precisions:
>
> (1) It will certainly not be me who denies the existence of the Antichrist, revealed in the biblical texts, since this is a reality that no Christian who has any knowledge of Sacred Scripture can deny. History through the centuries is a confirmation of the existence of an ill-omened role of the Antichrist in it.
>
> (2) Insofar as my interview by La Rocca, I must point out the context in which it was done and that neither the title nor the first few lines, attributed to me, do me justice. In fact, the context is the apparitions of Fatima, and in particular the so-called Third Secret of the Apparitions.
>
> It is in that well-defined context, therefore, that my responses should be read; they in fact relate to the possibility of identifying the Antichrist in these times relative to two totalitarian ideologies which devastated the last century. This was the theme of the discussion, in which I specified that there is no need to speak only of Antichrist, but of anti-man, because everything which is

---

[275] Blog, "Settimo Cielo," February 25, 2005 at www.espressonline.it.
[276] Apoc. 13:1-18.

against Christ is against man. Thus it is as if the Antichrist is "incarnated" in these two ideologies of Communism and Nazism, responsible for the killing of millions and millions of innocent people.

(3) Therefore, I think it necessary to repeat that I absolutely do not believe that the Antichrist is a fantasy or legend, but on the contrary believe firmly in his existence, certainly! His effects, on the other hand, are before the eyes of everyone.[277]

It is clear that the prelate is to some extent clutching at straws and seems to confound the ordinary role of Satan with the figure of the Antichrist. He is perfectly right to point to Stalin and Hitler as "antichrists," horrible followers of a series of bloody persecutors, but the Gospel and the letters of the New Testament warn against the Antichrist as well, above all when he is presented as a religious seducer. Jesus warns: "For many shall come in my name, saying, I am the Christ; and shall lead many astray." (Matt. 24:5). Also, Saint Paul warns that he will "sitteth in the temple of God, and proclaim himself God." (2 Thess. 2:4)[278] Therefore to insist—as does Cardinal Saraiva Martins—on substituting the term "Antichrist" with "Anti-man" is to present part of the truth, but it is also dangerous to risk substituting a threat to "the rights of God" represented by the Antichrist with a generic threat to "the rights of man."

On the idea of an Antichrist, no theologian (and perhaps no Churchman) has been more insistent than Cardinal Ratzinger in his many writings (while having himself also described Hitler as an antichrist).[279] The prelate, today Pope, taking as his starting point *The Account of the Antichrist* by Vladimir Soloviev, wrote: "A phrase of Soloviev's is illuminating. The Antichrist believes in God, but in the depths of his heart prefers himself."[280] Does the Third

---

[277] Blog, "Settimo Cielo," February 26, 2005.

[278] See, *L'anticristo*, Vol. I, *Il nemico dei tempi lontani* [*The Antichrist: The Enemy from Distant Times*] edited by John Luca Potesta and Marco Rizzi (Fondazione Valla-Mondadori, 2005); *Testi sull'Anticristo* [*Texts on the Antichrist*], Nardini, 1992. Gianni Baget Bozzo, *L'anticristo*, op. cit.

[279] Joseph Ratzinger, *La Mia Vita*, San Paolo, Cinisello Balsamo (Mi), 1997, p. 25.

[280] "The second temptation of Jesus, whose exemplary significance is not easily comprehended, is intended as a sort of vision in which is condensed a particular risk that threatens man and the mission of Jesus. What appears singular immediately is that it is the devil who cites Scripture, with the aim of pulling Jesus into his trap. He cites Psalm 91:11, where the protection that God assures His faithful is spoken of: 'For he

Secret put the Church on guard against the arrival of a personage of this kind, who believes in God (and perhaps has studied theology), but "prefers himself"?[281]

It is evident that, confronted by signs like the letter from Ağca and possible blackmail, the only defensive weapon is the truth—to speak the whole truth about the Third Secret. "The truth will make you free."

---

will give his angels charge over thee, To keep thee in all thy ways. They shall bear thee up in their hands, Lest thou dash thy foot against a stone.' These words assume a major significance because they are pronounced in the Holy City, in a sacred place ... The devil is thus a good connoisseur of Scripture. The colloquy is configured, therefore, as a debate between two experts on the Bible. This same theme is taken up by Vladimir S. Soloviev in his *Account of the Antichrist:* the University of Tubingen confers an honorary doctorate of theology on the Antichrist. If theology becomes purely a knowledge of Scripture and of the history of the Faith in order to adhere to other choices in life, then it is no longer at the service of faith, but rather destroys it. The debate between Christ and Satan focuses on the correct interpretation of the Bible, whose norms are not of a purely historical character. The question is how one reads the Bible, with what understanding one approaches Christ. And a phrase of Soloviev's is illuminating: The Antichrist believes in God, but in the depths of his heart he prefers himself." (Joseph Ratzinger, *On the Road toward Christ Jesus*, San Paolo, Cinisello Balsamo (Mi), 2004).

[281] A hypothesis of this kind is also found in the writings of Maria Valtorta, according to whom the 20th century would be the period of precursors of the Antichrist, who will manifest himself in the present day and will be an ecclesiastic. His arrival, which will be accompanied by a great falling away from the Church, is described thus: "Then will come the pastor-idol, who will be, and will stay, wherever his masters wish."

5. The "secret" meaning of the events.

"The historical event of the Church is accompanied by "signs" that are before the eyes of everyone, but which ask to be interpreted. Among these the Apocalypse presents the 'great sign' appearing in the sky, that speaks of the struggle between the Woman and the Dragon."

-John Paul II, *Ecclesia in Europa* (2003)

"The victory, when it comes, will be a victory through Mary."

-from *The Testament of John Paul II*

The "power" of the Pope

That day in 1917 there was a young Polish seminarian, Maximilian Kolbe, in Saint Peter's Square when a group of Masons, celebrating the 200th anniversary of the founding of the Grand Lodge, unfurled a banner which read: "Satan will rule the Vatican, and the Pope will be his slave."[282]

In 1914 there was initiated the violent explosion of Europe and

---

[282] In Aura Miguel, *Totus Tuus*, pp. 51 and 62. Among the images used by the Masons in Rome, aside from the written ones, must be recalled in particular—for the subversive iconographic and theological meaning it suggests—that in which Saint Michael the Archangel (victor over Satan and for this reason the protector of the Church) is represented beneath the feet of Lucifer.

the disintegration of Christianity. From their ruins shortly thereafter would be born the satanic monsters of totalitarianism and horror. On August 3, 1914, Edward Grey, Minister of Foreign Affairs of Britain, affirmed: "The lights are going out in all of Europe. I doubt that we will see them lighted again in the course of our life." And Winston Churchill during the same days: "All things tend toward catastrophe and collapse (as if) a wave of madness has struck the mind of the Christian world."[283]

Just elected on September 8, 1914, Pope Benedict XV, had raised his voice against the "useless slaughter" and called for the end of the war. But the carnage was only beginning and with it the epoch of the great anti-Christian persecution. And in 1915 there was perpetrated by Turkish Muslims the genocide of Armenian Christians (more than a million victims, and among them 48 bishops).[284] Shortly thereafter, the war erupted even more savagely. It was the first true global conflict. The first in which technology was put at the service of slaughter: more than 9 million soldiers died, and more than 29 million were wounded or missing. It was the end of the Hapsburg empire, the last vestige of the Holy Roman Empire,[285] the end of Russian Christianity (between the 12th and the 17th of March 1917, Czar Nicholas was constrained to abdicate by a revolution of a Masonic type), and the beginning of the collective insanity of ideologies (on April 16, 1917 Lenin and Trotsky arrived

---

[283] Both of these voices are cited by George Weigel in *The Cathedral and the Cube* (Rubbettino: Soveria Mannelli), (Cz) 2006, p. 32. The same author also cites the precious analysis of Alexander Solzhenitsyn, according to which this sudden collective insanity happened because men had forgotten God. "In the first years of the 20th century," notes the Russian writer, "Europeans were glorifying violence and some groups among them, in the last analysis, warned of the need for radical change ... At the same time a vision of Europe in the years between 1900 and 1914 would show that henceforth the Continent would be at the head of a scientific, technological and industrial revolution, a movement of almost unlimited energy that was transforming practically everything. I would show moreover that violence was endemic on the level of social, economic and political conflict between classes, national and ethnic, and that Europe had concentrated its energies on a breakneck arms race at a level that the world had never before known." (p. 33)

[284] *See* Antonio Socci, *I Nuovi Perseguitati (The New Victims of Persecution)*, op. cit., pp. 44-45.

[285] To understand the import (and the promoters) of this event, from which ruin was unleashed the madness of Nazism and therefore the Second World War, see Francois Fejto, *Requiem per un impero defunto* [*Requiem for a Defunct Empire*] (Mondadori: Milan, 1999).

at St. Petersburg where they began to assume leadership of the uprising).

On May 5, 1917—feeling himself impotent before the bloody end of Christianity, understanding that no kind of diplomatic action, speech, appeal or initiative could now avoid the consummation of the tragedy, and seeing the contempt and marginalization to which the international chancelleries had consigned the Holy See[286]—Pope Benedict XV did something that, to the eyes of the world, to the political analysts and the historians, would seem completely insignificant. He decided that the Church would add to the Litany of the Blessed Virgin Mary the invocation: "Queen of Peace, Pray for Us." In the letter in which he announced this, he writes:

> Our sorrowful voice, which calls for an end to this vast conflict, of this suicide of civilized Europe, remains unheard. Since every grace that the Fount of every good deigns to concede to the poor children of Adam, which by the loving design of His divine providence is dispensed through the hands of the Holy Virgin, we desire that the prayers of His most afflicted children can, above all in this most terrible hour, turn with lively faith toward the august Mother of God ....
>
> There is raised, therefore, toward Mary, Mother of Mercy and omnipotent through grace, this loving and devoted appeal from every corner of the earth, from the noblest temples to the last chapel, from the royal palace and from the mansions of the rich, as much from the most humble dwelling, from every place in which the souls of the faithful find refuge from the plains and seas red with blood. Bring to Her the anguished cries of mothers and spouses, the weeping of innocent little children, the

---

[286] The volume *Benedetto XV e la pace – 1918* [*Benedict XV and Peace – 1918*] (More-celliana: Brescia, 1990) (edited by Giorgio Rumi) gives an idea of the epochal transition during these months, and of the ideological hostility, mainly of Masonic origin, governments displayed toward the Vatican. The sage Alberto Monticone begins thus: "In the summer of 1914, as historiography has already amply documented, the diplomatic situation of the Holy See became extremely difficult. The histories speak of pontifical isolation in the context of international relations." The end of the conflict will see the consolidation of this *novus ordo* ideologically inimical to the Church, with "the Pope diplomatically defeated because his appeals to the heads of the belligerent nations produced no result, with the exception of the peace negotiations of the League of Nations."

longing of every generous heart. That her most tender and benevolent solicitude be touched and that the peace we seek for this devastated world be granted.

No historian, obviously, gives any importance to such an act, accomplished on May 5, 1917. But Heaven says Yes. Exactly eight days later, on May 13, 1917, precisely She, the Queen of Heaven and of earth, responds with concern to the invocation by the Pope and the Church and comes among us to assist the Church and humanity at the beginning of an hour among the darkest in history.[287] She chooses to appear at Fatima, in Portugal, called since ancient times "The Land of Holy Mary," which in 1917 has undergone a century and a half of Masonic domination,[288] but whose people are still authentically Catholic. As Paul Claudel will say: "Fatima is an explosion of the supernatural." There the Madonna promises that, after terrible trials, in the end victory is certain: "My Immaculate Heart will triumph."

Stalin—some years later—will ask mockingly: "How many divisions has the Pope?" The Pope does not have armies; he does not have any earthly power. His only power is to entrust himself to Her who is "omnipotent by grace"—who at Fatima prophesied all the events that would happen (from the communist revolution to the Second World War and beyond); the only one who can "bring down the power of thrones and raise up the humble."

To respond to the painful appeal by Peter and by the Church, She chose—according to Her "style"—the place and the people who were (apparently) the most insignificant, weak and vulnerable: three impoverished children from an isolated Portuguese village in Fatima, three simple and innocent little ones who did not even know how to read, but who had learned to pray and did it with diligence. Through them the Queen of Heaven did not limit Herself to predicting the horrible events that would happen, but also gave to Peter and to the Church the possibility of averting them. It is above all Peter who, consequent to his invocation, must entrust to Her the rescue he had requested. And with Peter the entire Church. And with the Church, humanity. Otherwise, everything will remain in the hands of the forces of darkness, and the Church will be the first

---

[287] Courtenay Bartholomew catches this "coincidence" of dates in *The Last Help Before the End of Time* (Queenship: Santa Barbara, California, 2005), p. 35.

[288] FM, vol. II, p. 305.

to endure the terrible persecutions which accompany the atrocities suffered by peoples.

All of the history of Fatima and of this century resides in this dramatic incapacity of Peter, of the men of the Church, and of humanity to entrust themselves fully to She who is "omnipotent by grace"—the incapacity to trust in Her truly and totally, almost as if the possibility of salvation could come from Peter (alone) by his own initiatives, from Vatican politics, from one's own projects of reform in the Church. At Fatima the Madonna shows with simplicity Her extraordinary theology of history. Let us try to understand it.

She enters into modern history, presenting Herself to three little children with these words: "Do not be afraid." Always—as Sacred Scripture attests—God enters into human history with this assurance: "Fear not." The Beautiful Lady seems to be around 16 to 17 years old. First of all She wishes to inform the three children—who had asked when the war would end—that the protagonist of history is not the one who wields power, the rulers or the revolutionaries who have armies or finance capital, but rather the beggar: "Christ begs the heart of man, and the heart of man begs Christ."[289]

It is thus She makes known Her own power and the power of he [Peter] who has no power on earth. The Madonna asks these three little children, insignificant according to the world, if they will "offer" their prayers and their sufferings "to obtain the conversion of sinners," that is, to save the world. "Yes, if You wish it," responds Sister Lucia with ardor. Thus the little and the simple become one with Christ and obtain glory and eternal felicity ("We must see ourselves in God..."). The little and the simple save the world, unknown by the newspapers, the intellectuals, and the chancelleries. The Madonna in fact asks them to recite the Rosary daily "to obtain peace in the world," the end of the first global conflict.

Two of these little children, Francisco and Jacinta, would be dead within the turn of a pair of years on account of the Spanish epidemic that mowed down millions of lives in Europe after the Great War. The Beautiful Lady, in the second apparition on June 13, tells them that She will come "soon to take them," and the

---

[289] These words and this extraordinary intuition are those of Father Luigi Giussani, who formulated them thus in Saint Peter's Square, at a gathering of religious movements before John Paul II in 2000.

two children will indeed offer with love all their sufferings for the intention that the Madonna had indicated, in order to collaborate with Her in Her work. Lucia, however, will collaborate with Her by remaining at length on the earth:[290] "Jesus wishes you to serve Him by making Me known and loved. He wishes to establish in the world devotion to My Immaculate Heart."[291]

The paradox—or better yet the scandal (for the wise and the powerful)—of this "madness" of God, who 2000 years ago came to establish His Reign with twelve down-at-the-heels individuals (mostly fishermen from a village at the periphery of the empire), is proposed again at Fatima. In 1917, in the face of the century of darkness, in the hour of a monstrous assault against the Church and humanity, God manifested His plan: to found the Reign of Mary to save the world from self-destruction, to save the Church from disappearance and humanity from eternal damnation. But which army would the Omnipotent put on the field for a work so colossal, to rout all of the powers of evil? Three children, two of whom would be dead in a little while and the third who would be a simple cloistered nun. With them He called forth the entire immense procession of the simple to offer their lives, their prayers, and their sufferings with love to the Heart of Mary.

Father Maximilian Kolbe—who personally endured the satanic horrors of the twentieth century—was certain of it: "The Reign of the Sacred Heart of Jesus will conquer the world through Her."[292] And She, appearing at Fatima, besides calling forth Her "army" of the little and the simple, would exhibit the other pillar of His plan: Peter. It is to the Pope—who has received from the Son the power of "opening and closing" the gates of Heaven—that the Madonna of Fatima hands the power to realize His design and therefore to save humanity from tremendous tragedy and the Church from persecutions and terrible trials.

She will reveal this to the children in the apparition of July 13,

---

[290] To Lucia, in order to console her, She said: "Do not be discouraged. I will never abandon you. My Immaculate Heart will be your refuge, and the way that will lead you to God."

[291] Luigi Gonzaga da Fonseca, *Le Meraviglie di Fatima* [*The Marvels of Fatima*], op. cit., pp. 32-33. The Madonna, concerning the devotion to Her Immaculate Heart, adds: "To whoever will practice it, I promise salvation. These souls will be favored by God as if they were flowers placed by Me before His throne."

[292] St. Maximilian Kolbe, *Lo Spirito Santo e l'Immacolata*, p. 98.

the fundamental one, where She will deliver to them the Secret that is precisely the "plan of Mary" to save us. After having recalled some prior recommendations,[293] the Madonna showed them, for a terrifying "instant," a vision of Hell. She explained to them that the end of life is to abandon oneself to God, thus saving oneself from the horror of eternal suffering. Then She revealed to them Her "plan." The theology of Mary is the only true "theology of liberation" for modern times. It involves the liberation of mankind from the nightmares and horrors of this epoch, on the earth, and from the nightmare and horror of eternal suffering.

To realize this plan, "the Lord wishes to establish in the world devotion to My Immaculate Heart. If what I ask is done, then many souls will be saved and there will be peace."

Otherwise, if men continue "to offend the Lord," just after the end of the Great War "another worse one will begin." It was difficult to imagine in 1917 a war worse than that in progress, but precisely this would happen. It will be "the punishment of the world for its sins, through war, famines, and persecutions against the Church and the Holy Father."

Here is a first oddity. That war and famines are a punishment of the world is obvious, "but the persecutions of the Church and of its Head Vicar," Paolini asks himself, "How can they be punishment for a world that is substantially hostile or indifferent toward the Church?"[294] Here there is a mysterious aspect according to which it would appear that God punishes the world through His silence, through His withdrawal, "so that everything goes to ruin." But according to the "Fatimists," there is also the punishment of the men of the Church whose errors and whose deafness fall upon the Catholic people and on the entire world as sufferings.[295] In fact, immediately afterwards the Madonna declares: "To prevent this, I will come to request the consecration of Russia to My Immaculate

---

[293] She had begun by repeating the invitation to recite every day the Rosary for peace and the end of the war (because only the Mother of Christ could come to their aid) and to offer sacrifices in reparation for the injuries committed against the Immaculate Heart of Mary.

[294] Solideo Paolini, *Fatima*, op. cit., pp. 232-234.

[295] Recall what Cardinal Ratzinger said of the Third Secret in the cited interview in *Jesus*. The prelate explained that it also concerns "the dangers threatening the faith and the life of the Christian and therefore of the world." That "therefore" seems to establish a causal connection between the two things.

Heart and the Communion of Reparation on the first Saturdays of the month. If My requests are heeded, Russia will be converted and there will be peace. Otherwise, she will spread her errors throughout the world, raising up wars and persecutions of the Church; the good will be martyred, the Holy Father will have much to suffer; various nations will be annihilated."

That this concerns prophecies which have already come true is before the eyes of everyone. Whoever objects that Lucia wrote these things *post eventum*, in 1941, forgets that the children at unexpected times had shown a knowledge of what would happen and that Sister Lucia had already made a first draft of the first two parts of the Secret in 1927. (Only under the orders of her confessor did she destroy it; but, in the face of critical observations, she pointed to it as evidence.)[296] In any case, there is a phrase in the Second Secret which has provoked much discussion. There the Madonna says: "If they do not cease offending God, during the reign of Pius XI there will begin another worse war (than that in progress)."

Naturally, that precise reference to Pius XI has stirred up all the adversaries of Sister Lucia and of Fatima. They ask: Pius XI died in February 1939, that is, before the first breaking out of the Second World War, which began on September 1, 1939, during the pontificate of Pius XII. Therefore, how is it possible that the Madonna had erred so sensationally? It is evident—they conclude—that this was an error by Sister Lucia which proves that it is not clear what, in the Secret as a whole, comes from Heaven and what comes from the visionary.

The fact is that to whoever made note of this "error" Sister Lucia always responded with conviction that she had written exactly what the Madonna said. In reality, what would seem to be a grave critical problem for the proponents of Fatima is on close examination actually a sensational confirmation of the authenticity of the apparitions and of the prophecies of the Virgin. Indeed, it is necessary to recall that Sister Lucia was writing *post eventum* in 1941. Hence at the moment she wrote she would have been able

---

[296] "Jacinta, who seemed to have had before her eyes the future war, repeated (January-February, 1920): 'If men do not amend their ways, Our Lord will send to the world a punishment the equal of which has never been seen; and first to Spain.' Then she spoke of great world events 'that would happen toward 1940' without specifying them." In Luigi Gonzaga da Fonseca, *The Marvels of Fatima*, op. cit., p. 44. See also FM, vol. II, pp. 117-123.

(thinking that she had misunderstood) to "correct" the Madonna's prophecy by writing "Pius XII," seeing that she knew that the war had begun under him. Instead, she wished to write precisely "Pius XI" because that is what the Madonna had said. This element in and of itself demonstrates that the text of the Secret was not written by the visionary on the basis of events that had already occurred, but with such a literal fidelity to the words of the Virgin as to transcribe even those which seemed to be errors.

Let us dwell on this point in order to understand if the Madonna really had "erred" in this prophecy. The proponents of Fatima attempt to respond by explaining that, in reality, the first flames of the Second World War were already lit before September of 1939 and therefore the Madonna was not mistaken. This is absolutely true, and historians have explained it well: the war had already begun with the annexation of Austria and the accord at Monaco. (Not by accident, the French ambassador to Warsaw, Leon Noel, was able to write that "the war of 1939 began four years earlier.") But this is not the point. The Madonna is not a professor of contemporary history who provides chronological notions, nor a political analyst who cavils over the initial sparks of conflict. No.

To understand the reason for that phrase of the Virgin of Fatima, it is necessary to keep in mind Her perspective and the nature of Her message: She thus intended to reveal that there is a causal connection between the response to Her appeals to the men of the Church and what will happen ("if what I ask is done, many souls will be saved and there will be peace", "if My requests are granted, Russia will be converted and there will be peace, if not she will spread her errors throughout the world, provoking wars and persecutions against the Church"). Therefore, there is no "historical" error by the Madonna; there is instead a sorrowful appeal to the men of the Church that they accept Heaven's extraordinary assistance. In this (terrible) sense She affirms that the Second World War began "under the pontificate of Pius XI."

The power they have renounced

Pius XI was elected pope in 1922. The Fatima apparitions are under the examination of ecclesiastical authority. The bishop officially recognizes their authenticity in 1930. In the meantime

Lucia has entered a monastery and awaits the signs from Heaven to evidence the will of the Madonna that She had expressed on July 13: "To prevent this [the punishments of the world and of the Church], I will come to request the consecration of Russia to My Immaculate Heart and the Communion of Reparations on the first Saturdays."

In fact, on December 10, 1925, at Pontevedra, Lucia had an apparition of the Virgin with Child which requested promotion of the devotion of the Five First Saturdays of the month.[297] The visionary immediately communicated this request to the superior and confessor of the monastery who ordered her to write everything down. But nothing happened. Then Lucia wrote to her confessor at the "Asilo de Vilar," but the letter was lost. On December 29, the superior informed Bishop da Silva, although in an imprecise manner, but nothing happened.

On February 15, 1926, Lucia had a new apparition of the Child Jesus who asked her: "Have you revealed to the world what the Heavenly Mother asked you?"[298] It is thus that the Immaculate Heart of Mary must begin to triumph in the world, and to open wide the arms of mercy for sinners. But the ecclesiastical hierarchy substantially ignored what Sister Lucia had attempted to make known. On May 29, 1930, after new interior locutions, Sister Lucia wrote to Father Goncalves: "It seems to me that the good God, in the intimacy of my heart, is insistent with me so that I will request from the Holy Father approval of the devotion of reparation, that God Himself and the Holy Virgin deigned to request in 1925."[299]

But, with Fatima, God does not entrust only the eternal salvation

---

[297] These are the words of the Virgin: "Look, My daughter, at My Heart, surrounded with thorns with which ungrateful men pierce It at every moment by their blasphemies and ingratitude. You at least try to console Me and announce in My name that I promise to assist at the moment of death, with all the graces necessary for salvation, all those who, on the first Saturday of five consecutive months shall go to confession, receive Holy Communion, recite five decades of the Rosary, and keep Me company for fifteen minutes while meditating on the fifteen mysteries of the Rosary, with the intention of making reparation to Me." (In FM, vol. II, p. 247.) The five Saturdays are to make reparation for the five types of offenses and blasphemies against the Immaculate Heart of Mary: "1. Against the Immaculate Conception; 2. Against Her perpetual virginity; 3. Against Her Divine Maternity, in refusing at the same time to recognize Her as the Mother of men; 4. Blasphemies by those who publicly seek to sow in the hearts of children indifference or scorn, or even hatred toward this Immaculate Mother; 5. Those who outrage Her directly in Her holy images." (Ibid., pp. 265-266.)

[298] Ibid., p. 251.

[299] Ibid., p. 271.

of sinning humanity to the Immaculate Heart of Mary, but also the history of the world itself and peace. It is in the monastery at Tuy, on June 13, 1929, that "Our Lord informed me," writes Sister Lucia, "that the moment had come. He willed for me to make known to Holy Church His desire for the consecration of Russia and His promise to convert it."[300] It is important to grasp the moment and to understand the importance of the question of Russia. 1917 was the year of a great turning point: the year of the apparitions at Fatima and of the Bolshevik Revolution. It is in the apparition of July 13 that the Madonna preannounces the Communist Revolution[301] which in fact will explode and triumph the following October 25th. In the words of the Madonna, it is Communism which installed in Russia the satanic element through which the great chastisement of the world and the Church will arrive.

Just a few days later began the anti Christian persecution in what was for centuries "holy Russia": On January 13, 1918, the Church is practically declared illegal. On June 4, 1918, by the will of Trotsky and Lenin, the first concentration camps are born. On August 9, Lenin commands the launching of "an implacable mass terror against the Kulaks, hooligans, and White Guards." From that point, according to the historians Nekric and Geller, "the concentration camp will become a universal means of terror"[302] (which 20 years later will be imported by the Nazis into Germany).

But Communism was not yet definitively installed in Russia. Notice the dates. It is precisely the year 1929 that is decisive: Stalin assumes total power. On April 16 a Communist Party conference launches the five-year plan and decides upon the first great Stalinist purge. On May 22 a modification of the Constitution qualifies "religious propaganda" as a crime against the state; "the ministers of cults and their families will be deprived of civil rights …, they will not have the right to ration cards, to medical assistance, to apartments for cohabitation, and their children will not have access to elementary schools or to higher education …, they will be constrained to renounce their parents if they wish to

---

[300] Ibid., p. 463.

[301] It is a remarkable discovery from the later documents and from the memoirs of the protagonists that it was precisely in July 1917 that Lenin decided the hour of armed insurrection: "Not later than autumn." (See Mikhail Geller-Aleksander Nekric, *Storia dell'Urss* [*The History of the USSR*] (Bompiani: Milan, 1984), p. 30.

[302] Ibid., p. 70.

live. Thousands of churches will be demolished, including certain historic monuments."[303] Finally, even Sunday is abolished.

It is the beginning of the greatest and bloodiest persecution in the two thousand year history of the Church. At the same time it is the beginning of the genocides. On November 7, Stalin publishes an article entitled "The Year of the Great Rupture." He thus launched the "liquidation of the Kulaks," that is, the deportation of 13 million people and the systematic and deliberate extermination through famine of 3½ million peasants, women and children included.[304] Here is why it is precisely in this year, on June 13, that Lucia receives the "communication" that the hour has come to save Russia and with it the Church and the world from horrible tragedies, now that even the Holy See was able to recognize and understand the satanic nature of Communism.

Here precisely is the message that Lucia transmits: "The good God promises to bring an end to the persecution in Russia, if the Holy Father deigns to make, and orders the bishops of the Catholic world to make as well, a solemn and public act of reparation and of consecration of Russia to the most Sacred Hearts of Jesus and Mary, and if His Holiness promises, having procured the end of this persecution, to approve and recommend the practice of the reparatory devotion already described [of the Five First Saturdays]."[305]

The background of this request and promise is the conversion of Russia and peace in the world. ("If My requests are heeded, Russia will be converted and there will be peace.") But this immense possibility of salvation given to the Pope (for the benefit of humanity and of the Church) was not seized; that powerful hand held out was not grasped; that salvific appeal was not heeded. And in August of 1931 arrived Heaven's reply: "Make it known to My ministers that, given they follow the example of the King of France in delaying the execution of My command, they will follow him into misfortune."[306]

It is clear that by the word "ministers" was necessarily intended above all the Pope, because "from the beginning of 1930 Our Lord

---

[303] Ibid., p. 258.

[304] Robert Conquest, *Raccolto di dolore* [*Harvest of Sorrow*] (Liberal: Rome, 2004), pp. 151-153.

[305] FM, vol. II, p. 465.

[306] Ibid., pp. 543-544.

had made known to His messenger that the two requests for the consecration of Russia and the devotion of reparation must be addressed together to the Holy Father in person."[307] But had the urgent appeal from Lucia reached Pius XI? The Vatican documents relative to these years remain inaccessible, but the reconstruction Frère Michel has conducted on the basis of the Fatima archives leaves no doubt: "Pope Pius XI knew of the request ... after the month of September 1930."[308] And he did not even give a response. Here is why the Madonna said that "another worse war" would begin "under the pontificate of Pius XI."

St. Maximilian Kolbe was among those who intuited that as to the "demons" unleashed on the earth in the 20th century (by which he himself would be martyred) one could offer opposition only through Mary: "Hell hates Her and trembles before Her." And to make understood the power of the humble young girl of Nazareth, he had recourse to the following paradox: "If Lucifer could invoke, for his own salvation, the Holy Virgin with the single word 'Mary,' he would reach Paradise in an instant."[309]

It is clear that the consecration of Russia requested at Fatima, with its characteristic solemnity and universality, would have been a grand and sensational public gesture. It would be a magnificent act of reparation and entrustment of all the Church and of all humanity to the Immaculate Heart of Mary, a great moment of conversion. An act of conversion away from a trust placed in our own initiatives and capacities in politics or in diplomacy, and toward a total trust reposed in Mary and thus in grace.

Indeed, what probably induced Pius XI not to heed this appeal was above all a political preoccupation. According to Frère Michel a solemn act [of consecration] would also have been a "formal doctrinal condemnation of Marxism-Leninism" and of the Soviet regime.

At any rate the Holy See—to tell the truth, even before the arrival of Pius XI—had committed, concerning the Bolsheviks who ascended to power, the same error committed by the Western powers

---

[307] Ibid., p. 524.

[308] Ibid., p. 509. Frère Michel also cites a subsequent letter from Lucia to the new Pope, Pius XII, in which the visionary explicitly affirms that her confessor in various ways had informed Pius XI (page 531).

[309] St. Maximilian Kolbe, *Lo Spirito Santo e L'Immacolata* [*The Holy Spirit and the Immaculate*], p. 39.

and which Solzhenitsyn denounced in his works. They sought the road of an agreement, of diplomatic rapport, by which the Western countries enabled the Soviet regime to survive and consolidate itself in those first years, precisely when it could have been swept away by the economic conditions of the country. Thus "Vatican *ostpolitik*"[310] was born. And if in the abstract this could be considered an attempt to limit evil, to ward off the worst consequences, in reality there was revealed a grave weakness and an incapacity to comprehend— so much so that the Soviet regime was utterly merciless toward Catholics, the Church, and the Soviet people.

Finally, what determined Pope Pius XI's refusal to Lucia was probably also something that was due to his own personal prejudices. Marco Tosatti has reported an "unpublished episode," attributing it to a "very authoritative Vatican source" who had lived for decades in the Sacred Palace: "Pius XI never wanted to hear any talk of Fatima. His then secretary, later to become Cardinal Carlo Confalonieri, then recounted ... that Pius XI preferred to sit alone at lunch to listen to the radio, which was then the great technological novelty of the epoch.... Pius XI received many letters, and he read them all; and there were not a few from sisters and women in general who recounted their mystical visions ... Pius XI read the letters, then lifted his gaze, putting his glasses on the table and uttering a pensive, 'Well!...' Finally he said in a lowered voice, as if he were speaking to himself: 'They say... they say that I am His Vicar on earth. If He had something that He wished me to know, He would tell it to me directly.'"[311]

Evidently this difficulty in understanding the method of God also reflects an insufficient theological reflection: According to the doctrine of the Church, the font of the charism of the Holy Spirit is not, in fact, the hierarchy, which is called instead to evaluate and recognize where it is manifested. The caution towards supernatural phenomena—which is more than healthy in the pastors of the Church—can never be allowed to become skepticism towards the liberty of the Holy Ghost. (St. Paul warns: "Do not extinguish the spirit; do not despise prophecies." 1 Thess. 5:19-20.) It was not by accident that it was precisely under the pontificate of Pius XI that there was launched and carried out the virulent ecclesiastical

---

[310] FM, vol. II, pp. 557ff.

[311] Marco Tosatti, *Il segreto non svelato* [*The Secret Not Revealed*], op. cit., p. 68.

persecution of a great saint like Padre Pio. It is necessary to admit that Pope Pius XI should have been more careful in guiding the Church during this period, which perhaps was the most terrible and grim of all modern history. But because that period was so terrible, with all the more reason he should have recognized the signs from Heaven.

We turn now to Fatima. According to a scholar as authoritative as Frère Michel, "from 1929 to 1931 everything depended on the Pope. If Russia had been consecrated to the Immaculate Heart of Mary, it would have been converted and neither the Second World War nor the dazzling expansion of Communism would have taken place. But since this did not happen, in place of the promises what arrived were the punishments that began to be realized, and misfortunes began to rain down on christendom."[312]

In fact here are the early warnings of current events: In 1931 the bloody violence begins in Spain which will provoke the civil war with a great massacre of Christians.[313]   Emblematic of this is Prime Minister Azana, who precisely on October 13, 1931 (the exact day of the last apparition at Fatima, where the Miracle of the Sun was produced) solemnly declared to the Cortes [the Spanish Parliament]: "Today Spain has ceased to be Catholic."

This was a dramatic proof of the veracity of the warning of the Madonna: "Russia will spread her errors throughout the world." At any rate, on January 30, 1933 Hitler takes power in Germany and thus all the demons are on the scene. (It has to be said that with Hitler was committed the same error that had been committed with the Soviet Communists: "Both the Western powers and the Church of Pius XI attempted to reach pacts with him, and thus, rather than domesticating him, they furnished him with time to consolidate and expand his power.) Communism and Nazism are two mirror-image demons, or rather the same monster with two heads, and—if we consider well the words of the Madonna at Fatima—the second would not have sprouted up without the first. In any case, the two monsters together launched the Second World War. (It was the Ribbentrop-Molotov Pact for the partition of Poland that caused the conflict to explode, and the two regimes remained allied for

---

[312] FM, vol. II, p. 607.

[313] Antonio Socci, *The New Victims of Persecution*, op. cit., pp. 45-49.

nearly two years, almost half of the conflict.)[314]

Throughout the 1930's Sister Lucia tirelessly launched appeals to the pastors. On January 21, 1935, she writes: "It is necessary to work so that the Holy Father realizes His [the Lord's] designs." And on May 18, 1936: "It is necessary to insist."[315] It is worth noting a passage of this letter of Lucia's to Father Goncalves which, in the face of the bloody events in Spain, explains the profound truth of the prophecies of the Madonna. Here are the words of the visionary:

Is it opportune to insist? I don't know. It seems to me that if the Holy Father were to do the consecration right now, God would accept it and would fulfill His promise; and without any doubt, through this act, the Holy Father would please Our Lord and the Immaculate Heart of Mary. I have spoken to Our Lord about this subject not too long ago, and I asked Him why He would not convert Russia without the Holy Father doing that consecration, and Jesus replied:

"Because I want My whole Church to acknowledge that consecration as a triumph of the Immaculate Heart of Mary so that it may extend its cult later on and place the devotion to this Immaculate Heart beside the devotion to My Sacred Heart."

"But, my God," I said, "the Holy Father probably won't believe me, unless You Yourself move him with a special inspiration."

"The Holy Father! Pray very much for the Holy Father. He will do it, but it will be late! Nevertheless, the Immaculate Heart of Mary will save Russia. It has been entrusted to Her."[316]

In 1937 events finally pushed the Bishop of Leiria to take formal

---

[314] See Ernst Nolte, *La Guerra civile europea 1917-1945)* [*The European Civil War: 1917-1945*] (Sansoni, Milan, 2004). Most significant is a dialogue in the novel *Vita e destino* [*Life and Destiny*] by Vasilij Grossman, where the Nazi says to the Soviet: "When we look at each other face to face, it is as if we are looking into a mirror. This is the tragedy of our time. Perhaps you do not recognize yourselves when you look at us? Perhaps the world is not to your liking? Perhaps there is something that makes you hesitate or stop [...]? You hate yourselves when you see yourselves in us [...] Our victory is your victory." (Jaca Book: Milan, 1984), pp. 393-395.

[315] FM, vol. II, p. 545.

[316] Ibid., p. 631.

steps with the Holy See. He accordingly wrote a letter to the Holy Father in March that was received on April 8.[317] But it was deemed not even worthy of a response. Thus, on January 25, 1938, arrived the *aurora borealis* that the Madonna had predicted as the signal for the unleashing of the war, which—according to Her words— would begin "during the pontificate of Pius XI." It is well that one comprehends the reason. Sister Lucia explains to the bishop and to her superiors the prophetic significance of that phenomenon which all the daily newspapers spoke about. On February 6, 1939, six months before the outbreak of the conflict, Sister Lucia writes to her bishop that "the war predicted by Our Lady is imminent," and she assures of the Madonna's protection of Portugal "thanks to the consecration to Her Immaculate Heart made by the Portuguese episcopate."[318]

In fact, both things will come true. Sister Lucia does what is possible, continuing to request with insistence and to petition the Vatican, through her superiors, that they perform the consecration of Russia and institute the "Communions of Reparation" on the first Saturdays. But in vain. In February Pius XI dies without having listened to the appeals from the visionary.

In March (or May), 1939, Sister Lucia receives a further communication from Jesus who tells her: "Ask, ask again insistently for the promulgation of the Communion of Reparation on the first Saturdays in honor of the Immaculate Heart of Mary. The moment approaches when the rigor of My justice will punish the crimes of diverse nations. Some will be annihilated. In the end the rigors of My justice will fall more severely on those who wish to destroy My reign in souls."[319]

On June 20, 1939, two-and-a-half months before the breaking out of the war, the words of Lucia become dramatic: "Our Lady has promised to delay the scourge of the war, if this devotion is

---

[317] According to Frère Michel that letter arrived precisely while Pius XI was preparing his encyclical *Divini Redemptoris*, and it influenced the draft (vol. II, p. 645). The Pope in fact formulates there a harsh condemnation of Communism which he describes as "a satanic scourge." He writes: "Communism is intrinsically perverse, and no one who would save Christian civilization may collaborate with it in any undertaking whatsoever." In the same year Pius XI also wrote an analogous encyclical against Nazism, a natural phenomenon equally satanic, entitled *Mit brennender Sorge*.

[318] FM, vol. II, p. 684.

[319] Ibid., p. 685.

propagated and practiced. We see that it can repel this chastisement in the measure in which we make an effort to propagate it. But I am afraid that we cannot do more than what we have already done, and that God, displeased, will lift the arm of His mercy and allow the world to be devastated by this chastisement, which will be horrible, more horrible than we have ever seen."[320]

On August 22 the Nazi and Soviet regimes signed the pact for the partition of Poland and of the Baltic countries, and on September 1 the invasion of Poland begins. On September 3, France and England enter the war and, formally speaking, the Second World War erupts. Pius XII had been elected pope a little earlier, on March 2, 1939. He loved to describe himself as the "Pope of Fatima" because of the strange temporal coincidence between his episcopal consecration (in the Sistine Chapel by Benedict XV) and the first apparitions at Fatima: on May 13, 1917, precisely at the same hour. But will he really be such?

In April of 1940 Sister Lucia writes to Father Gonçalves that "God is afflicted not only because of our great sins, but also because of our great laziness and our negligence in responding to His commands."[321] In the same month the same pontiff receives the first appeal from Sister Lucia to do the consecration of Russia according to "the will of God" who "is good and is always ready to use mercy." But from the Vatican the hoped-for response does not arrive. Lucia continues to pray for the Pope.

In September-October 1940, the visionary's confessors promise to make another approach to the Holy Father to propose a request held more acceptable by him, that is the consecration of the world (with a special mention of Russia) that had already been advanced by other parties. On October 22 Lucia receives the approval of the Lord for this request, but He reveals to her that this solemn act will not accomplish the promise of Fatima (the conversion of Russia and peace), but a more limited grace: "His Holiness will obtain an abbreviation of these days of tribulations."[322] (As certain proof, the visionary indicated the special protection that the Madonna accords to Portugal.)

Unfortunately, the letter to the Pope from Sister Lucia will be

---

[320] Ibid., p. 686.

[321] Ibid., p. 725.

[322] *Memoirs and Letters of Sister Lucia*, op. cit., p. 467, October 22, 1940.

distorted by Bishop da Silva, although it arrives at its destination. Two years later, on October 31, 1942, the Pope will finally perform this consecration of the Church and the world to the Immaculate Heart of Mary.[323] Sister Lucia, pleased by this, nevertheless makes it known that it was not the consecration that the Madonna of Fatima had requested to obtain the conversion of Russia and peace: "The Good Lord has already shown me His contentment with the act performed by the Holy Father and many bishops, although it was incomplete according to His desire. In return, He promises to end the war soon. The conversion of Russia (however) is not for now."[324]

Certainly the solemn gesture accomplished by the Pope represents a great thing—as Sister Lucia made known—to assist the Lord in "establishing in the world devotion" to the Immaculate Heart of Mary, and to draw down upon the Church and the world, on the brink of self-destruction, graces and blessings. There is one who has noticed—as a stunning insertion of the supernatural into history—that subsequent to the consecration of October 31, 1942 "God immediately kept His promise: November 3, 1942: defeat of the Germans at El Alamein, after ten days of terrible combat; November 8: the landing of the Anglo-Americans in North Africa; February 2, 1943: the capitulation of Stalingrad by the German Sixth Army; Churchill delivers the celebrated speech: 'The wheel of destiny has turned.'"[325]

In fact there was the impression of a sudden reversal of fate; and—in keeping with what had been indicated—the war soon ended, although one could not call "peace" that which began in 1945, with half of Europe ending up in Soviet hands, and the Communist nightmare, and the beginning of the "Cold War" that so

---

[323] It is necessary to keep in mind that the Pope was exerting every effort to avoid the Church being drawn into the conflict. There were in particular strong German pressures and threats, transmitted through the Italian fascist regime, because the Holy See had taken a position in favor of the war against the USSR. There was even "the risk that Hitler had already actuated his plan to invade the Vatican in 1941" while in 1943 "the danger of an invasion of the Vatican by the Nazis and the consequent deportation of Pius XII was anything but remote." (Angelozzi Gariboldi, *Pius XII, Hitler and Mussolini*, op. cit., pp. 192-194). All of this makes understandable the Pope's fear that a "consecration of Russia" could be considered politically as an alignment with Nazi-Fascism, perhaps because of fear of the threats. And the decision of the Pope to proceed with a "consecration of the world" must be read in this historical context.

[324] FM, vol. III, p. 61.

[325] Piero Mantero and Valentina Ben, *Fatima: The Prophecy Revealed*, op. cit., p. 52.

many historians have described as "the Third World War." Within the expiration of 15 years from 1945, besides the Communist occupation of Eastern Europe there had followed the Communist conquest of China, with the horror that attended it, the Korean War, the bloody repressions in the eastern countries (for example, the invasion of Hungary in 1956), the Cuban revolution with the missile crisis, and the beginning of the war in Vietnam.

Peace, in fact—true peace, with the conversion of Russia—was the promise that was linked at Fatima to the solemn consecration of Russia to the Immaculate Heart of Mary. Sister Lucia, while happy with that "incomplete act" of the Pope which was destined to shorten the war, now turned to sadly asking that the requests that the Madonna had confided to her be heeded.

But political-diplomatic reasons continued to prevail over this simple gesture of entrustment. Inexplicably, for decades the "ministers of God" have not listened to the Madonna and have not wished to accomplish that act, perhaps not believing completely in the "power" that Jesus has entrusted to Peter and of which the Madonna had come to remind us.[326] The popes have believed more in their diplomats than in the promises of Jesus and Mary.

Despite what some might superficially believe, Fatima is not a case of a conflict between charisms and institutions, but the contrary: Fatima is an authentic exaltation of the papacy[327] (and therefore of Catholicism) because it shows what immense power the Lord has

---

[326] In fact Jesus, after having invested Peter with the primacy and having promised that "the gates of Hell will not prevail against the Church," invested him with a singular power: "To you I give the keys to the Kingdom of Heaven; whatever you bind on earth is bound in Heaven." (Matt. 16: 19) Even more impressive is what recent studies have uncovered concerning this. In the evangelical episode at Cesarea Philippi, after the confession ("You are the Christ") and the installation of Peter, the episode concludes with a surprising order of silence from Jesus: "And He strictly charged them that they should not tell any man of Him." (Mk. 8:30) This is one of the passages that has induced modern theologians to concoct the theory of the Messianic secret, obviously absurd because it contradicts precisely the essential mission that Jesus entrusted to His apostles, that of preaching and carrying the good news throughout the world. Recent studies completed by the school of Madrid involving a recension of the Greek Gospels into the original language, Aramaic, have permitted a reconstruction of what seems to be the true contents of this passage of Mark. It should sound thus in the original: "And (Jesus) charged them always to see in him (in Peter) the Son of Man." (See Jose Miguel Garcia, *La vita di Gesu nel testo aramaico dei Vangeli* [*The Life of Jesus in the Aramaic Text of the Gospels*] (Rizzoli: Milan, 2005), p. 205.

[327] See Solideo Paolini, *Fatima*, op. cit., p. 252.

truly given to His vicar on earth. Except that Fatima also shows the human limits (and in certain historic cases the inadequacy) of the one who holds that ministry (limits evident in Peter himself) and exercises it with insufficient faith in the present operation of Christ, who guides and sustains His Church.

The solemn gesture by Pius XII nurtured in the Church a great popular devotion to the Immaculate Heart of Mary. Nevertheless, the historical facts obliged one to suggest to the pontiff that another step still had to be taken—the one requested at Fatima. The post-war period indeed realized precisely what the Madonna had predicted ("Russia will spread her errors throughout the world, provoking wars and persecutions") and what could have been averted: the worldwide expansion of Soviet Communism and the disappearance in the night of half of Christian Europe through persecution.

On July 15, 1946, interviewed by William Thomas Walsh, Sister Lucia returned to insisting: "What Our Lady wants is that the Holy Father and all the bishops of the world consecrate Russia to Her Immaculate Heart on one special day."[328] And, the following year, to someone who requested a precise clarification: "No, no! Not the world! Russia, Russia!"[329]

Pope Pius XII had extraordinary signs that encouraged his openness to the action of the Holy Virgin. One of the most sensational happened during the vigil of the Proclamation of the Dogma of the Assumption, the last Marian dogma, foreseen for the first of November, 1950. During the vigil, on the 30th and 31st of October (and then after the proclamation of the dogma), Pope Pius XII, walking in the Vatican gardens, saw happening the same miracle of the sun that occurred at Fatima on October 13, 1917. The pontiff, who was the only witness to the fact, referred to it in writing.[330] An interpretation of the miracle is assisted by three coincidences which do not at all appear to be fortuitous, but rather quite significant: It was the vigil of the proclamation of dogma; it was the anniversary of the solemn consecration of the world to the Immaculate Heart of Mary (October 31, 1942); it was precisely the 29th of October, the end of a long pilgrimage throughout the world by the statue of the Madonna of Fatima, which had just come to

---

[328] FM, vol. III, pp. 123-124.

[329] Ibid., p. 236.

[330] Ibid., pp. 283-286.

Rome during the hours of the solar phenomenon and was kept in the little church at Casaletto, precisely behind the Vatican gardens (territory of the Holy See).

It is therefore only right to interpret the phenomenon as a confirmation by Heaven of the proclamation of the dogma (which progressive theologians have instead opposed)[331] and as an invitation to heed the Madonna of Fatima by the consecration of Russia. Another sensational supernatural sign had comforted the Pope and moved him in this direction: on April 12, 1947 there occurred the apparition of the Madonna at the Three Fountains, that is, right in Rome in the center of Christianity, to Bruno Cornacchiola, both anticlerical and Protestant—an extraordinary event entirely centered on the papacy and personally followed by the Pontiff.[332]

Yet perhaps because of these sensational heavenly signs, the Pope decided that the closure of the holy year would take place at Fatima on October 13, 1951; and there Cardinal Tedeschini, revealing during the solemn celebration the miracle of the sun the Pope had witnessed, explained his interpretation: "Was this grace a reward for him? Was it a sign to show that the definition of the Dogma of the Assumption was sovereignly pleasing to God? Was it a heavenly testimony intended to authenticate the connection between the mystery of Fatima with the Center, the Head of the truth and of the Catholic Magisterium? It was all three things together."[333]

It is the Pope himself in his own message who—recalling that the miracle happened when the "pilgrim Madonna" had just arrived at the Vatican—celebrated the "miraculous statue" which from the sanctuary in Fatima has "visited Her entire realm during this Jubilee." And he explains: "with Her passage, in America as in Europe, in Africa as in India, in Indonesia as in Australia, the blessings of Heaven rain down, the marvels of grace are multiplied,

---

[331] And Joseph Ratzinger recalls the episode: "When the dogmatic definition of the bodily assumption of Mary into Heaven was imminent, the opinions of theological faculties throughout the world were requested. The response of our professors was decidedly negative. By this judgment was asserted a unilateral way of thinking which had a presupposition that was not only not very historic, but historicist" [i.e., the view that Catholic dogma is "historically conditioned" by the times and is not objectively true for all times]. (*La mia vita* [*My Life*], op. cit., p. 59.) It should be stressed that all of this had already happened by 1950—well before the Council.

[332] See Angelo Maria Tentori, *La bella Signora delle Tre Fontane* [*The Beautiful Lady of the Three Fountains*] (Paoline: Milan, 2000).

[333] FM, vol. III, p. 318.

so much so that we find it hard to believe our own eyes."[334]

In the face of all these signs it was expected that the "Pope of Fatima" would finally heed the requests of the Madonna. In October 1951 Sister Lucia, through Father Wetter, the rector of the "Russicum", was able to remind the Holy Father that "What Our Lady of Fatima requested has not yet been done." In May 1952 the Madonna again appeared to Sister Lucia and exhorted her: "Make known to the Holy Father that I am still awaiting the consecration of Russia to My Immaculate Heart. Without this consecration, Russia will not be able to convert, nor will the world have peace."[335] In the following month of June, Sister Lucia caused to arrive in Rome an umpteenth appeal.

Is it possible for Pius XII to doubt such a messenger after having seen so many signs? Or will he continue to listen to certain Roman theologians who maintain—even in published writings— that "it is impossible to do the consecration of Russia"? The Pope will choose—yet again—a middle way. On July 7, 1952, he will publish the Apostolic Letter to the people of Russia *Sacro vergente anno*. In it—heeding also many requests received from behind the Iron Curtain—he will finally consecrate Russia (named openly) to the Immaculate Heart of Mary. It was, however, yet again an incomplete act which did not take account of what the Madonna had demanded.

Frère Michel explains: Pius XII made no reference to the Virgin's request for "the reparatory devotion of the Five First Saturdays of the month," and then "the solemn act of reparation, requested jointly with the consecration of Russia, is suggested only indirectly in the Letter;" but "finally and above all the Pope had not dared to give to all the bishops of the world the order to unite themselves with him in this solemn act of reparation and consecration." In substance, there was no solemn act by the universal Church that responded to the desire expressed by Our Lord in the apparition to Lucia of May 1936: "I want My whole Church to recognize this consecration (of Russia), as a triumph of the Immaculate Heart of Mary, so as to extend its public veneration later on and place devotion to this Immaculate Heart beside the devotion to My Divine Heart."[336]

---

[334] Ibid., p. 319.

[335] Ibid., p. 327.

[336] Ibid., p. 335.

Because of this the promise of Fatima—the conversion of Russia and peace in the world—is not realized. Nevertheless, one can discern historically that yet again Heaven accepted this solemn act by the Pope and, as with the consecration of 1942, accorded to the Church and to the world exceptional graces and benefits.

We have the word of two unimpeachable lay historians: "The speech delivered by Stalin at the XIXth Congress, on October 14, 1952, was dedicated to ideological motivation for the imminent offensive in western Europe [...]. Stalin wanted to assist in the Soviet transformation of Europe during the course of his life. A new war was being prepared, but History raised its hand. At the end of February 1953, while he was in the final stages of preparation, Stalin was suddenly struck by a cerebral hemorrhage. On March 5 he died."[337]

Notice the dates: everything happened within the turn of eight months from the consecration of Russia to the Immaculate Heart of Mary. Who saved Europe from that projected and proclaimed Soviet invasion and "pulled down the tyrant from the throne"? The anonymous "hand of History" as the two historians say? Or the powerful hand of the Woman of the *Magnificat*, thanks to the solemn act by the Holy Father? There will be those who incline to the first answer, and those who incline to the second. In this second case, yet again, as with the consecration of 1942, we find ourselves before an act of the Pope that finds a hearing in Heaven, obtaining great graces, but which—being partial—does not obtain the realization of the extraordinary promises of Fatima. In fact it is true that the most bloody of the anti-Christian tyrants of the universe disappeared and that western Europe was saved from Communism, but Russia is far from converting, the Cold War continues and will become dramatic, and with the ascent of Khrushchev to power, the persecution of the Church of the East will continue. Pius XII will return no more to the consecration of Russia. According to Frère Michel, it is this foreclosure that underlies the umpteenth eloquent supernatural sign occurring during the pontificate of Pacelli: the tears of the Madonna of Syracuse. It is a sensational fact, which caused a sensation in the media and remains totally inexplicable from the scientific point of view. From August 29 to the first of September in 1953, in the humble dwelling of the day

---

[337] Nekric-Geller, *History of the USSR*, op. cit., pp. 582-583.

laborer Angelo Iannuso, at Syracuse, a high-relief of glazed plaster depicting the Madonna and showing Her Immaculate Heart (truly an extraordinary coincidence?) begins to weep from its eyes and will cry for four days. "The scientific investigation produced a disconcerting outcome: the tears were human, and no physical or chemical alteration was encountered in the plaster. The Church recognized the tears as supernatural. At fifty years distance it remains the only weeping phenomenon declared authentic by the ecclesiastical organs and inexplicable by science."[338]

What interpretation to give to this sign? There are those who remember two episodes referred to by Sister Lucia. Above all the apparition of December 10, 1925, at Pontevedra, when the Madonna said to the visionary: "Look, My daughter, at My Heart, surrounded with thorns with which ungrateful men pierce Me at every moment by their blasphemies and ingratitude without there being anyone to make an act of reparation to remove them. You at least try to console Me and announce in My name that I promise to assist at the moment of death, with all the graces necessary for salvation, all those who, on the first Saturday of five consecutive months shall confess, receive Holy Communion, etc."[338a]

And then the other apparition, on June 13, 1929, when yet again the Holy Virgin comes to request the consecration of Russia, showing Her Immaculate Heart pierced by thorns. Frère Michel asks himself rhetorically, concerning the weeping in Syracuse in 1953: "Is this not above all an anguished reminder of these two requests still unfulfilled?"[339]

Pius XII asks: "Will men understand the mysterious language of these tears?"[340] But perhaps he should have asked this of himself and of the men of the Church above all. That is, he should have asked whether they understood the meaning of these tears of the Mother of God— scattered, as noted, on Italian soil where the Holy See and the Pope are found—seeing that precisely in that same year, three months before the event at Syracuse, even in *Civilta Cattolica* (a semi-official publication of the Curia) Father Dhanis, the historic

---

[338] Saverio Gaeta, *La Madonna e tra noi. Ecco le prove* [*The Madonna is Among Us. Here is the Proof*] (Piemme: Milan, 2003).

[338a] FM, vol. II, p. 247.

[339] FM, vol. III, p. 344.

[340] Ibid, p. 398.

adversary of the Fatima apparitions, was able to cast doubt on Fatima with the passive consent of the Pope himself. The Madonna had Her sad reasons for shedding tears on papal territory. And, unfortunately, this extraordinary supernatural sign, the umpteenth, also remained uncomprehended and unheeded.

One has the sensation, in fact, of a distinct rigidification on the part of Pius XII, perhaps also because the contents of the Third Secret came to him in a secretive way. Indeed, in 1952 he had sent Father Schweigl to interrogate Sister Lucia and certainly had had information from him. Then, in May of 1955, he even sent Cardinal Ottaviani, his close collaborator and pro-secretary of the Holy Office, to question Sister Lucia privately concerning the Third Secret and the date it should have been revealed: 1960.

The prelate must have returned to Rome with information that was quite explosive, and shortly thereafter the Vatican demanded that all documents relative to the Third Secret be brought to it, and further decided to deposit the Secret in an inaccessible "dark well." Pius XII refused even to read that simple sheet of paper,[341] wishing to keep it to himself in a safe in his room.

In December 1957, speaking with Father Fuentes—as we have already seen—Sister Lucia will reveal all of the sorrow and pain of the Madonna: "The Holy Virgin is very sad because no one has paid attention to Her message, neither the good nor the bad. The good continue on their way, but without giving any importance to Her message." Then, speaking precisely of the Third Secret: "Based on the will of the Holy Virgin, only the Pope and the Bishop of Fatima are permitted to know it [before 1960], but they preferred not to know it in order not to be influenced."

Shortly thereafter, with the arrival of Pope Roncalli, provision would be made to "silence" Sister Lucia with a prohibition on meeting people or speaking without authorization; even John XXIII wanted to avoid being "influenced" by the Madonna. This disconcerting anxiety accords quite well with the incredible succession of events. According to the reconstruction by his secretary, Monsignor

---

[341] Even the addressee of the Secret, Bishop da Silva, always refused to read it with the singular motivation that "The secrets of Heaven are not for me. I don't want to take this responsibility upon myself." If a bishop says that the "secrets of Heaven" are not for him, how will the Church be able to ask all of humanity in modern times to lift its gaze to Heaven? Reading these words, what can we discern on the state of the ecclesiastical world and of the Church of the 20th century?

Capovilla, they were discussing the Third Secret with John XXIII, just elected pope. Cardinal Cento, former nuncio to Portugal who had physically carried the envelope to the Vatican in 1957, said to the Pontiff: "It is well that you take a look at it. Sister Lucia has approached me. She could deliver a message to the world. I don't know if it is opportune; in a little while you will hear what they say in the Secretariat of State."[342]

We are in the first days of January 1959. It is not yet clear today how and why Sister Lucia, usually very reserved and submissive, would immediately after the election of John XXIII (on October 28, 1958) think of an initiative as sensational as a radio message to the world. The year 1960 had not yet arrived. What was she afraid of? What did she know? What urgency did she feel? It would never be known. Because in the first days of January 1959 an alarmed summit met in the Vatican and, faced with the prospect that the visionary of Fatima would reveal to the world something the Madonna had said, by the will of the Pope there issued the prohibition on the sister, and her substantial isolation from the entire world.

Then it was thought to read the Third Secret immediately, but John XXIII said: "No, wait." First he wanted to announce the convocation of Vatican Council II, almost as if to place before Heaven a *fait accompli*. It was Sunday, January 25, 1959. (Curiously, on January 25th there also occurred the *aurora borealis* which, according to the prophecy of the Madonna of Fatima, would signal the breaking out of the war, the great punishment of the world.) It is not that the idea of a council was a negative in itself. Anything but. (The great thing would have been if precisely that solemn assembly had made the consecration requested at Fatima, as sought by a petition of 510 bishops, and if the Third Secret had been revealed.) But John XXIII was worried and had stubbornly wished to postpone the reading of the Secret in case it contained something that advised against that announcement. Evidently, Roncalli wanted to take that enormous decision for the Church without being "influenced" by the Mother of Good Counsel, without being illuminated by the Queen of the Apostles, without being assisted by the Mother of God, by the Mother of Divine Grace, by the Help of Christians. Therefore, once the announcement had been made, once his own will had been done, John XXIII gave his consent: Now that everything had already

---

[342] See Marco Tosatti, *The Secret Not Revealed*, op. cit., pp. 70-71.

been decided, one could read what the Madonna of Fatima had said.

After having read it, in the face of the Madonna's request that Her words be revealed to the world in 1960—the message of the Queen of Prophets not being to his liking—Pope Roncalli decided to do exactly the opposite: He decided to bury the message and not to give any explanation, either to the Church or to the world. Finally, as we have seen, he caused to be attached to the envelope from Sister Lucia his heavy opinion, destined to weigh down upon his successors, according to which the message "could be a manifestation of the divine and could not be."[343] As if to insinuate that it involved the fantasies of a nun.

Nevertheless, it was precisely in 1959 that signs and news of extraordinary graces continued to be linked to a pilgrimage in Italy of the statue of the Madonna of Fatima,[344] the coldness of Roncalli was evident. "The statue of the Madonna of Fatima," writes Frère Michel, "arrived at Rome on September 14. It remained there until the 17th. During these three days, great solemn ceremonies were conducted at the Flaminio Stadium, at the Church of the Immaculate Heart of Mary, and at the Basilica of St. John Lateran. The Mayor of Rome welcomed the Virgin of Fatima. The crowds flocked in to see Her. But Pope John XXIII did not move. He did not pronounce even a single word of welcome to the Virgin, who visited his diocese at the end of a triumphal voyage around the world."[345]

Pope Roncalli did not even wish to receive the proposal by the Bishop of Leiria to renew the consecration of the world to the Immaculate Heart of Mary performed by Pius XII.[346] Even Cardinal

---

[343] Ibid., pp. 71-72.

[344] A sensational episode whose protagonist was Padre Pio who at the same time was enduring a new harsh persecution from the ecclesiastical world. Between May and June of 1959 the holy priest suffered from a very serious form of pleurisy. During those days the statue of the Madonna was being brought to the major towns in the south. On August 6 it arrived at San Giovanni Rotondo. Padre Pio was able to pray for a long time before it, and at a certain point he wanted to kiss the statue, and "in that precise instant, as he later revealed to his confreres, the Capuchin felt as if a shiver had run up and down the length of his body. A few instants later he suddenly ceased to feel any symptoms of the diagnosed illness, notwithstanding that all of the doctors declared themselves skeptical concerning such an improbable recovery." (Maurizio Ternavasio, *Padre Pio*, op. cit., pp. 119-120.) All of this happened at Gargano, ten days after Pope John, at Castelgandolfo, opened the envelope containing the Third Secret, and then resealed it with the attestation of his doubts.

[345] FM, vol. III, p. 563.

[346] Ibid., p. 612.

Lercaro, presiding on May 13, 1960 over the celebrations at the Portuguese sanctuary, had to recognize that there was a serious problem: "We have come here, not out of an anxious curiosity to know what other secrets the word of the Mother has reserved to the world, but as penitents concerned for not having taken account of Her admonitions and not having followed Her clear indications, nor having heeded Her loving requests."[347]

Apart from the fact that among Her "clear indications" there also was not followed the publication of the Secret in 1960 (and the desire to know such a providential aid from Heaven cannot be described as "anxious curiosity"), it must be asked where is the "worried repentance" of an ecclesiastical class which, while recognizing that it has not heeded the "loving requests" of the Madonna, obstinately persists in not accepting them and even in discrediting and "gagging" the witness to them.

John XXIII inaugurated the Council in October 1962 with a discourse that remains celebrated for its infelicitous irony concerning the children of Fatima: "To us it seems necessary to disagree with these prophets of doom who are forever forecasting calamity, almost as if the world's end were imminent."[348]

Evidently, Roncalli felt that his "prophetic spirit" was much more acute than that of the "Queen of Prophets." In fact, he announced a splendid springtime for the Church, and we have seen that a dark and freezing winter arrived.

The message of Fatima evidently was felt to be profoundly embarrassing by one who was preparing to agree to what he thought to be a masterpiece of diplomacy and ecumenism: a pact with the Kremlin to have two Russian Orthodox observers at the Council, guaranteeing to that regime, in exchange, that the Council would not formulate any condemnation of Communism

---

[347] In Aura Miguel, *Totus Tuus*, op. cit., p. 134.

[348] In that solemn discourse Pope Roncalli added: "The Church today prefers to use the arms of mercy, instead of the arms of severity" and to give "teachings rather than condemnations." He then affirmed: "Not that there are lacking false doctrines, opinions, and dangerous concepts [...] but [...] now it seems that men are of themselves inclined to condemn them." (Allocution at the opening of Vatican Council II, *Gaudet Mater Ecclesia*, October 11, 1962.) Apart from the "prophetic talent" that Pope Roncalli here demonstrates (shortly thereafter 1968 will explode, and the entire world will become drunk with terrifying ideologies), taking these words of the Pope literally one would deduce that there is no longer any need of the Church as Mother and Teacher.

or the Soviet system.[349] Beyond the judgment (the worst possible) that one must give to this compromise of the "moral liberty" of the Catholic Church and of the Council itself, and moreover in return for a mess of pottage (two orthodox observers well-chosen and controlled by the KGB), one remains horrified in the face of a Council—what is more, a "pastoral" council, and thus one occupied with the historical reality of the Church—that pronounces itself on everything, but does not proffer a single word on the ideology of a regime that since 1917 had realized (and was still realizing in those years) on a planetary scale the most immense and bloody work of eradication, extermination, and persecution of the Church in its bimillenial history."[350] Pius XII was attacked furiously for years because, according to his critics, he did not formulate clear and public condemnations of Nazism during the war (which is, however, untrue). But John XXIII has received only applause for having contracted this "silence" with the Kremlin. How is this explained?

[349] The steps toward this unheard-of accord were the voyage of Monsignor Willebrands to Moscow, from September 27 to October 2, 1962 (see Zizola, *John XXIII*, op. cit., pp. 210-211) and the so-called Metz Pact, sanctioned in the springtime of 1962 between Cardinal Tisserant and Metropolitan Nikodim. Events had it that the two observers arrived at the Council precisely on October 13, 1962, the anniversary of the great miracle of Fatima during the last apparition. "The written intervention against Communism on the part of 450 Council fathers was 'lost' mysteriously after having been delivered to the Secretary of the Council, and those Council fathers who insisted on denouncing Communism were gently invited to be seated and remain silent." (Father Paul Kramer, *The Devil's Final Battle*, op. cit., p. 57.) Documentation of this history is furnished also by Romano Amerio, *Iota Unum* (Ricciardi: 1985, pp. 65-67) who writes that "the initiative for the meetings was taken personally by John XXIII at the suggestion of Cardinal Montini, and Tisserant 'received his formal orders, both for the signing of the accord and overseeing its exact execution during the Council.'"

[350] I am reminded of this extraordinary admonition that Padre Pio is said to have made public to his spiritual brothers in 1963, where he speaks of Fatima and of the tears of the Madonna. It provokes much reflection precisely in reference to the Metz Pact and the Madonna of Syracuse: "Because of the spreading injustice and the abuse of power, we have arrived at a compromise with atheistic materialism, denying the rights of God. This is the chastisement preannounced at Fatima [...] All of the priests who maintain the possibility of a dialogue with the deniers of God and with the Luciferian powers of the world are mad, they have lost the faith, they no longer believe in the Gospel! They thus betray the Word of God, because Christ came to bring to earth a perpetual alliance only with men of goodwill, but not to ally Himself with men thirsty for power and domination over their brothers…The flock is dispersed when the pastors ally themselves with enemies of the Truth of Christ. All of the forms of power made deaf to the will and the authority of the heart of God are rapacious wolves who renew the Passion of Christ and cause the tears of the Madonna to pour forth." (*Avvenire*, August 19, 1978.)

And—to return to Fatima—how does one explain the date chosen for the revelation of the Third Secret? Why did Sister Lucia say that in 1960 it would be "more clear"? Paolini observes: "What new event is dated in 1960 if not Vatican Council II, convoked in 1959, and whose preparatory commission will be launched in precisely that year (1960)?"[351]

The decisions and choices of John XXIII were also followed by his successor Paul VI, who—for his own part—added the annoyed and public rejection of Sister Lucia: "It is said that Lucia that day at Fatima asked for a meeting with the Pope," recalls John Guitton, who was his friend and confidante. The Pope responded brusquely: "Address yourself to your bishop." According to his French friend, "Paul VI had a sort of generic aversion for visionaries. He maintained that, since revelation is complete, the Church has no need of these things, to which one must not give an exaggerated importance."[352]

Are the "little ones" chosen by Mary despised? Are prophecies despised? Aura Miguel has observed that on the day he rejected a meeting with Sister Lucia, the last living visionary of Fatima, at the Portuguese sanctuary, Paul VI "received that evening civil and military authorities, members of the government and the diplomatic corps. The Pope also held an audience with the Portuguese episcopate, with representatives of Catholic Action and with other Christian churches. Returning to the Monte Real Airport, he found the time to make a visit to the monastery of Batalha."[353]

Why did he have time for everyone except she whom the Madonna had chosen as Her messenger? Fifteen days later in response to a question by John Guitton: "What impression do you have of Lucia?", Pope Montini gave an answer in which everything shows through: "Oh, she is a very simple girl! She is a peasant without complications." The aristocratic Montini, the intellectual of French formation, did not mention that the Madonna had chosen that girl as a depository of Her exceptional message to the Church and to humanity. He saw in Lucia only "a peasant."[354]

To tell the truth, on September 13, 1964, Pope Montini confided

[351] Solideo Paolini, *Fatima*, op. cit., p. 115.

[352] Interview with Stefano Maria Paci in *30 Giorni* [*30 Days*], March 1990.

[353] Aura Miguel, *Totus Tuus*, op. cit., p. 61.

[354] John Guitton, *Paolo VI segreto* [*The Secret Paul VI*], op. cit., p. 85.

to the same French friend that he expected to see "lay people animated by the spirit of prophecy," but he expected them as "fruits of the Council,"[355] not by the election (and gift) of Heaven as with the children of Fatima. We are still awaiting the "prophets" born of the Council. On the other hand, there were soon seen other "fruits" of the Council—terrible fruits.

It was precisely Montini—the Pope according to whom "the Church does not have need" of the extraordinary assistance of the Madonna and can do without Her maternal aid—who shortly thereafter had to recognize dramatically that, within a few years of the Council's conclusion, the Church was in the process of "autodemolition." Paul VI even shouted out desperately his apocalyptic feeling that "from somewhere or other, the smoke of Satan has entered the temple of God." Then he added bitterly: "It was believed that after the Council there would come a day of sunshine in the history of the Church. Instead there came a day of clouds, tempests, of darkness."[356]

Pope Montini hinted at some self-criticism ("The opening to the Church became a true and proper invasion of the Church by worldly thinking. We have perhaps been too weak and imprudent."). However, it was seen quite clearly who had opened the door to the world and to the "smoke of Satan." In fact, he persisted in error: The most devastating of the errors was the traumatic "coup d'etat" by a "minority revolution" that imposed the liturgical reform (with its thousand abuses), hailed by Paul VI but clearly not blessed by God.[357] The prohibition of the millennial Latin liturgy of the Church

---

[355] Ibid., p. 61.

[356] Discourse of June 30, 1972, in Romano Amerio, *Iota unum*, op. cit., pp. 7-8.

[357] Even more embarrassing is the response that he will give to his friend Jean Guitton in November 1976. During a private meeting Guitton, confronted with the disastrous product of the liturgical reform with its many permitted abuses, indicated to Paul VI the irrationality and authoritarianism with which it was proceeding: "The general opinion cannot admit that all Masses are allowed except that of St. Pius V, the Mass that all of the bishops said during the Council." Then he said to the Pope that "It would be auspicious…to annul the interdiction in France of the Mass of St. Pius V that the Council had never pretended to abolish." The response by Montini is peremptory and chilling: "This never!" Even more incredible is the motivation: "This Mass, as we have seen at Ecône, became a symbol of condemnation of the Council. I will never accept that one can condemn the Council by means of a symbol." (John Guitton, *The Secret Paul VI*, op. cit., pp. 144-145.) It is useless to underline, as Guitton did, that the Council had not at all wanted to abolish that Mass, that the new liturgy has been disastrous for the Church, and that it was an authoritarian imposition by Paul VI himself, who

was effectuated by a decision that contravened even the documents of the Council.[358] The modality and contents of this "coup d'etat" have had disastrous effects on the orthodoxy and faith of the people, while—as the writer Guido Ceronetti has noted—that folly "pleased Communist authorities... who were not stupid, having in their bestial ignorance of the sacred perceived that a crack had been opened."[359] Paradoxically, even then the enormity of the error was recognized more by the world of culture, even lay culture,[360] than by the ecclesiastical class, who were sometimes modernists, and in other cases superficial and ignorant, or opportunistic and cowardly. The harshest factual judgment on the methods and contents of this reform was given by a pastor as conciliar as Joseph Ratzinger: "I am convinced that the ecclesial crisis in which we find ourselves today depends in great part on the collapse of the liturgy, which

---

should have taken responsibility instead of offering the excuse of the Council. Pope Montini was stubborn and did not wish to give a victory to Ecône and to his other critics. While watching the Church "auto-demolishing" itself, he did not wish to admit that he had erred. Thus he remained until the end.

[358] In reality, the Council never decreed the sudden and unjustified banning of the sacred liturgy with which the Church for 2000 years had expressed its creed. In fact, the destruction of the Latin liturgy contradicts precisely Article 36 of the Conciliar constitution on the liturgy. It contradicts the Apostolic Letter *Sacrificium laudis* by Paul VI; it contradicts *Veterum sapientia* by John XXIII ("no innovator should dare to write against the use of the Latin language in the sacred rites"); and it contradicts *Mediator Dei* by Pius XII, which reaffirmed "the unconditional obligation of the celebrant to use the Latin language." It contradicts, in sum, all of Catholic tradition.

[359] Ceronetti offered these considerations in an open letter to the new pope, Benedict XVI, which appeared in *La Repubblica*, in which he asked that "the sinister gag suffocating the Latin voice of the Church be removed."

[360] It is a forgotten, or better yet censored, story that has just been recalled by Francesco Ricossa in the book *Cristina Campo, o l'ambiguita della Tradizione* (Centro: Librario Sodalitium). With the subversive season in full bloom—that is in 1966 and in 1971— there were published two manifestos in defense of the traditional Mass of St. Pius V. And they were signed by personalities of exceptional prominence. To cite a few: Jorge Luis Borges, Giorgio De Chirico, Elena Croce, W. H. Auden, the directors Bresson and Dreyer, Augusto Del Noce, Julien Green, Jacques Maritain (the intellectual dearest to Paul VI, with whom the Pope delivered, at the end of the Council, the document addressed to intellectuals), Eugenio Montale, Cristina Campo, Francois Mauriac, Salvatore Quasimodo, Evelyn Waugh, Mario Zambrano, Elemire Zolla, Gabriel Marcel, Salvador de Madariaga, Gianfranco Contini, Giacomo Devoto, Giovanni Macchia, Massimo Pallottino, Ettore Paratore, Giorgio Bassani, Mario Luzi, Guido Piovene, Andres Segovia, Harold Acton, Agatha Christie, Graham Greene and many others, ending with the famous editor of the *London Times*, William Rees-Mogg. Curiously, precisely the Conciliar Church, which made dialogue with the world and modern culture its keynote, took no account of them.

sometimes comes to be conceived 'as if God does not exist': as if it no longer matters whether God is there and is seen and heard in it. But if in the liturgy there no longer appears the communion of the faith, the universal unity of the Church and of her history, where does the Church appear in her spiritual substance?"[361]

A terrifying balance sheet for a season that John XXIII had opened with his euphoric "prophecies" according to which there was about to arrive, thanks to the Council, "a new springtime for the Church," and "a new Pentecost." Instead, the dark and frigid winter arrived.

The unimpeachable witness, Henri De Lubac, who even took part in the cause, made this terrible diagnosis:

> The drama of Vatican II consists in the fact that instead of having been conducted by saints, as was the Council of Trent, it was monopolized by intellectuals. Above all it was monopolized by certain theologians, whose theology started off with the preconception of updating the faith according to the demands of the world and to emancipate it from a pre-supposed condition of inferiority with respect to modern civilization. The place of theology ceased to be the Christian community; that is, the Church became the interpretation of individuals. In this sense the post-conciliar period represented the victory of Protestantism

---

[361] Joseph Ratzinger, *My Life*, op. cit., p. 115. In these pages the future Pope recalls "the publication of the Missal of Paul VI, with the almost complete prohibition of the preceding missal." Ratzinger comments: "I was dismayed by the prohibition of the old missal, since nothing of the sort had ever happened in the entire history of the liturgy. The impression was even given that what was happening was quite normal. The preceding missal was produced by Pius V in 1570, in keeping with the Council of Trent; it was therefore normal that, after 400 years and a new council, a pope would publish a new missal. But the historical truth is otherwise. Pius V limited himself to making a revision of the Roman Missal then in use, as had always happened in the living history of the Church down through the centuries…without ever substituting one missal for another. This has always involved a continuous process of growth and purification, in which, however, continuity had never been destroyed… Now instead," writes Ratzinger, "the promulgation of a ban of the Missal which had developed over the course of the centuries, from the time of the sacramentaries of the ancient Church, has produced a rupture in the history of the liturgy whose consequences could only be tragic. Pieces of the old edifice were taken and a new one constructed from them… What is dramatically necessary for the life of the Church is a renewal of liturgical conscience, a liturgical reconciliation, which returns to recognizing the unity of the history of the liturgy and understands Vatican II not as a rupture, but as an evolutionary moment." (pp. 113-115.)

within Catholicism.[362]

The victory of Protestantism within Roman Catholicism? Is this not already an apocalyptic event? And the sign of this Protestant victory was precisely the hostility (Pelagian, modernist and activist) against Mary which was manifested during the Council and in the post-conciliar Church. It is also seen in the hostility to Fatima and the hard-fought battle which had been waged against the recognition of Our Lady's titles—"Mediatrix of All Graces and Co-redemptrix"[363]—which spring forth from all Catholic Tradition.

Yet, in the tempest of the post-Conciliar period, only one thing has descended into crisis: the Marian sanctuaries which represented the lifeboat for rescuing the faith of the people, so despised by theologians precisely because they are linked to Mary, "Help of Christians."

At any rate, by a curious phenomenon which Catholics ascribe to the assistance of the Holy Spirit, both Montini and Roncalli, while making decisions opposed to their own words, taught clearly that the door to salvation was and is Mary. John XXIII, in February 1959, pronounced these words: "In our time the august Mother of God makes Her presence felt in human events in a special way … Thus one would put at risk his own salvation if, when he is assailed by the tempests of the world, he refuses to welcome Her rescuing hand."[364] He then spontaneously asked himself whether, as Pope, he had grasped that maternal hand, or rather had not wanted it. For his part, Paul VI said at the Angelus of December 5, 1972: "We also exhort you, dearest sons, to look for the 'signs of the times' which seem to precede a new coming of Christ among us. Mary, the bearer of Christ, could be our teacher, but on the contrary She Herself awaits His coming."

---

[362] "The true Council and who has betrayed it," in *Il Sabato*, July 12-18, 1980.

[363] As a theologian of the 20th century, Hans Urs von Balthasar, has observed: "no one aspired less than the Mother of God to personal 'privileges'; She is gratified uniquely insofar as these redound to the benefit of all the children of the Church." Without Mary "Christianity threatens to dehumanize itself inadvertently. The Church becomes functionalist, soulless, a feverish work incapable of stopping, dissipated in noisy projects. And since in this world dominated by men there is a continuous succession of ideologies which supplant each other, everything becomes polemical, critical, bitter, flat and finally boring, while the people remove themselves *en masse* from a Church of this sort." (In *Nuovi punti fermi* [*New Firm Points*] (Jaca Book: Milan, 1980), cited in *Maria* by the Base Community (Mondadori: Milan, 2000), pp. 1065-1067.

[364] FM, v. III, p. 615.

In fact the true sign of the times, although misunderstood and unheeded, was Mary at Fatima. That Roncalli and Montini in particular indicated entirely different signs of the times to the Church, trying to "bury" the true sign of the Message of Mary and to elude its assistance, leads one to think that these teachings of the Popes are the judge of their own historical deeds. Fatima, therefore, is a great sign of contradiction that makes evident a kind of blinding of the pastors.

With John Paul II the declared hostility to Fatima finally ended. The Pope of *Totus Tuus*, especially protected precisely by the Madonna of Fatima—who saved his life on May 13, 1981—will go on pilgrimage to the Portuguese sanctuary no fewer than three times. It will be he who beatifies Jacinta and Francisco, and in that context will publish a part of the Third Secret (although with a hypothetical interpretation that is unconvincing and rife with twisted readings of the text).

Unfortunately, not even John Paul II will be able to do everything he had in his heart to respond finally to the requests of the Madonna, because by now—after fifteen years of post-Conciliar devastation—the "Protestant victory within Catholicism" (as De Lubac called it) was crushing, and by then there was consolidated in the ecclesiastical ranks a formidable anti-Fatima deployment with which even the Pope had joined hands.

"With Wojtyla we knew since the years of the Council," recalls Monsignor Pavel Hnilica to Andrea Tornelli. "I had occasion to greet him a few days after the election, and I said to him: 'God has called you because your first work must be the consecration and conversion of Russia.' He answered me: 'I am willing to do it even tomorrow. If you convince the bishops.'"[365] After the assassination attempt, on December 8, 1981 the Pope pronounces these words in Saint Mary Major: "Mary, to You we entrust the fate of humanity." Monsignor Hnilica was present, and recounts: "After the ceremony, while in the sacristy, I said to the Pope: 'Holiness, an entrustment does not suffice. What is needed is a consecration.' He answered me: 'I know, but many theologians are opposed.'"[366]

The following year the Pope did the consecration, but it was not a solemn act in communion with all the bishops and addressed

---

[365] Andrea Tornielli, *The Secret Revealed*, op. cit., pp. 109-110.
[366] Interview in *Il Giornale*, May 18, 2000.

to Russia in particular. Sister Lucia, consulted by the Apostolic Nuncio to Portugal, Monsignor Portalupi, declared on March 19, 1983: "The consecration of Russia has not been done as Our Lady of Fatima requested."[367]

Finally, the consecration of March 25, 1984, which has already been analyzed. It appears that Sister Lucia commented thus: "The Pope did everything that he could do."[368] It is a phrase that brings to mind something the same pontiff had said concerning the previous consecration of 1982, when he affirmed that he had "done everything possible in the concrete circumstances."[369] What does this mean? Perhaps the Holy Father was not able to do everything he had wished? By whom or what was he impeded? What did Sister Lucia know?

A flash that illuminates these questions with a sinister light is provided by Hamish Fraser, a writer converted to Fatima, in November 1985: "Concerning one thing there are no doubts: the Holy Father is acutely aware of the need for the collegial consecration of Russia ... given that within the space of two years he has consecrated the world three times ... and the third time (March 25, 1984) he invited the bishops to unite themselves to him ... in accomplishing the act of consecration. Beyond this, on each occasion he indicated that he knew the consecration requested by Our Lady had not yet been done. Therefore no one can pretend that this is not something that remains in the heart of the Holy Father."

And here is the disturbing explanation: "Given the anxiety of the Holy Father concerning the consecration ... and, on the other hand, the scandalous hostility aroused by his request for episcopal participation in the solemn act of 1984, it can be deduced with moral certainty that until now one thing in particular has impeded the Holy Father from ordering the bishops of the universal Church to unite themselves with him in the consecration of Russia: his fear that it could really provoke a formal schism."[370]

---

[367] On that occasion Sister Lucia added a very significant phrase concerning her condition since 1960: "I could not say so [before now], because I did not have permission from the Holy See." (Laurent Morlier, *The Third Secret of Fatima*, op. cit., p. 93.)

[368] Quoted by Monsignor Hnilica in the interview in *Il Giornale*, op. cit.

[369] In Francis Alban and Christopher A. Ferrara, *Fatima Priest* (Good Counsel Publications: Pound Ridge, New York, 2000), p. 500 (Italian edition); translated from *Fatima Priest* hardcover edition (Good Counsel Publications, 1997), p. 357.

[370] Ibid., p. 100 (Italian edition); pp. 88-89 (English edition).

Is this perhaps a fear due to his knowledge of the entire Third Secret? Is it preannounced in the words of the Madonna that are still secreted? Certainly Fraser is right to affirm that "many bishops literally turn red when the Message of Fatima is mentioned." At any rate, Cardinal Stickler, who was very close to the Pope, confided on November 26, 1987 that the Pope had not been able to perform the consecration he would have wished because "the bishops do not obey him."[371] And this leads to the intuition that perhaps there is already in progress a silent schism with respect to Catholic truth. Or—as De Lubac said—that Protestantism has triumphed within Catholicism. And the great sign of contradiction is inevitably Mary—who, as the Fatima event demonstrates, hears and assists Popes in every way. Mary is the "vanquisher of all heresies," as Cardinal Ratzinger underlined in *Maria, Chiesa nascente* (p. 19).

Turning to the consecration of 1984, it very much brings to mind the consecrations of the world performed by Pius XII in 1942 and 1952. As with these—as shown by the words of Sister Lucia—that solemn act was incomplete and has not permitted realization of the promise made by the Madonna at Fatima, but would however obtain a positive response from Heaven. And a generous, unimaginable response!

The visionary has affirmed (very probably thanks to the apparition of 1985 of which Cardinal Bertone has also hinted) that this act spared the world a catastrophic war that should have erupted precisely in 1985. Naturally, we find ourselves on a supernatural plane and thus there is no historical "document" containing this "news." However, there are surprising clues: It is startling to reconstruct the situation during the months between 1984 and 1985 in order to understand what happened.

It is a fact that these were the years of the grave crisis of the Euromissiles. At the Kremlin, Andropov was succeeded by Chernenko. During the period 1983-84, according to historians, the conflict between NATO and the Warsaw Pact reached its height. The Euromissile crisis is perhaps the most dramatic moment of the post-war period. The USSR was losing the conflict because of the extreme socioeconomic crisis of the system and because it was not able to keep up with the competition and the challenge launched by Reagan with his "Star Wars" missile defense shield. Thus, facing the

---

[371] Ibid., p. 502 (Italian edition); p. 358 (English edition).

prospect of collapse and military vulnerability, for the first time the Kremlin took under consideration the military option, that is, the possibility of a "preventive" attack on Western Europe.

All indications are that this would have involved an atomic conflict, a road with no return. (In forty years of cold war 130,000 nuclear arms had been produced, a quantity sufficient to destroy the planet thousands of times.)

It is at this white-hot moment that, on March 25, 1984, in Saint Peter's Square in Rome, before the statue of the Madonna, John Paul II pronounces his dramatic and solemn consecration of the world to the Immaculate Heart of Mary.[372]

What happened? Within the span of a very few months, the Kremlin puts aside the option of war. It is as if a terrible storm is about to arrive, and at the very moment when the sky is darkest the sun suddenly comes out and a powerful wind disperses the threat. Many years later there would come to be understood a fact which—according to the experts—appears to have determined this reversal. Alberto Leoni, an expert in military history, has recounted the

---

[372] *And therefore, O Mother of all men and of all peoples,* You who know all their sufferings and their hopes, You who maternally feel all the struggles between good and evil, between light and darkness, which afflict the modern world, accept our cry which We, moved by the Holy Spirit, address directly to Your Heart. *Embrace* with your *love,* O Mother and Handmaiden of the Lord, this human world of ours, which we entrust and consecrate to You, for we are full of deep concern for the earthly and eternal destiny of men and of peoples....

Entrusting to You, O Mother, the world, all men and peoples, we also *entrust* to You *this same consecration of the world,* placing it in Your motherly Heart.

O Immaculate Heart! Help us to conquer the menace of evil, which so easily takes root in the hearts of men of today, and in its immeasurable effects already weigh down upon our present life and seem to block the paths towards the future!

From famine and war, *deliver us.*

From nuclear war, from incalculable self-destruction, from every kind of war, *deliver us.*

From sins against the life of man from its very beginning, *deliver us.*

From hatred and from the demeaning of the dignity of the children of God, *deliver us.*

From every kind of injustice in the life of society, both national and international, *deliver us.*

From readiness to trample on the commandments of God, *deliver us.*

From attempts to stifle in human hearts the very truth of God, *deliver us.*

From the loss of consciousness of good and evil, *deliver us.*

From sins against the Holy Spirit, *deliver us, deliver us.*

Accept, O Mother of Christ, this cry *laden with the sufferings* of all men, *laden with the sufferings* of all society.

"incident" which ruled out the use of the Soviet military potential in 1984: the explosion of the arsenal at Severomorsk on the North Sea. "Without that missile apparatus that controlled the North Sea," explains Leoni, "the USSR did not have any hope of victory. For this reason the military option was canceled."[373]

Well then, that decisive event happened two months after the solemn rite of consecration in Saint Peter's Square—exactly on May 13, 1984, the first anniversary and feast of the Madonna of Fatima and the attack on the Pope. Will there also be in this case the "invisible hand" of history or the extreme particularity of the date of the event to suggest that it involves, yet again, the hand of Mary Immaculate of Fatima, to whom the Pope had so ardently entrusted the fate of humanity?

Indeed, this was only the beginning of the "thank-you's" raining down from Heaven after March 25, 1984. In fact, with the military option canceled there remained only the desperate option of reform of the Soviet system. Hence with the death of Chernenko a few months after the consecration performed by the Pope, Mikhail Gorbachev was called to power. The man of reform was able to sign the first fundamental treaty with the United States for the reduction of armaments and the elimination of Euromissiles, thereby moving away from a nuclear Apocalypse. (According to the "Bulletin of the Atomic Scientists" there was fixed the maximum total of nuclear warheads for both sides, around 70,000.)

Well then, as "luck" would have it, that signature—after which, according to Sister Lucia, war was averted—was affixed precisely on December 8th of 1987, when the Church celebrates the Feast of the Immaculate Conception. Moreover, it was Gorbachev himself who, on the vigil, made this surprising declaration to *Time* magazine: "I am sure that God, up there in the heights of Heaven, will not refuse us the necessary wisdom to find the ways of understanding." In effect, around that accord there was also noticed a curious intertwining of interventions by the Madonna.[374]

The cancellation of the military option and the discovery that the system was irreformable (the man of *perestroika* could have done very little) brought on, within the turn of a few months, the collapse

---

[373] *Il Domenicale*, August 7, 2004.

[374] For the role of one of the visionaries of Medjugorje, Marija Pavlovic, see Antonio Socci, *Mistero Medjugorje*, cit., pp. 143-144.

of the Soviet Union and the dismantling of the entire communist empire. One thing above all astonishes: that the most terrible and durable of totalitarianisms disintegrates in a few days without any violence, without victims and without traumas. If there are and can be identified a thousand historical, political and economic causes which provoked and explain this collapse, no one has yet succeeded in explaining how it was possible that it happened without any spilling of blood and without any violence.

We know (from what Lech Walesa has said) that in the first years of the 1980s John Paul II's appeal to non-violence, launched at the outdoor Mass for Solidarity, was decisive: a violent revolt in Poland would certainly have given a bloody and tragic turn to the events. But how and why the subsequent disintegration of the communist system consummated itself without a single broken window pane remains a mystery.

Catholics discern in all of this a special and providential protection of Heaven precipitated by prayer and—not least—by the solemn act of the Pope in the consecration of 1984. Secular people will maintain that all of this is unprovable; however, there are "traces" left by the invisible hand that guided the events, traces that amaze and cause one to think that what is involved is a hand that is very readily identifiable. Yet again it involves the dates, with their illuminating and inexplicable coincidences.

Indeed, as "luck" would have it, the liquidation of the USSR in 1991 (which becomes the CIS, while Leningrad returns to calling itself St. Petersburg) was consummated on yet another 8th of December, the Feast of the Immaculate Conception, and the lowering of the Red Flag by the Kremlin (that is, the end of the regime that perpetrated the worst massacre of Christians in history) happened on December 25, 1991, the day of the Birth of Our Lord. A mere happenstance? A banal coincidence?

When a Korean bishop, Monsignor Angelo Kim Nam-su, said to the Pope: "Holiness, thanks to you Poland was able to liberate itself from communism," the Pope replied: "No, not thanks to me; it was done by the Virgin, as She said at Fatima..."[375] That there was a beneficial intervention of the Madonna, therefore, is what the Pope

---

[375] In *Notizie Cattoliche* [*Catholic Notes*], November 11, 1990 (in Caniato-Sansonetti, *Maria, alba del Terzo millennio* [*Mary, dawn of the Third Millennium*], Ares, 2001, p. 391).

and the Church think. And also Sister Lucia, who when questioned concerning this by *Thirty Days*, declared: "I am completely in accord with what the Holy Father has said... I believe this involves an action of God in the world, to liberate it from the danger of an atomic war that could destroy it, and an insistent call to all of humanity for a more lively faith."

Nevertheless, neither she nor the Pope has ever maintained that the promise of Fatima has been realized: there is, in fact, not a trace of the "conversion of Russia" and true "peace." The evolution of the post-communist countries is not very reassuring for the Church. But certainly the continuing recurrence of May 13 and December 8, the liturgical Feast of the Immaculate Conception, in the events of the collapse of communism prompts us to recall the Madonna's promise at Fatima: "In the end, My Immaculate Heart will triumph." Which sounds like a biblical warning: "Oh if Israel listens..." If the consecration of 1984, like those by Pius XII, has yet again brought great benefits to the world, how much greater would they have been had the Madonna been heeded?

Perhaps it is no happenstance that the pontificate of John Paul II—who did so many similiar things in regard to Our Lady of Fatima as the other "Pope of Fatima", Pope Pius XII—was also marked, at its decline, by a supernatural sign so similar to the tears of the Madonna of Syracuse: Civitavecchia.[376] Another statue of the Madonna which weeps, but sometimes weeps blood. And weeps at the doors of Rome. Is the Third Secret about to come true?

Mea culpa of a Pope

The Great Secret of Fatima fittingly mentions the Pope about ten times. According to Frère Michel "we must reread the text attentively to discover (perhaps to our astonishment) to what extent the role of the Sovereign Pontiff is absolutely necessary for the success of the providential grand design"—that is, the design of Divine Mercy for our century, which "clearly underlines the supreme responsibility of the Holy Father, on whom everything depends in the final analysis."[377] In the apparitions after 1917—in which Heaven demands the concrete realization of God's design—

---

[376] See *Lacrime di sangue* [*Tears of Blood*] by various authors (Sei: Turin, 2005).

[377] FM, vol. III, p. 694.

the role of the papacy is even more vital and essential.

Studying well the Message of Fatima, one understands also that, despite a long deafness, "from the Pope will come, in the end, salvation." Thus does Frère Michel interpret the epilogue of the Message: "In the end, My Immaculate Heart will triumph. The Holy Father will consecrate Russia to Me, which will be converted, and a period of peace will be granted to the world." However—always basing himself on the words heard from Lucia—Frère Michel maintains that "the Popes will undergo punishments for their disobedience". (Obviously, our thoughts return to the terrible words of Jesus to Sister Lucia: "They did not wish to listen to My request. Like the King of France, they will repent and they will do it, but it will be late... The Holy Father will have much to suffer.")

But is the comprehensive interpretation given by this Fatima scholar plausible? Do there exist precedents in the history of the Church that could support this theology of history, according to which the infidelity or deafness of the pastors of the Church brings persecutions to the Church and terrible disasters to the world? There is a resounding precedent which corresponds—not by accident—with the other great collapse seen by the Church in her two thousand years: that of the Protestant schism. It was Pope Adrian VI, the last non-Italian Pope before John Paul II, who formulated a courageous *mea culpa* that provides an interpretative key for subsequent events quite consonant with that which the Madonna will utter at Fatima.

The Protestant "bomb" had exploded and, addressing himself in 1523 to the delegates to the Imperial Diet meeting at Nuremberg, he declared:

> We freely acknowledge that God has permitted this persecution of the Church because of the sins of men, and in particular of priests and prelates. The hand of God has not, in fact, been withdrawn; He could save us; but sin separates us from Him and prevents Him from hearing us. All of Sacred Scripture teaches us that the errors of the people have their origin in the errors of the clergy... We know that for many years abominations have been committed even in the Holy See: trafficking in sacred things, transgression of the commandments in such measure that everything is turned to scandal. One should not be surprised that the sickness has descended from the head to the members, from the popes to the prelates. All of

us, prelates and ecclesiastics, have strayed from the path of justice. For a long time no one has pursued the good. For this reason all of us must honor God and humble ourselves before Him. Each one of us must examine himself to see in what way he has fallen short, and must examine himself much more severely than will God on the day of His wrath. We must all consider ourselves committed to do this because the entire world thirsts for reform.[378]

The pontificate of Adrian VI came, in fact, after that of Leo X and a series of objectively unworthy Popes (I recall only Pope Borgia, that is, Alexander VI), whose errors had led to an extremely grave crisis in the Church and finally to the tragedy of the Protestant schism. The pontificate of Adrian VI lasted only two years (1522-1523) and the events which happened afterwards will confirm his "diagnosis."

In 1527 the punishment struck Rome itself: twenty thousand mercenaries in the service of Charles V swooped down on the heart of Christianity and devastated it at length—a scourge made of sacking, assassination, fire and destruction. The Lutheran schism (with those that followed) inflicted on Catholicism the gravest wound in its history, pitting half of Christian Europe against Rome and the papacy (a situation that perdures today, moreover with a grave secularization of Protestant countries), and launched a war of religion that set Europe aflame for more than a century and devastated it irremediably, producing the conditions that gave birth to secular thought. Finally, Protestantism planted the seeds of modern ideologies with all the disasters that accompanied them, above all in the 20th century.[379] Therefore we can say that the "punishment" was much greater than Adrian VI himself had imagined, developing itself over centuries.

---

[378] In Liddia Maggi and Angelo Reginato, *La Riforma Protestante tra passato e presente* [*The Protestant Reform from the Past through the Present*] in "Sette e Religioni" [Sects and Religion], 5 (2004) 37, p. 20.

[379] "Modernity is a result of the Protestant heresy… From which is born the absolutization of the State, the rebirth in the 1800s of a political paganism, founded on the myth of the nation and the State, which will give birth to the crisis of Europe. It is the first great attempt to destroy the Church: what follows is modern totalitarianism in which Communism and Nazism will try to extinguish radically the memory of Christ. The Protestant heresy was not ecclesially innocuous, because the redivinized State is a consequence of the rejection of the Church as Body of Christ, of the Church as one, holy, Catholic and apostolic." (Gianni Baget Bozzo, *The Antichrist*, op. cit., p. 133.)

This notwithstanding, however, one is made to feel the maternal presence of the Madonna to protect from worse disasters, limiting the damage and opening new horizons. It suffices to consider a coincidence. The year 1531—when the Schmalkaldic League, the Lutheran anti-imperial alliance, was formed, that is, the moment in which the Lutheran revolution had truly exploded in Europe—was also the year of the apparition of the Madonna of Guadalupe in Mexico. It is the first Marian apparition of the modern epoch and the beginning of that action of Mary in aid of the Church which will have its maximum expression in the 20th century, the century of great conflicts.

The apparition of Guadalupe—according to the general acknowledgment of historians—was what attracted the Indians to Christianity. Therefore, it was precisely Guadalupe that gave birth to Latin American Christianity.[380] It was not born of ecclesiastical projects (which, on the contrary, were being met with hostility from the indigenous populations), but from the initiative of Heaven, manifested through Mary. Precisely at the moment in which the Church in half of Europe was being mutilated by a heresy that, among other things, was profoundly hostile to the Holy Virgin, the Madonna gifted to the Church an entire continent, which today is the greatest Catholic continent in the world. The apparition happened—notice the coincidence—on the Feast of the Immaculate Conception (which in those times was celebrated on the 9th of December, not the 8th). This is the Feast of the Woman who crushes the serpent's head.

In the following years were witnessed other decisive events that allow one to glimpse the succoring hand of Mary, which aids the Church. First of all, the birth of the Society of Jesus on August 15, 1540, Feast of the Assumption: the Jesuits were the invaluable troop chosen by the Church to repel the assault of Protestantism and of modernity. (St. Ignatius of Loyola, the head and founder, was converted at the sanctuary of the Black Madonna of Montserrat, depositing his sword and shield on the altar of the Virgin.) And then the Council of Trent (1545-1563) which—against the theories

---

[380] See Gonzalez, Sanchez, Rosado, *El Encuentro de la Virgen de Guadalupe y Juan Diego* [*The Encounter of the Virgin of Guadalupe and Juan Diego*] (Editorial Porrua, 2000); Manuela Testoni, *Guadalupe* (San Paolo, Cinisello Balsamo: Milan, 1998); Donal Anthony Foley, *Il Libro delle apparizioni mariane* [*The Book of Marian Apparitions*] (Gribaudi: Milan, 2004).

of Luther—defined the dogma of Original Sin, proclaiming the unique exception, preserved by a special grace of God from all sin, even venial: Most Holy Mary.

Pope Pius V, a great saint and a great Pope, applied the Council throughout the Church and in 1571, confronted by the menace of a new and (this time) devastating Muslim invasion, succeeded in convincing the Christian sovereigns to ally themselves together and create a fleet equal to that of the Turks (250 ships). On October 7, 1571 the Christians, at Lepanto, with minimal losses, routed the Turkish fleet, putting an end to the myth of Islamic invincibility on the seas. Not only was Europe saved, but there was also involved an historical turning point, because from there began the decline of the Turkish threat to Europe.

The historian Fernand Braudel: "The victory signaled the end of a destitution, the end of a real Christian inferiority complex, the end of a just as real Turkish supremacy. The Christian victory barred the road to an adversary whose looming threat was very dark and near."[381] But this victory remains in the memory of the Church a victory by Mary because of two events. First, Charles V donated to the admiral, Prince Doria of Genova, an image of the Madonna of Guadalupe; and it is recounted that at the darkest moment—when his ships were cut off and he feared the worst—he knelt desperately, commending himself to the Virgin, and there was a sudden reversal of fortune.

But above all it is recounted that during the battle, hundreds of miles distant Pius V in the Vatican had a vision of the Madonna that assured the Holy Father of victory: "While working intently with his cardinals, he suddenly opened the window, fixed his gaze on Heaven and then invited those present to unite themselves with him in gratitude to God for the great victory he had just obtained. Pius V did not hesitate to attribute this great victory to the prayers of the confraternity of the Rosary, spread throughout Rome and beyond, and he ordered that Lepanto be commemorated every year. Initially known as the "Feast of Holy Mary of Victory," this celebration then became the Feast of Our Lady of the Rosary, a feast that in the 20th century was extended to the entire Church. Neither was this the last

---

[381] Fernand Braudel, *Civilita e imperi del Mediterraneo nell'eta di Filippo II* [*Civilization and Empires of the Mediterranean in the Age of Phillip II*] (Einaudi: Turin, 2002), p. 1283.

time that it could be said that Christianity was saved from the threat represented by Islam: the crucial victory of Vienna carried off by the Polish King John III (Sobieski), in 1683, is a further example of the intercessory power of the Madonna of the Rosary.[382]

The Rosary thus assumed a great importance in the prayer of the Church. The Rosary is historically the prayer of the poor, from which arises the idea of a Psalter for the illiterate, for the people. It is the cry of the poor in spirit to the Mother of Jesus, and thus a prayer that is especially heeded and efficacious. And in the 20th century the Madonna Herself will recommend it as a most potent weapon, attributing to it at Fatima the power to bring an end to the war.

In our time, however, the Rosary is not limited to this. It is worth rereading the words of Lucia to Father Fuentes:

> She said to my cousins as well as to myself that God is giving two last remedies to the world. These are the Holy Rosary and devotion to the Immaculate Heart of Mary. These are the last two remedies, which signify that there will not be others.... God, always before He is about to chastise the world, exhausts all other remedies. Now, when He sees that the world pays no attention whatsoever, then, as we say in our imperfect manner of speaking, He offers us "with a certain trepidation" the last means of salvation, His Most Holy Mother. It is "with a certain trepidation" because if we despise and repulse this ultimate remedy this means we will not have any more forgiveness from Heaven because we will have committed a sin which the Gospel calls the sin against the Holy Spirit...

> Look, Father, the Most Holy Virgin, in these last times in which we live, has given a new efficacy to the recitation of the Holy Rosary. She has given this efficacy to such an extent that there is no problem, no matter how difficult it is, whether temporal or above all, spiritual, in the private life of each one of us, of our families, of the families of the world, of the religious communities or even of the life of peoples and nations, that cannot be resolved through the prayer of the Holy Rosary. There is no problem, I tell you, no matter how difficult it is, that we cannot resolve through the recitation of the Holy Rosary. Through the Holy Rosary we will save ourselves. We will sanctify ourselves.

---

[382] Donal Anthony Foley, *The Book of Marian Apparitions*, op. cit., pp. 76-77.

We will console Our Lord and obtain the salvation of many souls. Finally, devotion to the Immaculate Heart of Mary, Our Most Holy Mother, consists in considering Her as the seat of mercy, of goodness and of pardon, and as the sure door through which we are to enter Heaven.

What does all of this mean? Does it not give an excessive importance—as many theologians, modern and modernist, say—to She who is still only a human creature?

The overthrow of "power"

"She is the most beautiful person that I have ever seen,"[383] confides the little Francisco Marto to someone who questions him. The marvelous Lady, who in reality, based on the testimony of the children, was a girl between the ages of 15 and 18, appears thus—extraordinarily sweet and beautiful—in all of the modern apparitions. What is signified by a sign so profound theologically and so universally comprehensible (because whoever is human is moved and attracted by beauty)? Why does God wish to break into history with these public and prophetic apparitions, with this "eternal youth," this absolute Beauty, in modern times? What is the motive and what is the hidden message?

Fatima is the most sensational, the most public, and the most "political" of the modern apparitions. It is Heaven's answer to a two-hundred-year-long revolution and to the final attempt, in the 20th century, to eradicate Christ from the heart and the history of man, annihilating the Church.

Can one say that God has revealed at Fatima His very special "plan" for these times of ours? Yes, this is emphasized from the beginning with the apparition of the angel to the three children in preparing them for the apparition of the Blessed Virgin: "The most holy Hearts of Jesus and Mary have designs of mercy on you." Then the Virgin Herself openly reveals this plan to them: "God wishes to establish in the world devotion to My Immaculate Heart." And Our Lady makes it known that—notwithstanding the deafness of men— the plans of God will always be accomplished; in fact the Message of Fatima concludes with the prophecy of a factual certainty: "In the end, My Immaculate Heart will triumph."

---

[383] Luigi Gonzaga da Fonseca, *The Marvels of Fatima*, op. cit., p. 69.

This Our Lady announces after making a series of historico-political prophecies (all of which, as we have seen, came to pass: revolutions, persecutions and wars); therefore the "triumph" prophesied by Mary will have a resounding historical, and even cultural and political, obviousness. Like the victory at Lepanto, but much greater.

We find ourselves before a prophecy that announces a radical and extraordinary change in the world, an overthrow of the mentality dominating the modern world, probably following dramatic events for humanity. (The Third Secret could coincide with the events contained in the "Ten Secrets" of Medjugorje, which will be announced in advance, and whose realization concerns the years in the near future.)[384] Thus, a total change in modern history through the Hearts of Jesus and Mary, which is here prefigured. Further, the "requests" made by the Madonna to the Church acquire—as can readily be seen—a much clearer significance.

They remind the Pope of the divine power of which he is truly the depositary. From these pages emerge perhaps a heavy judgment on the choices of many Popes of the 20th century. The "Fatimist" literature, still worse, is often implacable. Are we not being—while in different ways—ungenerous and one-sided? Does it make sense to focus totally and exclusively on Fatima, as if every pontificate should be judged solely according to its response to the requests at Fatima? And these requests by the Mother of God, are they not interpreted—by Fatimists, but also on these pages—in a manner too literal and rigid, almost as if God and the Holy Virgin would demand nit-picking attention to every "quibble" of their requests, as harsh judges, under penalty of terrifying punishments?

Ultimately, what Father Rene Laurentin writes is true: "Never have the popes been pushed so far to obey, at the level of the universal Church, the request of a visionary."[385] However, this is true above all for John Paul II and Pius XII. For the others, no. And it is also true that the words concerning the "ministers" of the Church who do not listen to Heaven and act like "the King of France" were heard by Sister Lucia during an apparition, and therefore are decisively authoritative. However, on the other hand, the visionary was always exhorted by Heaven to pray and do penance for the Popes, and to

---

[384] See Antonio Socci, *Mystery of Medjugorje*, op. cit.

[385] In Aura Miguel, *Totus Tuus*, op. cit., p. 98.

request always from her superiors what Heaven had indicated to her, while recognizing always their authority and central role.[386]

From her superiors she scarcely requested a nit-picking respect for all of the particulars, but rather a total change of heart and of ecclesiastical mentality. For example, the consecration of Russia should have been—based on what Lucia says—an immense event for the whole Catholic Church, which in every corner of the planet would share in a great rite of expiation and consecration for that unfortunate nation, entrusting itself universally to the Immaculate Heart of Mary. What is extraordinary is the coincidence between the prophecy of Fatima and the "prophecy" by Saint Louis Marie Grignion de Montfort, who was providentially (not accidentally) made known to the whole Church by John Paul II, who drew from him the motto *Totus Tuus*.[387] Here is the striking prophetic intuition of this saint of the 17th century:

> By means of Mary the salvation of the world began; again by means of Mary it must have its fulfillment. During the first coming of Jesus Christ, Mary was almost invisible, so that men, still little instructed and illuminated concerning the Person of His Son, would not drift away from the truth, attaching themselves too sensibly and coarsely to Her. This certainly would have happened—had She been known—because of the marvelous enchantment that God had also conferred on Her exterior aspect. Thus it is quite true, as Saint Diogenes the Areopagite observed, that when She lived She would have been taken for a deity because of the secret charms and the incomparable beauty She possessed, if the faith, in which [the Church] was very firm, had not taught the contrary.

> But during the Second Coming of Jesus Christ, Mary must be known and revealed by the Holy Spirit in order that Jesus Christ be known, loved and served by means of Her ... In these last times, therefore, God wishes to reveal and manifest Mary, the masterpiece of His hands.

---

[386] And the same Frère Michel emphasizes: "Our Lady never ordered Sister Lucia to write or to disclose this or that part of the Secret... No, She has willed that the initiative come from the Church: confessors, bishop, or pope." FM, vol. III, pp. 52 and 467-479 (2001 edition).

[387] As for the importance in the life of Karol Wojtyla of this author, Montfort's *Treatise on True Devotion to Mary*, it has been diffused throughout John Paul II's book *Dono e mistero* [*Gift and Mystery*] (Libreria editrice vaticana: 1996), pp. 37, 38.

With almost these same words the Madonna of Fatima announces that the time predicted by Montfort has arrived: "God wishes to establish in the world devotion to My Immaculate Heart," and, after a great conflict that corresponds to our times: "In the end, My Immaculate Heart will triumph."

In 1973 a Catholic intellectual and French academic as great as Jean Guitton, in a study dedicated to the apparitions of 1830 at Rue du Bac, perceived that this time of Mary is coming: "One of the themes of Grignion de Montfort is that the devotion to Mary would grow toward the end of time, that the progress of this cult would be a sign of the end times… If we are drawing near to a crisis without precedent, or if instead we find ourselves at the threshold of a new phase in the growth of the Church, in either case it is possible that 'the time of the Virgin' is near."[388] (It certainly makes an impression to think that only eight years later began the apparitions of Medjugorje, "the greatest post-conciliar mass movement of Catholics".)[389]

The perception of the mission that the Madonna is carrying out really and personally in our time, declared publicly at Fatima, was shared by two great men of the Church, two Popes who have collaborated closely: Karol Wojtyla and Joseph Ratzinger. The latter, commenting on *Redemptoris Mater* by John Paul II, observed that it does not involve only a meditation—as with the Mariology of the past—on "the privileges of the Mother of God," or "Her great titles." The novelty suggested by Pope Wojtyla, according to Cardinal Ratzinger, does not concern contemplating the "static mysteries" of Mary, but rather, transmitted through Her, the "understanding of the dynamic history of salvation, involving us and pointing to our place in history, bestowing gifts and imposing demands upon us. Mary does not reside only in the past," the Cardinal writes, "but also in the heights of Heaven, in intimacy with God; and She remains present and active in the current historical moment; She is here and now an acting person. Her life does not stand only behind us, nor simply above us; She precedes us, as the Pope stresses continually. She explains to us our historical hour, not through theories but by

---

[388] Jean Guitton, *La medaglia miracolosa* [*The Miraculous Medal*] (San Paolo: Cinisello Balsamo, Milan, 1995), pp. 126 and 128.

[389] Vittorio Messori and Rino Cammilleri, *Gli occhi di Maria* [*The Eyes of Mary*] (Rizzoli: Milan, 2001), p. 243.

acting and indicating to us the road that lies ahead."[390]

It is natural, reading these words, to think that these two men of the Church had precisely Fatima in mind. (I personally think that these words are perfect also for Medjugorje.) This is the time in which Peter finds the special assistance of Mary as the "guide" who "points out the road."[391] John Paul II said this with very clear words, speaking precisely of Fatima (and quoting almost to the letter St. Louis de Montfort): "When I entered into the problems of the universal Church with the election to the papacy, I brought with me a similar conviction: that is, even in this universal dimension, the victory, if it comes, will be carried off by Mary. Christ will be victorious by means of Her, because He wishes that the victories of the Church in the contemporary world and in the future be united to Her."[392]

As Saint Bernard had said already in the Middle Ages: "Such is the will of He who has willed that we should obtain everything through Mary." But modern times seem to have been destined—to the fury of the Enemy in a thousand ferocious forms—to know in a very special way the regality of Mary. Perhaps precisely because Satan hates men viscerally and in our time has frightfully loosed himself, God wishes to counterpoise to him the elevation of one human creature, the most sublime, the only innocent, whom He even crowns Queen of Heaven and earth, above the angels.

Indeed, "hell hates Her and trembles before Her,"[393] declares Saint Maximilian Kolbe, a paladin of the Immaculate and who died at Auschwitz (on August 14, 1941), victim of one of the modern demons that he conquered with his love for Christ and for His Mother, and therefore for all men. "We do not yet know Mary, and

---

[390] Joseph Ratzinger, *Mary, the Church Rising*, op. cit., pp. 36-37. Ratzinger continues, explaining that therefore "Mariology becomes a theology of history and of the imperative to act... The encyclical presents Mary as guide of history, sign of the times" and as "prophetess" (pp. 42 and 61).

[391] "Mary the Virgin gave birth, having given birth to her Son, to the end of time... We poor sinners invoke her at the hour of our death: she is the 'doorway to heaven,' and is much more than Peter the 'heavenly door-keeper' who makes the presence of her Son accessible to us: through Mary to Jesus (*per Mariam ad Jesum*). She is the aid of which we have need so that our birth will succeed... until we reach heaven." (Von Balthasar, *New Firm Points*, op. cit., pp. 1067-1069.)

[392] Vittorio Messori and Karol Wojtyla, *Crossing the Threshold of Hope*, op. cit., pp. 242-243 [Italian edition].

[393] Saint Maximilian Kolbe, *The Holy Spirit and the Immaculate*, op. cit., p. 39.

for this reason we do not even know Christ in the way we should," Montfort explained. Mary indeed came to Fatima to open our eyes to the infinite value of our existence and of the blood of He who has redeemed it. First of all She showed us, for a chilling instant, Hell, thus reminding all men of the great drama of their liberty. Then—as we have seen—She invited the "ministers" of Christ to exercise the "power" that Christ has conferred on them to prevent vast throngs from being lost forever in horror.

But She came also to exalt the power of simple Christians and to appeal to them. It is often said that thanks to Vatican Council II the place of the laity was recognized in a Church that up until then had been suffocated by clericalism. But if the Council created a dispute over rules and power, clericalism has, however, remained. And is it not understood that it was precisely the Madonna, well before the Council, who pointed out the road at Fatima: something more revolutionary—in a Church totally centered on priests and hierarchical power—by the Mother of God appearing to lay people, indeed to three children who, apart from Lucia, had not even made their First Communion, as was the case with Bernadette of Lourdes? And the Queen of Heaven and of Earth called precisely them to the highest of missions, to exercise, therefore, the power for which we are qualified by a simple Baptism, which transforms every human being into "priest, king and prophet."

An "investiture" that no power—neither clerical, nor theological, nor worldly—can impugn, even if it is difficult for the cleric to accept the free choices of Mary and of the Holy Spirit and to acknowledge being only servants and not masters of the work of God. Precisely these three children, insignificant according to the world to the point of being insulted and threatened by the political authorities, and unimportant even for a certain ecclesiastical world, were recognized by the Madonna as "priests, kings and prophets," and sent forth to exercise their immense and precious power.

The sacerdotal power: When the Madonna invited them to "say the Rosary every day with devotion to obtain peace in the world," She recognized in them an immense power, the power of priests, who can speak directly to God, are admitted into His presence, and offer to Him, sanctifying it, their own life and the whole world (they can even baptize), thus manifesting the power of God in reality (indeed with prayer one can obtain even peace). It is a power—as one can discern in history—that not even a head of State possesses. Yet every simple Catholic graced by Baptism has it.

Then the royal power: When the Virgin asks these little children (two of whom will die shortly thereafter in the "Spanish epidemic," as will so many others) if they wish to accept the sufferings of life and offer them "for the conversion of sinners" and for the liberation of souls from Purgatory, She recognizes in them the royal power that Jesus had on the Cross. From there, crowned by the suffering of the thorns, on the throne of wood to which He was nailed, the Son of God manifested His total lordship over the world and over history, freeing men from the slavery of the Malignant. It is a power that can not only change the face of history and the lives of individuals, but extends even to the next world, being able to liberate forever suffering masses, entire peoples. It is the one true movement of liberation that brings happiness to the suffering. Finally, to reign means to serve (in fact She who is described as "servant of the Lord" is the Queen of Heaven and of Earth).

Third, the prophetic power. The Madonna delivers to the children the "secret" that makes them properly prophets in the biblical sense. But they are this above all because they are baptized, through the power every one of the baptized has to announce Christ to the world and give testimony of Him unto martyrdom. At times with charisms and special missions. For example, the Madonna says to Lucia: "Jesus wishes you to serve Him by making Me known and loved. He wishes to establish in the world devotion to My Immaculate Heart."

After all, the words of the little Jacinta, on her death bed, are also the words of a prophetess, full of a wisdom that is not hers: "When you must speak, do not hide yourself. Tell everyone that God grants us graces through the Immaculate Heart of Mary, to whomever asks them from Her; that the Heart of Jesus wishes that at His side be venerated the Immaculate Heart of Mary. If I could put into the hearts of everyone the fire that I feel here inside, that makes me savor so much the Heart of Jesus and the Heart of Mary!"

Thus it is right to conclude—from the complicated history of the unheeded requests of the Madonna of Fatima—that all of us Christians (not only the pontiffs) bear responsibility for the fate of the world. And it is thanks to the prayers of the simple that the Madonna has until now been able to protect humanity, because the simple have always loved Her as their Mother and their help.

Since the episodes of the Gospel, Mary is She who succors everyone, always ready and merciful; She who hastens caringly, who embraces tenderly, who consoles and heals. It is not by accident that before Fatima there was the great event at Lourdes where the Holy Virgin manifested to modern humanity the infinitude of Her compassion for the suffering, the desperate, and for each human being. The "Beautiful Lady" of Nazareth, courageous and so sweet, is She who always defends everyone; She who stands in humble silence and wishes only that men know Her Son; She who lived literally taking on Herself the sufferings of the Son together with Him; She who serves; She who sees need and hastens even before help is asked of Her; She who never abandons anyone; She who gladdens and dries tears; She who is illumined by joy, singing the marvels of the God who has mercy on all, who "exalts the humble" and "fills the hungry with good things." "In the centuries it has never been heard," writes Saint Bernard, "that anyone who has made recourse to Her protection, implored Her help, or sought Her assistance has ever been abandoned by Her." She never abandons anyone. "It is never too late," Sister Lucia is heard to say, "to entrust oneself to the Sacred Heart of Jesus and to the Immaculate Heart of Mary."

Places and circumstances of this book

I wrote some of the pages of this book while sitting on a promenade in Tuscany. Waving above me, in the red of the sunset, was an Italian flag, a remnant of the world soccer championship. How soon were faded the flags that waved from the windows, the terraces and the bars. They were once so bright. Now they are unsightly. One sees some of them frayed and torn by the wind, others consumed by the sun, still others stained by rain. It is incredible how soon the flags came to ruin. All of the flags. There was no time to become covered in cracks for those which had already become indecent tatters. From living and triumphal symbols they had become in a short time sad and colorless rags. It is the inevitable course of events for the things of this world. And also of dreams. Even of loves. It is a universal wasting away.

Clothes become wrinkled, yesterday's newspaper is already

yellowed and illegible, the fields gold with grain seem already to be autumnal steppes. The flowers fade. "If they are roses they will fade," declares a scathing remark of Montanelli's. An impalpable dust settles incessantly on everything. A house seems solid and robust, yet even if it is a castle it has need of constant maintenance, because everything ages, breaks down and is corrupted. Everything tends toward disorder, everything decays and falls apart, says a fundamental principle of the physical. Everything wears out.

Usually we distractedly avoid thinking of this in order not to despair. But the first thing to decay, wear out and break down is our own body. The vigor and voluptuous harmony of young bodies, proudly exhibited, within the span of a few years will have to surrender to the force of gravity: over the decades the body wears down and gets out of shape. The earth calls the body toward itself. Dust you are and to dust you will return. And so begins the mighty effort at continuous maintenance. It is the obsession of this fatuous epoch: to dye graying hair, to lift up falling buttocks, to stretch out those wrinkles, not to consume fat in excess, to erase those bags under the eyes. Interminable efforts, continuous, costly, tireless—as if to put up each day a wall that collapses at night. And then the visit to the ophthalmologist because one cannot read well without glasses. And the hair that falls out. And those little pains in the back.

One tries (vainly) to stop aging in every way. One would prevent the moment like Goethe's Faust, but even millennial empires vanish, reminding us of the fate of individual mortals. "All the world passes, almost without leaving a trace," warns Leopardi. This is the weight of fallen nature. Even the young daily invest superhuman efforts in the exhausting, however vain, work of maintenance: to "sculpt" themselves in the gym, to perfume and tan themselves. Poor little ones, as if to build a castle of sand, as if to write the name of a beloved at the water's edge, this illusory flight from the insult of time. In the end it is the carnality of our being that terrifies us. Everything reminds us of its continuous corruption. To sweat is a sign of the biological degradation to which we are subject; the odor of the body itself must be banished. Our society is antiseptic: sweating is prohibited; bodies must emit only perfume; there must be no sign of putrefaction.

The most "materialist" and hedonistic epoch, which is ours, in reality has a horror of the flesh. We are all Gnostics without knowing

224

it. This is shown by the enormous growth in our expenditures for cosmetics, by the horror we have for the ailing body, for the suffering flesh. The disturbing Crucifixion by Grünewald, the most dramatic in all the history of art, was conceived by the German painter of the 1400s for the sufferers of leprosy and "Saint Anthony's Fire,"[393a] who desperately crowded the hospital chapel at Isenheim to pray, finding in the devastated flesh of the Man-God their own tears, their own agony.

In the end, only triumphant "materialists" are Christians. As Tertullian says, "It is Flesh that saves flesh." In *The Brothers Karamazov* Dostoevsky recounts the story of a parricide who is more than a parricide. The old Fyodor Pavlovich Karamazov, father of three brothers, expresses in fact the maximum of the terrestrial carnality that causes horror: he is described as vulgar and violent, mean-spirited and cynical, a "miserable buffoon." Physically he is bald, big-nosed, large-mouthed, double-chinned. He provokes physical repulsion in the three sons.

But while Ivan and Dmitri despise him openly, Alexei becomes a monk and thinks to avoid hatred of the flesh by choosing the spirit and a "spiritual father" like the Starec Zosima. But in fact the monk gives him the most important lesson in dying: his body immediately begins to emit a foul odor. Alexei is at first shocked and upset by this, but then learns the great lesson: Even that saint is made of flesh like his father. Then he leaves the room, bursts into uncontrollable weeping, and that night, throwing himself to the ground, he embraces all of Creation. He understands that faith in Christ is not a flight into the spiritual, but is the certainty of the only God who has taken human flesh and whose suffering has overcome the gravitational weight of fallen nature, who has manifested with His miracles His dominion over Creation, over sickness and even over the putrefaction of the flesh with the Resurrection. The risen Jesus is the beginning of a "new Creation" no longer subject to the dominion of death.

Alexei comprehends that the destiny of man is not the dark and desperate decomposition of the flesh, and is not even only the "salvation of the soul," but the glorification and "divinization" of our

---

[393a] The colloquial name for ergotism, a disease caused by the ingestion of a fungus that grows on rye grass. The symptoms include hallucinations, unbearable pain, and the loss of fingers, toes and limbs to gangrene.

entire being. And he understands that this force has entered into history and that this new history has already begun—with Christ, and with the first creature who already lives this glorification of the flesh, this eternal youth, this beauty which is not corrupted and does not pass away: Mary, She who was assumed body and soul into the glory of Heaven.

Her presence among us, in this our time, is so constant as to permit us to trace as if with an Identikit Her mysterious and fascinating beauty. The children of Medjugorje (and other visionaries) have done so: She is a "marvelous lady who appears about 18 years old, about five feet seven inches in height, a slender figure, wavy, black-chestnut hair, markedly blue eyes (of an extraordinary blue, never seen on earth), delicate, normal eyebrows. Her face has regular features, slight red in the cheeks, a small and well-proportioned nose. There is a light that accompanies Her always and emanates from Her: She is the most beautiful creature ever seen."[394] Her voice is a harmony impossible to imagine. She is a dazzling beauty, "so attractive," recounts Melanie of La Salette, "that it made me melt," like "Her gaze, so sweet and penetrating." This marvelous child is the Queen of Heaven and of Earth. Her beauty speaks to all of us of the true world to which we are destined. Her eternal youth preannounces the annulment of death and final happiness.

Today, Her presence among us, Her goodness, Her maternal assistance, Her appeals and also Her prophecies truly qualify Her as the Mother of Mercy. She has been sent to us because Jesus Himself wishes to make known His mercy especially in our time. As He confided to the Polish mystic Saint Faustina Kowalska:

> I desire that My Priests announce My great mercy for the souls of sinners. The sinner should not fear to approach Me. Even if a soul were like a cadaver in the state of putrefaction, if humanly there were no remedy, it is not so before God. The flames of mercy consume Me, and I desire to send them forth to the souls of all men. I am all love and mercy. A soul that has trust in Me is happy, because I Myself will take care of him. No sinner, be he an abyss of degradation, will ever exhaust My mercy, for the more it is drawn from, the more it grows. My daughter,

---

[394] Antonio Socci, *Mystery of Medjugorje*, p. 114.

do not cease to announce My mercy; doing this, you will bring refreshment to My Heart, which is consumed by the flames of compassion for sinners. How painfully I am wounded by the lack of trust in My goodness! I have all eternity to punish, but now I prolong the time of mercy for them. Even if his sins were as black as night, by turning himself toward My mercy the sinner glorifies Me and honors My Passion. At the hour of his death I shall defend him with that same glory. When a soul exalts My goodness, Satan trembles before it and flees into the depths of Hell. My Heart suffers, because even consecrated souls ignore My mercy, and treat Me with distrust. How greatly this wounds Me! If you do not believe My words, believe at least My wounds!

Appendix

The third part of the Secret of Fatima: paleographic examination, analysis of the Vatican edition, linguistic and translational aspects.

Mariagrazia Russo[394a]

The Third Secret of Fatima is a testimony-memoir written on January 3, 1944 by Sister Maria Lucia of Jesus and the Immaculate Heart by order of His Excellency the Bishop of Leiria and by "Vossa e Minha Santissima Mãe" [your and my Most Holy Mother] concerning what the three shepherds had seen and heard on July 13, 1917. The text (at first kept in a sealed envelope by the Bishop of Leiria then delivered on April 4, 1957 to the Secret Archive of Holy Office) was made public by Pope John Paul II during the passage from the second to the third millennium. In Italy a photostatic copy of the text, with a translation in Italian, was published by the Congregation for the Doctrine of the Faith in the volume *The Message of Fatima*. (It is to this that reference will be made within this contribution.) This documentation is introduced by a brief "Presentation" by then Archbishop emeritus of Vercelli and Secretary of the Congregation for the Doctrine of the Faith, Tarcisio Bertone, and commentated theologically by then Prefect of the same Congregation, Cardinal Joseph Ratzinger.

The Codicological and Graphological Level

The third part of the Secret was written by Sister Lucia on a paper base, using four sides of a folio without pages numbered, each side with 16 lines. The authoress habitually uses all the lines, with the exception of the first page on which she leaves two lines blank between the opening initials and the title of the document,

---

[394a] Established researcher and associate Professor of Languages and Portuguese and Brazilian translation on the Faculty of Languages and Modern Foreign Literature of the University of Tuscany at Viterbo; Professor of Romance Philology at Lumsa University in Rome.

and another line blank between the title of the document and the beginning of the body. At the end of the testimony Sister Lucia writes another three lines occupying the final non-ruled space on the page. The writing is kept neatly and fully within the line, respecting the right and left margins. The text is therefore written in an accurate and linear manner, slowly and calmly, and would appear to have been copied from a preceding rough draft.

The writing proceeds with a strong pressure of the nib on the paper (it is not possible from a photocopy to determine the color—perhaps black—nor the nature of the ink used), with letters attached to each other and words well separated; capitals demarcated and average graphical flow; a light slope to the right and round vowels rather open: elements which denote a very scholastic handwriting. Altogether the writing appears neat and clear, devoid of confused thickening and tangling of letters.

At the web site of the Vatican Congregation for the Doctrine of the Faith, http://www/vatican.va/roman_curia/congregations/cfaith/doc_doc_index_it.htm, appears the Portuguese transcription of the handwritten Portuguese text. **Despite the importance of the document, however, it is revealed there that in many parts the transcription was not conducted with methodological rigor, in that the spelling is at times updated and modernized, while in parts the system of spelling utilized by the authoress is faithfully retained.** Among other things, the transcription is not accompanied by a critical apparatus, nor by an introduction which specifies the spelling criteria adopted. We indicate as follows the interventions in a normative direction effected by the Vatican:

1. Folio p. 1, line 5, *parecia* instead of what Sister Lucia writes: *parcia.*
2. Folio p. 2, line 16, *vêem* instead of *vem.*
3. Folio p. 3, lines 5 and 6: *religiosos* and *religiosas* instead of *relegiosos* and *relegiosas.*
4. Folio p. 3, line 7 and folio p. 4, line 2, no *cimo* instead of no *simo.*
5. Folio p. 3, line 9, *Cruz* (with a capital) instead of *cruz* (with lower case); moreover no correction is made to the same word at folio p. 4, line 13 where the authoress writes first lower case, and then corrects with a capital.

6. Folio p. 3, line 14, *trémulo* instead of *tremolo.*
7. Folio p. 3, line 14, *vacilante* insead of *vassilante*
8. Folio pp. 3-4, line 16/1, *cadáveres* instead of *cadavers.* The Vatican does not intervene, however, to correct other words which today would be accented, such as *Mártires.*

The Phonological and Orthographical Level

The text evidences some hypercorrect forms which lend support, on the one hand, to the remarkable effort of she who writes and, on the other hand, the minimal schooling to which the authoress must have been subjected.

1. The complex Portuguese vowel system, which foresees for the same graphic sign different phonetic realizations, is such that the authoress of this testimony, evidently little familiar with writing, proceeds to the phenomena of hypercorrectness,[394b] that is, intervenes erroneously concerning vowels such as the /i/ and the /u/—rendering them "e" and "o"—which she believed to be incorrect by apparent analogy to other forms where the "e" and the "o" are effectively pronounced /i/ and /e/, or not pronounced at all inasmuch as they are pretonic.[394c] We find ourselves presented with the following cases:

a. oscillation between "e" and "i" in the word *rel̠egioso/-s, religioso/-s:* folio p. 3, lines 5 and 6; folio p. 4, lines 9 and 10;

b. "e" rather than "i" in the case of *ce̠ntilar* for *ci̠ntilar*, with the meaning of "scintillate," folio p. 2, line 4; and of *emensa* for *imensa*, folio p. 2, line 14;

c. "o" instead of "u" in *tremolo* instead of the correct form *trémulo*, folio p. 3, line 14.

2. Different, however, is the case in which Sister Lucia follows her own phonetic system:

a. there is the case, for example, of the errorneous *ju̠elhos* instead of *jo̠lhos*, with the meaning "knee" (folio p. 4, line 3);

[394b] An improper usage arising from a faulty analogy to formal usage because of a desire to be especially correct: e.g., "on behalf of my parents and I," instead of "my parents and me."

[394c] The syllable before the primary stressed syllable in a word.

b. the suppression of the pretonic vowel where required graphically, even if phonetically;

c. tending to disperse, as for example in *parcia* instead of the correct *parecia* (folio p. 2, line 5).

3. A separate discussion is warranted of Sister Lucia's graphical realization of the <u>sibilants</u>. In the North of Portugal, the place of origin of the authoress of the text, these consonants are in fact realized differently from the central-southern zone: in the speech of Alto Minho there exists today a complex system of 4 sibilants: an unvoiced apicoalveolar,[394d] a strong apicoalveolar, an unvoiced predorsodental, and a strong predorsodental. Standard Portuguese, which for its system of sibilants which follow instead the simplified central-southern structure with only two consonants (the unvoiced and strong apicoalveolar), is such that a northern speaker, little schooled, can at times confuse some graphemes.[394e] This phenomenon is even more widespread in the first decades of the 20th century. Thus in the writing of Sister Lucia we witness the following cases of departure from the graphic standard:

-*vós* instead of *voz* (the first with the meaning of "you" plural which, however, would not make sense in context; the second instead with the meaning of "voice"), folio p. 2, line 11.

-*simo* instead of *cimo*, folio p. 3, line 7 and folio p. 4, line 2;

-*vassilante* instead of *vacilante*, folio p. 3, line 4.

4. Yet to be pointed out at the orthographic level is the lack of <u>accents</u> compared with current Portuguese. One observes, however, that the system of written accents at the beginning of the 20th century was still rather irregular. The lack of accents, therefore, is not to be considered a departure from the norm:

a. the case of the hiatus[394f] *ai* instead of *aí* (folio p. 3, line 12) and *ruinas* instead of *ruínas* (folio p. 3, line 13);

b. in words stressing the antepenultimate syllable: *cadavers* (folio pp. 3-4, line 16/1), *martires* (folio p. 4, lines 15-16) and *varios/varias* (folio p. 4, lines 6, 10 and (twice) 11).

[394d] A sound "articulated with the apex of the tongue touching or near the alveolar ridge, as (t), (z), (n), and (l)."

[394e] The letters comprising the phonemes, or sounds, that make up a word.

[394f] "The occurrence of two vowel sounds without pause or intervening consonantal sound."

The morphosyntactic level

The missing contraction or elision of the preposition *em/n'* with the determinate and indeterminate article or with the personal pronoun *ele* is a part of the *usus scribendi* [written usage] of the epoch: <u>*em a mão*</u> *esquerda* (folio p. 2, line 2), *n'uma* and *n'um* (folio p. 4, line 15 and folio p. 2, lines 14 and 16); *n'êles* (folio p. 4, line 15).

But Sister Lucia runs into graphic confusion, writing the third person plural of the verb VER = to see (*vêem*) as if it were the third person plural of the verb VIR = to come (*vem*) (folio p. 2, line 16).

From what has been examined here, it can therefore be shown that within the text one does not encounter lexical or morphosyntactical problems due to regionalism or provincialism. Moreover, the departure from the standard relative to the system of sibilants could constitute only a diatopic [phonetical style] variant. The orthographic errors or variants present in the text are, therefore, to be attributed more to lack of familiarity with writing, at the elementary stage of the education of the authoress, and to problems of a diastratic type, rather than to diatopic variants relative to Sister Lucia's place of origin.

The translational level

In the examination of the complete version of the text there can finally be brought to light some problems of a translational nature.

The periphrastic verbal form in Portuguese comprised by the auxiliaries (*estar, andar, continuar, vir, ir…*) followed by the gerund represents a process underway, the duration and development of an action in its progressive element. In Italian this verbal form could be realized as well with a simple imperfect indicative, with some periphrastic structures better defining such a course, as for example the verb *stare* followed by the gerund or other combinations that define the process. One observes at folio p. 3, line 6 the expression referring to the "Holy Father" who "antes de chegar aí, atravessou uma grande cidade meia em ruínas, e meio trémolo com andar vassilante, acabrunhado de dôr e pena, *ia orando* pelas almas dos cadáveres que encontrava pelo caminho [before reaching there the Holy Father passed through a big city half in ruins and half trembling with halting step, afflicted with pain and sorrow, he prayed for the souls of the corpses he met on his way]." The phrase presents within itself two verbs of movement—*chegar* ("to arrive") and *attravessou* ("traversed")—as well as a substantive, *andar*, which indicates the "step," the "walk." **The phrase "ia orando," if translated with the imperfect verb "pregava" (he prayed), as it was translated in the volume of the Congregation for the Doctrine of the Faith, loses all the force of the image of movement, of distance, which it appears Sister Lucia wished to confer on the action of the Holy Father. Rather than "he prayed" *tout-court* [without qualification or explanation] it therefore would have been more opportune to translate with a periphrastic structure of movement such as, for example, "he advanced solemnly, praying," or "he proceeded praying."** That is, the translator should have been able to find a more elaborate form to diminish the translational residuum.

In the same phrase (lines 1-2) the binomial "pelo caminho" (along the road) is translated "nel suo cammino" ("on his way"): to the articulated preposition *nel* the translator added the possessive adjective *suo* ("his"), not present in the text. Rather than working in the adjectival element (inserting an element that is lacking), it would perhaps have been more opportune to confer on this simple phraseological connection the idea of movement, as for example "lungo il cammino" (along the road).

The same periphrastic formula composed of the verb IR (to be) plus the gerund is present at folio p. 4, lines 7-8: "Foram morrendo uns trás outros" (there were dying one after the other). The translator provides a dry rendition of this phrase as "morirono gli uni dopo gli altri" (there died one after the other). Lacking yet again in this Italian rendering is the action in progress, the process that is slow to happen, so that if it were not possible to render this action through verbal forms, it would have been necessary to use further images that would clarify its contents. For example: "they died slowly, one after the other."

The stylistic choice made by the translator at folio p. 3, line 15 for rendering the adjective *acabrunhado* settles on the adjective "afflito." So that the reader will understand completely the valence [range of connotations] of this attribute, in its place there can be considered other Italian synonyms that could be linked to it: "avvilto" (disheartened, discouraged), "oppresso" (oppressed), "umiliato" (humiliated), "mortificato" (mortified), some of which perhaps better represent the state of the soul of the Pope as seen by the young shepherdess Lucia.

But the most notable translational choice within this text is found at folio pp. 1 and 2 where one reads: "vimos ao lado esquerdo de Nossa Senhora um pouco mais alto um Anjo com uma espada de fôgo em a mão esquerda; ao centilar, despedia chamas que parecia iam encendiar o mundo; mas apagavam-se com o contacto do brilho que da mão direita expedia Nossa Senhora _ao seu encontro_ (emphasis added)."

This passage was translated thus in the following passages:

In Italian: "Abbiamo visto al lato sinistro di Nostra Signora un poco più in alto un Angelo con una spada di fuoco nella mano sinistra; scintillando emetteva fiamme che sembrava dovessero incendiare il mondo; ma si spegnevano al contatto dello splendore che Nostra Signora emanava dalla sua mano destra _verso di lui_."

To this version are linked all the other translations:

In French: "Nous avons vu sur le côté gauche de Notre-Dame, un peu plus en hauteur, un Ange avec une épée de feu dans la main gauche; elle scintillait et émettait des flammes qui, semblait-il, devaient incendier le monde; mais elles s'éteignaient au contact de la splendeur qui émanait de la main droite de Notre-Dame _en direction de lui_."

In English: "We saw an Angel with a flaming sword in his left hand; flashing, it gave out flames that looked as though they would set the world on fire; but they died out in contact with the splendor that Our Lady radiated _towards him_ from Her right hand."

In Spanish: "Hemos visto al lado izquierdo de Nuestra Señora un poco más en lo alto a un Ángel con una espada de fuego en la mano izquierda; centelleando emitía llamas que parecía iban a incendiar el mundo; pero se apagaban al contacto con el esplendor que Nuestra Señora irradiaba con su mano derecha dirigida _hacia él_."

In German: "Haben wir links von Unserer Lieben Frau etwas oberhalb einen Engel gesehen, der ein Feuerschwert in der linken Hand hielt; es sprühte Funken, und Flammen gingen von ihm aus, als sollten sie die Welt anzünden; doch die Flammen verlöschten, als sie mit dem Glanz in Berührung kamen, den Unsere Liebe Frau von ihrer rechten Hand _auf ihn_ ausströmte."

It is likely that the other translations began with the Italian version: all of them in fact depict the Virgin extending Her arm against the Angel. But concerning this some considerations are necessary:

1. first of all, the Portuguese possessive adjective _seu_ (underlined in the text) can refer morphosyntactically[394g] to either the Angel or the flames (the adjective possesses the same form);
2. Moreover, the adjective _seu_ is in the lower case and not the

---

[394g] Meaning the internal structure of a word and the way it is put together with other words in a sentence.

upper case: If Sister Lucia had wished to refer to the Angel rather than to the flames she would have used the upper case out of deference;

3. the verb *expedir* presupposes the will of the one who accomplishes the action, that is "spedire, inviare, espellere, allontare (to send, to expel, to move away from)." The Madonna does not "emanate" that splendor (as in a static picture on a holy card), but seems of Her own accord to intervene to stop the flames;

4. at the morphosyntactic level the last element cited by the authoress are the flames and not the Angel.

The passage could therefore be interpreted in two ways: either the Madonna sends Her splendor toward the Angel (and this is the reading all the translators have given the passage, but we suppose that the original error was exclusively by the Italian translator, who then influenced the other translators) or the Virgin sends Her splendor toward the flames to arrest them. **In the context it seems in fact to be much more plausible that the Madonna[394h] extends Her hand not against the Angel, but rather against the flames that issue from his sword, to stop them.** While in the Portuguese text the ambiguity created by the adjective *seu* is resolved by the context, however in the Vatican's official translation the formulation used also annuls the ambiguity, but the attribution to an erroneous and illogical referent[394i] [the Angel rather than the flames] creates grave confusion in the vision that the seer had.

[394h] Incidentally, "Our Lady" could be translated more elegantly from the Portuguese *Nossa Senhora* as "the Madonna".

[394i] A person or thing to which a linguistic expression refers.

Select Bibliography

Alban, Francis and Christopher A. Ferrara, *Fatima Priest*. Pound Ridge, New York: Good Counsel Publications, 1997, Second Edition.

----------, *Il sacerdote di Fatima* (*Fatima Priest*). Pound Ridge, New York: Good Counsel Publications, 2000, Italian edition.

Congregation for the Doctrine of the Faith, *The Message of Fatima*. (English edition). Vatican City: Libreria Editrice Vaticana, 2000.

Kramer, Father Paul, *The Devil's Final Battle*. Terryville, Connecticut: The Missionary Association, 2002.

----------, *La battaglia finale del diavolo* (*The Devil's Final Battle*). Buffalo: The Missionary Association, 2004, Italian edition.

Michel de la Sainte Trinité (Frère), *The Whole Truth About Fatima*, Volume I, *Science and the Facts*. Buffalo: Immaculate Heart Publications, 1989.

----------, *The Whole Truth About Fatima*, Volume II, *The Secret and the Church*. Buffalo: Immaculate Heart Publications, 1990.

----------, *The Whole Truth About Fatima*, Volume III, *The Third Secret*. Buffalo: Immaculate Heart Publications, 1990, republished in 2001.

----------, *Toute la vérité sur Fatima: La science et les faits* (*The Whole Truth About Fatima*, Volume I). Saint-Parres-lès-Vaudes, France: La Contre-Réforme Catholique, 1984, French edition.

----------, *Toute la vérité sur Fatima: Le Secret et l'Église* (*1917 – 1942*) (*The Whole Truth About Fatima*, Volume II). Saint-Parres-lès-Vaudes, France: La Contre-Réforme Catholique, 1984, French edition.

----------, *Toute la vérité sur Fatima: Le Troisième Secret* (*1942 – 1960*) (*The Whole Truth About Fatima*, Volume III). Saint-Parres-lès-Vaudes, France: La Contre-Réforme Catholique, 1985, French edition.

Paolini, Solideo, *Fatima: Non disprezzate le profezie*. (*Fatima: Do Not Despise Prophecy*). Tavagnacco (Ud): Edizione Segno, 2005.

Tornielli, Andrea, *Il segreto svelato (The Secret Revealed)*. Milan: Gribaudi, 2000.

Tosatti, Marco, *Il segreto non svelato (The Secret Not Revealed)*. Casale Monferrato (AL): Edizioni Piemme Spa, 2002.